Urs Widmer

Vom Fenster meines Hauses aus

Prosa

Diogenes

Inhalt

I

Vom Fenster meines Hauses aus

I

Vom Fenster meines Hauses aus, an dem ich an einem Holztisch sitze, sehe ich, hinter Telefondrähten, die voller Schwalben mit zitternden Schwänzen sind, die Giebel der Dächer der Häuser von Sesenheim. Wenn ich einatme, pfeifen meine Lungen. Gewitterwolken stehen über der Rheinebene, und hinten bei Sesenheim, das heute Sessenheim heißt, grollt es. Ich weiß, dort, wo jetzt eine Erntemaschine durchs Getreide rast, dort standen Goethe und Friederike, die sich küßten, und es war der letzte Kuß im Leben Friederikes. Es donnerte über dem Schwarzwald. Als Friederike starb, etwa 20 Kilometer südlich von Sesenheim, war das Elsaß immer noch ein stilles Land mit krähenden Hähnen, Störchen, Fachwerkhäusern, Blumen, aber Goethe war ein großes Tier geworden, mit dicken schweren Füßen, einem breiten Mund, fetten Händen und einer öligen Nase. Drei alte Freundinnen gingen hinter dem Sarg her. Sie weinten wasserlose Trä-

nen und warfen mit ihren dürren Händen Erd-
krümel in das Grab. Sie hatten Friederike ge-
mocht. Sie hatte nie von Goethe gesprochen.
Dieser wandelte zu dieser Stunde durch einen fran-
zösisch angelegten Park und sagte gerade zu seinem Eckermann: Begreif er, Eckermann, ein jeder
hat einen schwarzen Abgrund in seinem Innern,
auch ich. Zuweilen, wenn ich in den unendlichen
Nachthimmel hinaufsehe, dröhnt in mir das
wilde Pochen einer längst vergangenen Schuld,
notier er sich das, Eckermann.

Ein Zahnarzt aus meiner Bekanntschaft zum
Beispiel hat einen Teil der Leiche Napoleons im
Keller, ein Bein, auf einer Apfelhurde. Er zerstö-
ßelt es in einem Mörser zu feinem Pulver und
analysiert dieses und stellt fest, daß Napoleon
eine Überdosis Arsen enthält. Ich, ich schrecke
manchmal nachts hoch und denke, mein Bruder
ist tot und liegt in meinem Keller. Aber ich habe
gar keinen Bruder, oder ist gerade das der Beweis? Ich mache nie Licht im Keller, d. h. ich gehe
nie in den Keller. Ich sitze an meinem breiten
Holztisch am Fenster und sehe über die Rheinebene hinweg. Bauern und Bäuerinnen stehen in
den Stoppelfeldern und sehen zum Himmel
hinauf. Es donnert. Ich schlage auf die Tasten
meiner Schreibmaschine, auch wenn ich nach Sesenheim hinüberschaue, ich schreibe blind. Ich erin-

nere mich, daß Gottfried Keller eine lebenslange Angst hatte, lebendig begraben zu werden. Es ist entsetzlich, wenn man in eine helle klare Luft eingemauert ist wie in einen Glassarg.

Es ist sowieso bekannt, daß die Lebenswege aller Menschen von ihren Namen beeinflußt werden. Das ist die letzte magische Macht, die die entmachteten Zauberer noch ausüben. Aber die meisten Menschen machen schier übermenschliche Anstrengungen, ihrer Bestimmung zu entgehen. Herr Keller wurde, auch auf Kosten seines Glücks, Schriftsteller. Herr Bauer. Herr Falk. Herr Lenz. Herr Sommer. Herr Wiener. Herr Bayer. Herr Hesse. Herr Essig. Herr Kluge. Herr Kaiser. Herr Graf. Herr Bürger. Herr Mann. Herr Klopstock. Was soll die Auflehnung gegen unsre Namen? Wer einmal einer Susanne im Liebesrausch Irma ins Ohr geflüstert hat, weiß, wovon ich spreche.

Der erste Schriftsteller, den ich kennenlernte, war ein Kriegsblinder. Er hatte den Krieg nur gehört. Er hatte eine junge Frau, die jeden Tag ein neues Halskettchen für ihn anzog und seine Gedichte in einer zierlichen Schrift in einen Blindband eines Romans eines Freundes des Schriftstellers schrieb, der von den Leiden der Deutschen in Rußland handelte. Als ich zur Tür hereinkam, kam mir der Schriftsteller mit weit ausgebreiteten Armen entgegengeeilt. Er schüttelte meine Hände und führte mich in sein Arbeitszimmer und öffnete, während er etwas über den neuen Roman seines Freunds sagte, nämlich, er habe ihn nicht gelesen, eine Rotweinflasche. Ich saß auf der Vorderkante eines Stuhls und sagte, ich auch nicht, und sah, er war taub, nicht blind. Eine Granate war im ersten Kriegsmonat vor seinen Ohren explodiert. Jetzt schrieb er seine Gedichte mit Filzstiften auf große Papierbögen, und abends las seine Frau sie ihm vor. Er hing an ihren Lippen. Er wußte genau, an welcher Stelle sie war. Wenn sie einmal einen Text sagte, der nicht von ihm war, verstand er nichts. Ratlos starrte er sie an und schüttelte den Kopf. Schließlich nahm sie ein Papier und einen Filzstift und schrieb etwas darauf und gab es ihm. Sie rannte zur Tür hinaus und schlug sie hinter sich zu. Der Dichter zuckte zusammen. Er las das Geschriebene. Seine Augen füllten sich mit Tränen. Er sah mich an. Langsam wurden seine Haare weiß, oder meine.

Eines Morgens, als ich aufwachte, waren meine Haare wirklich weiß. Ich hatte die Nacht mit einem stämmigen Dichter verbracht. Wir waren auf einer gemeinsamen Fahrt. Ich sah auf seine bebenden Nasenflügel. Ich hörte das Schnarchen, das ich schon die ganze Nacht gehört hatte. Ich bringe ihn um, dachte ich. Ich packte ihn an den

Beinen, den Dichter, und zerrte ihn durch lange Korridore. Sein Kopf schlug die Treppenstufen hinunter. Im Keller legte ich ihn auf eine Apfelhurde. Ich sah ihn genau an. Er sah widerwärtig aus, ganz anders als seine Gedichte. Er öffnete ein Auge. Ich rannte die Treppen hinauf, an verdutzten Stubenmädchen und Hotelburschen in grünen Schürzen vorbei, mit weißen Haaren. Das war in Kufstein, wo alle Bauern Zither spielten und jede Bäuerin vielfarbige Stickereien auf ihren großen milchweißen Brüsten hatte.

Gottfried Kellers Lieblingstiere waren Katzen. *Er* war es, der seinen Bruder umbrachte und in den Keller schleifte. Kein lebender Bruder ist in Gottfried Kellers Leben nachweisbar. Obwohl Gottfried Keller nicht an die Reinkarnation glaubte, ist es bei dieser so, daß, wenn man sich gut benommen hat, man im nächsten Leben ein hochentwickelter Säuger wird, war man ein Lump, ein Wurm. Im Alter wurde Gottfried Keller schlohweiß. Er saß jeden Abend in einem Weinkeller in Zürich und trank und brummte vor sich hin. Man verstand nie, was er sagte, aber man nahm an, daß es unflätige Bemerkungen über den Magistrat waren. Einmal träumte er, er sei über Nacht völlig schwarz geworden, ein Neger, oder, wie man heute sagt, ein Schwarzer. Gottfried Keller hatte in seiner Jugend Mühe mit dem Atmen, dann nicht mehr, dann im Alter wieder.

Ich besitze ein Sechstel des Hauses, aus dem ich über die Rheinebene hinwegsehe, jetzt in eine schwarze Regenwand hinein. Die Erntemaschine ist weg, und die Bauern rennen über die Stoppelfelder. Die Bäuerinnen schlagen die Röcke über die Köpfe. Im Estrich unsres Hauses sind Hornissen, die bei Gewittern besonders nervös sind. Der Estrich gehört zu meinem Sechstel, in den untern Sechsteln, in denen gemütliche Lehnstühle und geheizte Öfen stehen, sind die andern fünf Inhaber meines Hauses, z. B. ein hagerer älterer Herr, der Versicherungsaquisitör ist. Sein Hobby ist das Beobachten von Hornissen. Stundenlang liegt er in dicke Tücher eingehüllt und mit einer Skifahrerbrille über den Augen in meinem Sechstel des Hauses. Einer der fünf andern Hausbesitzer ist ein Hund. Ihm gehört das schönste Zimmer. Der Keller gehört allen. Nie geht jemand hinunter, und wenn, etwa um Wein zu holen, mit geschlossenen Augen. Er riecht säuerlich. Immer wieder schauen wir, ob einer von uns fehlt oder ob in der Zeitung von einem vermißten Schriftsteller geschrieben wird.

Mich interessiert eher das, was ich nicht kann. Ich bewundere z. B. Revolutionäre, die fette gesunde stinkreiche zynische mörderische Diktatoren erstechen. Wir, meine Frau und ich, haben statt dessen ein Pferd angeschafft, erstens, weil meine Frau glaubt, es könnte die Seele von Gottfried Kellers Bruder beherbergen, zweitens, weil der Verkäufer sagte, es frißt Hornissen. Es steht oben im Estrich. Als ich jetzt eben, auf Zehenspitzen, in den Estrich hinaufstieg, fand ich den Satz bestätigt, daß zwei Hornissen ein Roß töten. Von entsetzlichen Stichen übersät gelang es mir, das röchelnde Tier in den Keller zu schleifen. Wir sahen, wie es starb. Es krümmte sich vor Schmerz. Es schnaubte. Susanne, meine Frau, versuchte, die Seele von Gottfried Kellers Bruder beim Entweichen in einer Plastictüte aufzufangen, vergeblich. Wir ließen die Pferdeleiche auf der Apfelhurde liegen, auch, weil mein Herzschlag plötzlich aussetzte und Susanne wie ein Teufel mit eingeschalteten Scheinwerfern ins Spital rasen mußte, wo der Arzt mir Kalziumspritzen gab. Sie haben eine Konstitution wie ein Roß, sagte er, als ich aus meiner Bewußtlosigkeit aufwachte. Sie haben mindestens zehn Stiche und leben noch. Ich nickte. Susanne, zu der ich im Vergeß zuweilen Irma sage, nahm mich bei der Hand. Wir gingen in ein Café, in dem wir uns mit Cognacs vollpumpten, bis wir genügend Mut hatten, noch einen Weinkeller zu besuchen.

Dort sagte Susanne, ich sei blöd. Blöd, blöd,

blöd. Ich sagte: Das kann schon sein, daß ich blöd bin, aber ich glaube nicht an die Vererbung. Mein Vater war ganz anders blöd. Er stand um vier Uhr früh auf, setzte sich an seine Schreibmaschine an seinem Tisch in seinem Haus und schrieb wie rasend auf ihr herum bis um acht Uhr abends. Seine Werke sind verschollen, sie liegen in irgendeinem Keller. Dein Vater war nett, sagte Susanne, der war gar nicht so blöd wie du Blödian immer meinst. Wie dem auch sei, sagte ich, meine Mutter war so blöd: sie stand um sieben Uhr früh auf und putzte bis acht Uhr abends all das sauber, was wir schmutzig gemacht hatten. Ich, heute, schreibe kaum je, nie, so viel und so schnell wie heute. Sonst sitze ich eher am Fenster und schaue auf die Rheinebene und den fernen Schwarzwald, wenn ich nicht gerade in meinem Stadthaus in Frankfurt bin und telefoniere oder fernsehe. Manchmal brülle ich auf und schlage die Fäuste gegen die Zimmerwand. Jahrelang hatte ich eine Schreibmaschine, deren L abgebrochen war. Was ich noch sagen wollte, sagte ich zu Susanne, die inzwischen, wie ich, betrunken war, manchmal sucht mich mein Vater heim. Er kommt aus dem Keller. Plötzlich ist er da. Er trägt ein Manuskript unter dem Arm. Keinem von uns ist ganz klar, ist es eines von seinen oder von meinen. Mein Vater kann die Gesichter in

Sekundenschnelle von jung auf uralt wechseln. Ich bin zwar tot, sagt er dann, aber heute habe ich Ausgang. Dann gehen wir ins Kino, wie früher, wie früher sehen wir uns einen Schießfilm an mit unzähligen Leichen. Unser Lieblingsfilm war eine Geschichte, in der Peter Lorre zwei Leichen in einem Keller hatte und an ihnen herumoperierte, ich weiß nicht mehr was und warum. Ich rief nach dem Wirt und bestellte nochmals eine Flasche. Ich leckte meine Hornissenstiche. Susanne hatte glänzende Augen und schrie, der einzige wirkliche Mann für eine wirkliche Frau sei ihr Vater. Das kann sein, sagte ich, jedenfalls, nachher aßen mein Vater und ich ein Eis, und dann war sein Urlaub abgelaufen und er mußte zurück, in den Himmel oder in die Hölle, blöderweise habe ich vergessen, ihn zu fragen.

Ich wohne in einem Haus, über dem die Nato Formationsflüge übt. Es sind Kanadier, die die Elsässer vor den Russen beschützen. Sie rasen im Tiefflug über die Rheinebene. Ich fühle, wie ich langsam taub werde. Irgendwann einmal werde ich die Flugzeuge nur noch sehen. Ich könnte natürlich beim fernsten Düsengeräusch in den Keller rennen und den Angriff abwarten, aber erstens sind die Flugzeuge schneller als ich und zweitens will ich nicht in den Keller. Der Vorbesitzer des Hauses hat die Tragebalken des Hauses vom Keller aus mit Baumstämmen abgestützt, denn schon zu seinen Zeiten war Krieg. Er sah aus dem Kellerfenster, wie deutsche Panzer über die Rheinebene gerollt kamen, und vorbei, und am nächsten Tag kamen amerikanische aus der andern Richtung, und vorbei. Der Vorbesitzer war schlohweiß geworden. Er hatte jahrelang im Keller gelebt. Nun grub er den alten Wein aus, und das Geld, und er rief und rief nach seiner Frau, und dann trank er alle Flaschen auf einen Ruck aus. Vollständig betrunken fanden ihn die Befreier, und als wir ihn, dreißig Jahre später, kennenlernten, war er immer noch betrunken, oder wieder. Er verkaufte uns das Haus, in dem er ein Leben verbracht hatte, mir einen Sechstel, Susanne einen Sechstel, dem Versicherungsaquisitör einen Sechstel, seinem Hund einen Sechstel, und zwei weiteren Personen, die ich noch nicht vorgestellt habe, die letzten zwei Sechstel. Diese zwei Personen sind ein Gelehrter und seine Frau. Der Gelehrte lehrt Steuerrecht an der Akademie für Management in Baden-Baden. Jeden Tag fährt er mit seiner Mobylette über die Grenze, aber abends wühlt er sich hinter komplizierte Partituren und erforscht das Leben tauber Komponisten. Er erzählte mir einmal, wie Beethoven mit einem starren Gesicht vor seinem Orchester stand und die neunte Sinfonie dirigierte. Als die

Musiker ihre Instrumente absetzten und die Sänger die Münder schlossen, hörte auch er mit dem Dirigieren auf. Er drehte sich um und nahm den tosenden Applaus entgegen, bis er sah, daß niemand mehr im Saal war. Seine Haushälterin führte ihn ins Künstlerzimmer und heim. Die Frau des Gelehrten hat zwei Kinder, die gut hören, und wir hören sie auch gut. Wenn sie und die Nato gleichzeitig angreifen, gehe sogar ich in den Keller. Ich setze mich auf die Romane meines Vaters, und die Füße stelle ich auf das tote Pferd. Susanne legt sich auf die Apfelhurde. Gemeinsam warten wir, bis das Gewitter vorüber ist. Dann steigen wir wieder an die Oberwelt. Im Salon steht der Steuerrechtler mit einer Partitur, er dirigiert still vor sich hin, mit einem Cognacglas in der Hand. Ich sehe, daß er seine Lippen bewegt. Was? sage ich. Diesmal konzentriere ich mich auf seine Mundbewegungen. Hast du dir die Haare färben lassen? sagen seine Lippen. Auch Irma sieht mich entsetzt an.

Ich schreibe dies am 22. Juli 1976, hauptsächlich weil mein Schwager auf Besuch ist. Er sitzt im Fauteuil und löst Kreuzworträtsel. Er weiß, daß man arbeitende Menschen nicht anspricht. Ich darf keine Sekunde aufhören zu schreiben, sonst fragt er mich nach einer Stadt ohne Autoverkehr mit sieben Buchstaben. Nur wenn er einschläft, schaue ich zum Fenster hinaus auf die Schwalben, die auf den Telefondrähten sitzen und sich die weißen Federn unter den schwarzen Flügeln putzen. Sie haben zwei Nester an den Tragebalken des Kellers, seit dem Krieg. Immer lassen wir das Fenster offen. Später will ich meinen Schwager fragen, ob er sie sich ansehen will. Bei seinem letzten Besuch ruinierte ich meine Schreibmaschine, indem ich hunderte von Seiten mit großen und kleinen Ls füllte. Die Taste brach ab. Deshalb schreibe ich jetzt einen richtigen Text mit einem richtigen Sinn, damit die mittlere Buchstabendichte, auf die hin die Maschine konstruiert ist, richtig auftritt. Die Garantie für die Maschine ist längst abgelaufen, es ist die, auf der schon mein Vater geschrieben hat.

Mein Schwager ist aufgewacht. Er sitzt mit offenem Mund bolzgerade im Sessel, gerade jetzt, wo mir der Stoff ausgeht. Ich schreibe jetzt irrsinnig schnell. In meiner derzeitigen Form könnte ich Gabriele Wohmann zu einem Wettschreiben herausfordern. Allerdings kenne ich Gabriele Wohmanns derzeitige Form nicht. Sie ist viel trainierter als ich, sicher hat sie eingespielte Helfer, jemanden, der ihr Kaffee bringt, und Mechaniker, die eine Schreibmaschinenwalze in dreißig Sekunden auswechseln können, wenn sie einmal an die Boxen muß. Inzwischen sind alle

Schwalben weg vom Draht. Vielleicht enthält eine die Seele von Gottfried Kellers Bruder. Wer beschreibt meinen Schreck, als ich jetzt sehe, daß mein Nachbar, Herr Schnabel, ein Maurerpolier, auch seinen Schwager zu Besuch hat. Herr Schnabel schaut mich mit traurigen Augen an, während sein Schwager auf ihn einredet. Er nickt mir zu. Dann nimmt er seinen Schwager sanft beim Arm, langsam steigen die beiden die Kellertreppen hinunter. Gleich höre ich auf zu schreiben. Sowieso ist es jetzt Zeit, meinem Schwager einen Apéritif anzubieten. »Hubert«, sagt meine Stimme jetzt, »wie wär's mit einem Apéritif?« Ein Leuchten geht über Huberts Gesicht. »Das wäre schön«, sagt er leise. »Obwohl ich die Stille sehr genossen habe. Wir wollen uns vors Haus setzen und kein Wort sprechen und schweigend über die Rheinebene bis zu den Giebeln von Sesenheim schauen. Morgen müssen wir ja sowieso in die Stadt zurück, in den Lärm und den Dreck.« Ich nicke. Als ich einatme, höre ich, daß meine Lungen pfeifen. Die ersten Regentropfen fallen. Ein ferner Reiter reitet in einem wilden Galopp über das weite Stoppelfeld.

Vom Fenster meines andern Hauses aus, dem in
Frankfurt, könnte ich das andere Haus Goethes,
das am Großen Hirschgraben, sehen, wenn nicht
so viele andere Häuser dazwischenstünden. Früher nannte man solche Häuser Wolkenkratzer.
Irgendwie bin ich nie dazugekommen, Goethes
ehemaligen Wohnsitz zu besuchen, obwohl man
dort vergilbte Liebesbriefe von Friederike lesen
kann und einen Tintenklecks bewundern, der davon herrührt, daß Goethe, als er den Faust
schrieb, einer eintretenden Magd ein Tintenfaß
entgegenschleuderte, weil er meinte, sie sei der
Teufel. Ich bin bei jedem Versuch, sein Haus zu
besuchen, abgelenkt worden. Ich fand mich dann
im Kaufhof wieder, oder in der Deutschen Bank,
oder bei Montanus. Ich blättere dort manchmal in
der Deutschen Waffenzeitschrift oder im Play-
boy.

Vom Fenster meines Stadthauses aus, das gar
nicht mein Haus ist, sondern einem Hersteller
von Verpackungsmaterial gehört, der mit seinem
PVC so viel Geld verdient, daß er mir eine völlig
humane Miete abverlangt, vom Fenster meines
Stadthauses aus sehe ich auf eine Straße mit
Kopfsteinpflaster. Früher rumpelten Kutschen
und Biertransporte darüber. Man sieht heute

noch die mit Teer verschmierten Geleise der Straßenbahnen, die von schweren Gäulen gezogen wurden. Heute gleiten, bei Regen, die Radfahrer auf ihnen aus. Um die Autos nicht allzu deutlich zu hören, spiele ich Platten mit Klaviersonaten von Beethoven. Wenn ich zuweilen in ein Konzert gehe, in den Musiksaal der Deutschen Bank zum Beispiel, lehne ich mich wie alle Konzertbesucher zurück und genieße die Wucht der Tonsprache, aber irgendwie fehlen mir immer die begleitenden Bässe der Automotoren.

Gegenüber von meinem Haus steht eine Trinkhalle mit einer niederen Mauer, auf der fast immer Männer mit Bierflaschen sitzen und trinken und reden. Manchmal, ich schaue ja nicht ununterbrochen auf meine Kollegen, kracht es dann plötzlich, und einer der Männer hat in der Hitze seiner Argumentation seine Flasche auf den Boden gedonnert. Scherben und Bierlachen sind am Boden, und die Trinker, die dann laut reden, sind naßgespritzt. Der Trinkhallenpächter, ein Jugoslawe, kommt vor die Tür und sagt etwas Serbokroatisches oder Serbisches oder Kroatisches. Je nachdem wird die Stimmung sanfter oder aggressiver. Nachts verlagert sich die Auseinandersetzung in die Gastwirtschaft, die auch vom Trinkhallenpächter betrieben wird, der sie übernehmen konnte, weil vor zwei Jahren einer der

Serbokroaten oder Serben oder Kroaten sein Bier mit einem Revolver bestellte und der damalige Wirt dann genug davon hatte, mit einem Bein im Gefängnis und mit dem andern im Grab zu stehen. Er wußte, so nahe war er dem Grab noch nie gewesen. Sein Gast ist inzwischen aus dem Gefängnis heraus und sitzt wieder auf der Mauer vor der Trinkhalle. Nachts dann, wenn Susanne und ich schon schlafen, herrscht zuweilen ein plötzliches Gebrüll, dann stehen wir auf und gehen ans Fenster. Zuerst hören wir die serbokroatische Auseinandersetzung nur, oder die serbische, oder die kroatische, Glas splittert, Holz kracht, Schreie schreien, dann geht die Tür auf und, wie aus einem Dampfkessel, in dem ein Überdruck herrscht, zischen vier oder fünf Serbokroaten oder Serben oder Kroaten heraus, fassen auf dem Kopfsteinpflaster wieder Fuß und stürzen sich in das unsichtbare Getümmel zurück. Meistens ruft dann jemand, der nicht ich bin, die Polizei. Sie kommt, und dadurch wird das Ganze auch nicht besser. Ich glaube, die vom Haus gegenüber rufen an, da ist so eine Sauna für Manager, wo man einen Martini on the Rocks schlürfen kann, während einem eine Thailänderin zwischen den Beinen krault.

Ich werde nie vergessen, wie meine Mutter, die eine Dame ist und mit Messerbänkchen auf dem

Tisch aufgewachsen, neben mir in der Gaststätte saß. Wir tranken einen Wein, Susanne war auch dabei, und dann begann plötzlich und unerwartet eine Schlägerei, viel früher als sonst, und schon flogen Stühle durchs Lokal, und die Männer hatten rote Gesichter. Meine Mutter saß strahlend an ihrem Tisch. Irgendwie hatte sie begriffen, daß sie unverletzbar war, und tatsächlich zischten alle Geschosse an ihr vorbei. Sie saß da wie in einem besonders guten Film. So etwas hatte sie schon lange nicht mehr erlebt, und ich auch nicht.

Vor einiger Zeit wurde ich auf der Straße, direkt vor meinem Haus, von einem Herrn, der einen Hund ausführte, mit einer Pistole bedroht, weil ich etwas über seinen Hund gesagt hatte. Der Herr war sehr betrunken, ich ein bißchen. Der Hund war ein Chow-Chow. Ich trug eine dunkelrote Indianerjacke, die ich heute nicht mehr trage. Damals war 1968. Der betrunkene Herr versprach mir den sofortigen Tod, und es war seltsam, das Klicken des Entsicherungshahns zu hören. Ich hatte das Geräusch vorher nur im Film gehört. Der betrunkene Herr, der, physiognomisch gesehen, etwas von einem Zuhälter an sich hatte, schlug mir im Rhythmus seiner schnellen Worte den Revolver um die Ohren. Ich hielt den Atem an und sprach beruhigend auf ihn ein.

Neben mir standen Susanne und der Versicherungsaquisitör. Susanne sagte nichts, d. h. ich hörte nicht, was sie sagte, und ich war froh, daß der Versicherungsaquisitör nicht seinen Stockdegen zog, denn er ist einer, der zu Husarenstücken neigt. Erst als ich oben in meiner Wohnung saß, versagten die Beine unter mir. Noch nie im Leben und bisher nie wieder habe ich einen Schnaps nötiger gebraucht. Das war übrigens nicht in dieser Wohnung hier, obwohl man von ihr aus das Haus Goethes auch nicht sah. Jenes Haus gehörte einem Herrn, der uns die Wohnung mit dem Argument kündigte, ich sei ein maoistischer Advokat und Susanne ein Flittchen. Dabei ist Susanne mit mir verheiratet, ich habe Germanistik studiert, und Mao ist tot.

Meine jetzige Wohnung zittert, wenn ein Omnibus vorbeifährt. Überhaupt hört man bei uns zu Hause viel mehr als man sieht. Oben hört man die Spanier, unten die Oma des Hausbesitzers, und man riecht die Küchen von beiden. Autos hört man überhaupt immer, die höre ich schon gar nicht mehr, auch wegen Beethoven. Susanne sagt zuweilen, wenn wir nicht einschlafen können, daß man sich an alles gewöhnt. Ich sage dann, daß man sich an Schwefel in der Luft, PVC im Essen und Arsen im Wasser nicht gewöhnt. Manchmal beneide ich Schriftsteller wie

Goethe, die zu einer Zeit lebten, wo die sozialen Ungerechtigkeiten für alle klar und deutlich waren, wie Holzschnitte. Männer, Frauen und Kinder verhungerten auf der Straße. Goethe mußte nur aus dem Fenster schauen. Erstaunlicherweise schrieb er dann doch Hermann und Dorothea. Wie dem auch sei, heute ist auch alles voll von Gegnern und sozial Schiefgelaufenem, aber alles ist auch diffuser und unfaßbarer, weil niemand verhungert, sondern alle einen Opel haben und glücklich sind. Ich habe auch ein Auto, ich bin auch glücklich, ich habe das Auto schon nur, um von diesem Haus hier in mein anderes zu kommen, das bei Sesenheim, das mir zu einem Sechstel gehört.

Vor einiger Zeit saß ich am Fernseher, und das Fernsehen zeigte ein brennendes Hochhaus, und ich dachte, ja Herrgott, das kenne ich doch, und da endlich drehte ich mich um und sah das brennende Hochhaus unserm Haus gegenüber. Irgendwer hatte es angezündet, weil der Besitzer ein Perser war oder ein Kapitalist oder beides. Das Hochhaus wurde dann gelöscht, und ein Kranführer, der mit seinem Kran durch die Flammenwand hindurchgefahren war und das Haus gerettet hatte, bekam vom Perser oder Kapitalisten persönlich einen Scheck über 5000 DM überreicht. Ich sah das Foto der Schecküberrei-

chung in der Zeitung, der Perser oder Kapitalist
lächelte und drückte dem Kranführer die Hand.
Er sah dabei in die Kamera. Der Kranführer, der
einen Plastic-Helm aufhatte, sah den Perser oder
Kapitalisten an. Er hatte ein ernstes Gesicht und
keine Augenbrauen mehr.

Oft gehen wir ins Bahnhofsviertel. Als wir das
erste Mal da waren, steckte Susanne einen Groschen in den Schlitz einer Glücksmaschine, und
vierzehn Mark rasselten heraus. Wir gingen auch
in eine Bar, in der alle Gäste Neger oder
Schwarze waren und zu je einem Drittel Heroin-
händler, Heroinkunden und Heroinfahnder.
Man sagte mir später, daß alle Weißen in dieser
Bar ein Messer in den Rücken gesteckt bekämen,
und seither gehe ich nicht mehr hin. Ich war dafür kürzlich in so einer Fickbierbar, in der unzäh-
lige Kurzfilme gezeigt wurden, die das Wunder
der Liebe nicht, wie im Kino, in Spielhandlungen
kleideten zum Beispiel, der Briefträger bringt
einen Eilbrief, und die Hausfrau duscht gerade
etc. –, sondern die sofort und ausschließlich den
Rausch der tiefsten Leidenschaften zeigten. Ich
hatte in allen Zeitungen immer wieder gelesen, es
komme täglich vor, daß Geschäftsleute aus Würz-
burg oder Kuweit für ein Bier 700 Mark bezahlen mußten, aber wir bezahlten 2,50 pro Flasche
und wurden von einer netten Frau in einem Ho-

senanzug bedient. Jeden Tag lese ich von Erschos-
senen und Angeschossenen. Kein Mensch sieht bei
uns aus dem Fenster, wenn ein Schuß kracht. Erst
eine auf Serie geschaltete Maschinenpistole läßt
uns aufspringen, denn das ist die Polizei, nur die
Polizei kann sich solche Waffen leisten. Früher,
als sie die Anarchisten noch öffentlicher als heute
jagte, pflegte sie um sechs Uhr früh mit Nagel-
schuhen unsre Wohnungstüren einzutreten, und
wenn dann einer von unsern Freunden nackt
nachsehen ging, was denn da los war, wurde er in
Notwehr erschossen.

So gesehen, bin ich froh, daß ich früher einmal
bei der Schweizer Armee war. Ich habe gelernt,
unsere Ostgrenze gegen unsere Feinde zu vertei-
digen. Wenn der Krieg im Raum Oensingen
stattfindet, schwöre ich, daß kein Russe einer
Schweizer Frau ein Leid antun wird, solange ich
dastehe mit meinem Karabiner in der Hand. Ich
bin auch an der Leuchtpistole ausgebildet, das ist
ein Instrument, mit dem man einen chemischen
Scheinwerfer in den Himmel schießen kann. Für
etwa eine Minute verwandelt sich die Nacht in
einen diffusen Tag, und man kann auch den
schleichendsten Russen genau erkennen. Manchmal bedaure ich, daß ich alle Waffen abliefern
mußte, als ich ins Exil ging, besonders die Leuchtpistole hätte ich gern. Ich wohne direkt neben

dem Palmengarten, der uns im Sommer immer mit Sommernachtsfesten erfreut. Da schießen sie dann Raketen in den Himmel, die Sterne machen. Dann habe ich immer Lust, mich mit meinen Leuchtpatronen einzumischen. Ohh, würden die Frankfurter Bürger rufen, was ist denn das für ein Licht, das da im Osten aufstrahlt? Mit den andern Waffen, die ich beherrsche, wüßte ich heute weniger anzufangen. Ich war ein mittelmäßiger Karabinerschütze. Das gibt mir heute zuweilen trotzdem den Mut, am Wäldchestag auf eine Rose zu schießen, für Susanne. Meistens habe ich sie tatsächlich in ein zwei Schüssen. Am letzten Wäldchestag, wir hatten einen gemeinsamen Kummer und tranken reichlich Apfelwein, traf ich sogar einen mikroskopisch kleinen Knopf, der ein Blitzlichtgerät und eine Polaroidkamera auslöste. Man sieht uns zwei auf dem Foto, mich mit einem zugekniffenen Auge und dem Gewehr, Susanne mit einem ernsten Gesicht und einem Teddybären im Arm. Ich lernte auch Handgranaten werfen. Wir mußten das Deckelchen am Stielende abschrauben, die Kordel fassen, sie mit einem satten Ruck abziehen, bis zehn zählen und die Granate wegwerfen. Die Rekruten aus Bern mußten nur bis fünf zählen. Meistens allerdings warfen wir nur so Metallklötzchen, da war es egal, wie schnell man zählte. Die letzte Waffe, die ich beherrsche, ist eben die Maschinenpistole. Wenn wir mit ihr übten, sahen wir wie ganz viele Bankräuber aus. Die Schüsse ratterten aus den Maschinenpistolen heraus, bevor wir den Abzug auch nur anfaßten, und daß einige von uns noch leben, ist ein Wunder. So gesehen, kann ich keinem Polizisten einen Vorwurf daraus machen, daß er einen unbewaffneten nackten Freund von mir erschossen hat.

Ich weiß nie recht, was ist die widerwärtigere Form von Gewalt, das Stellmesser eines Kneipengasts oder eine vierspurige Autobahn. Uns gegenüber, wenn ich ans Küchenfenster gehe, steht ein Bürohaus. Es ist vollklimatisiert und hat riesige Fenster. Ich kann in die Büros hineinsehen, und die Büroleute in meine Küche. Manchmal, wenn ich um sieben Uhr früh schlaftrunken aufs Klo tappe, sehe ich zu meinem Entsetzen, daß in allen Büros schon Leute sitzen und Briefe tippen oder Brote auswickeln oder Zeitung lesen. Manchmal, wenn es mit meiner eigenen Arbeitsmoral nicht so weit her ist, setze ich mich ans Küchenfenster und schaue denen im Bürohaus zu. Ich sehe dann, daß die Angestellten zwar alle immer da sind, daß sie aber überhaupt nichts arbeiten. Nur die Sekretärinnen tippen. Sie haben Stöpsel in den Ohren, und wenn sie allein im Büro sind, öffnen sie ihre Handtaschen und machen sich frisch. Ich versuche zu erraten, wer mit wem telefoniert. Wenn zwei Telefonierer in ihren Zimmern gleichzeitig aufhängen, nehme ich an, daß es *ein* Gespräch war. Es gibt zuweilen Dramen. Da war zum Beispiel ein weißhaariger Herr, der immer eine Arbeitsschürze trug und auch wenn ich um sechs Uhr aufs Klo tappte schon in seinem Büro saß. Oft zitierte er jüngere Mitarbeiter zu sich. Er sprach dann viel und hatte einen roten Kopf, während die Mitarbeiter schweigend dastanden. Er schlug mit der flachen Hand auf Pläne oder Gutachten. Eines Morgens stand in seinem Büro ein zweiter Schreibtisch, seinem gegenüber, und daran saß ein jüngerer Herr in einem gutsitzenden Anzug. Der Mann in der Schürze wirkte jetzt ganz klein, und vierzehn Tage später war er verschwunden. Ich bin sicher, er ist tot, obwohl ich keinen Leichenwagen habe vorfahren sehen. Es gibt auch einen großen Saal mit Zeichentischen, vor denen Männer in weißen Schürzen stehen. Das heißt, meistens stehen sie am Fenster und warten darauf, daß ein Radfahrer auf den Geleisen ausgleitet. Einmal stand an einem der Zeichenbretter ein Neger oder Schwarzer, er trug einen knallroten Pullover und hatte weiße Zähne, wenn er lachte. Am nächsten Morgen trug er einen grauen Pullover, am dritten eine weiße Schürze, am vierten war er nicht mehr da. Ich vermute, er wurde nach

Ghana zurückgeschickt, wo er rote Pullover tragen darf. Dafür wurde er vielleicht inzwischen auf einem Marktplatz öffentlich aufgehängt, weil er nach ein paar Bieren abschätzige Bemerkungen über den Staatschef gemacht hatte. Ich weiß nie sicher, welche Gewalt die ekligere ist, das Aufhängen in roten Pullovern oder das Lebenlassen in grauen.

Übrigens ist die Möglichkeit, durch langes Hinüberschauen eine Bekanntschaft anzuknüpfen, gering, denn die Menschen im Bürohaus sind immer wieder andere. Kaum jemand bleibt länger als ein paar Monate. Nur ich bleibe ständig in meiner Wohnung. Kaum nicke ich einer Sekretärin zu, während ich am Mittag meinen Quark löffle, ist sie auch schon entlassen oder geht. Auch habe ich immer noch keine Ahnung, was da drüben hergestellt oder verwaltet wird. Franz Kafka würde sich nach seinen gemütlichen Amtsstuben sehnen, wenn er das sähe. Ein Büromensch zu seiner Zeit wußte, was für einen traurigen Job er hatte, und das bißchen Bestechungsgeld war das mindeste, was sein Leib und seine Seele brauchten. Im Bürohaus meinem Haus gegenüber herrscht jedoch immer eine gute Laune. Ständig wird irgendein Betriebsgeburtstag gefeiert. Ich bin ja überhaupt nur Schriftsteller geworden, weil ich Betriebsgeburtstage hasse. Früher, als man dafür

Geld bekam, konnte jeder zweite über ein Drahtseil von Kirchturm zu Kirchturm gehen. Jeder achte stürzte ab, aber die andern hatten ein gutes Leben, die Frauenherzen flogen ihnen zu, wenn sie wieder unten waren, und der Bürgermeister spendierte ihnen ein Essen. Dann zogen sie ins nächste Städtchen weiter, möglichst in eines mit nicht allzu hohen Türmen, denn kein einziger Seiltänzer war schwindelfrei. Erfinder erfanden Dinge, die es überhaupt noch nicht gab und die sie trotzdem verkaufen konnten. Zigeuner schleppten riesige Magneten und Kühlschränke mit sich übers Land, und staunende Menschenmengen zahlten einen Groschen, um zu sehen, wie die Zaubermaschine Nägel aus Särgen riß und wie Eisberge mitten in den Sommer hineinwuchsen. Wandersleute zeugten Töchter mit Frauen, deren Vornamen sie nicht genau kannten. Zwanzig Jahre später kamen sie dann in das Dorf zurück und drehten sich nach jedem jungen Mädchen mit blonden Zöpfen um. Sie versuchten sich zu entscheiden, welche es sei, sie entschieden sich auch, aber dann setzten sie sich doch still in die Kneipe und tranken ein paar Biere und reisten wieder ab. Sie wollten einsam bleiben, und sie hatten ja auch anderswo Töchter. Schmuggler schmuggelten Reissäcke über Gebirge und verkauften den Reis von Tür zu Tür, und wenn sie

ihn nicht loswurden, sammelten sie im Wald
Pilze und Holz und kochten einen Risotto. Piani-
sten traten zu Wettkämpfen an, wie heute Boxer,
einer war dann der Sieger und kam eine Runde
weiter. Mozart hat tausende von Hammerkla-
vierspielern auf dem Gewissen, aber die starben
auch nicht daran, sondern verdienten sich ihr
Brot in Bierbars und Bordellen, wo sie *Ah vous
dirai-je Maman* und ähnliches spielten. Manchmal kam Mozart und trank ein Bier, und nach
dem vierten Bier spielten sie vierhändig *Ah vous
dirai-je Maman,* und beide spielten plötzlich
genau gleich gut oder schlecht. Ich kenne heute
nur noch etwa zwölf Personen, die ein bißchen so
leben. Wenn mich Irma, meine Tochter, besucht,
sagt sie, daß die Bafög und die Beihilfe und die
Ersatzkasse und die Rentenversicherung und die
Studienplatzunterstützung und die Begabtenför-
derung und die Alters- und Hinterbliebenenkasse
sie im Stich gelassen hätten. Von 1000 Mark im
Monat könne niemand leben. Da ich auch nicht
von 1000 Mark im Monat lebe, nicke ich, gebe ihr
hundert Mark, und wir gehen in ein italienisches
Restaurant Spaghetti essen.

III

Im Himmel über meinem Haus fliegen Flugzeuge, in ihren Luftkorridoren hoch über Rhein-Main. Ich sehe sie, ihre allmählich verflatternden weißen Schweife, aber sie sehen mich nicht, sie sehen nur die gleißende Sonne und unter sich die Staubdecke über Frankfurt. Hier unten kommt es vor, daß ich nicht atme. Es kommt vor, daß ich ein heißes Bad mit Fichtennadelschaum nehme. Trotzdem habe ich zuweilen einen verspannten Rücken und ein schmerzendes Kreuz, wegen meiner Wut.

An manchen Tagen trinke ich Chianti aus Doppelliterflaschen. An andern Tagen wage ich es nicht, an einem Korken auch nur zu riechen. Manchmal sitze ich da an meinem Fenster und denke, daß in der nächsten Zehntelsekunde ein Atomblitz am Horizont sichtbar wird, und noch eine Zehntelsekunde später wird mich die Druckwelle erreichen. Weißwein macht mich dann böse, Bier macht mich dumm, und Rotwein traurig. Entweder starre ich dann dumpf in eine Ecke, oder ich schreie, Schluß jetzt, ab sofort greife ich an.

Oft bin ich auch froh und weiß nicht warum. Alles stimmt. Geht aber alles allzu lang einen allzu ruhigen Gang stillen Glücks, werde ich immer sirriger. Ich würde dann jede Gefahr auf mich nehmen, um von einer bestürzenden Schönheit überrumpelt zu werden, fast jede Gefahr.

Nachts lausche ich manchmal auf die Atemzüge Susannes und lege mein Ohr auf ihr Herz. Dann stehe ich am Fenster und suche die Milchstraße. Tagsüber arbeite ich. Unten, vor der Trinkhalle, sind vor ein paar Wochen Schilder montiert worden, auf denen, wenn man sie herunterklappt, Smog steht. Man muß dann Hessen 3 einschalten, und die Sprecherin wird uns sagen, in welchem Rhythmus wir atmen müssen.

Ich kann mir denken, daß der Reiter über den Bodensee tot zusammengebrochen ist, weil er plötzlich Festland unter sich spürte. Er hatte immer gewußt, daß die Ebene, auf der er galoppierte, ein See war. Er hatte gehofft, der See sei unendlich.

Früher, als meine Eltern jung waren, war überall auf der Erde so viel gleichwertige Luft, daß sie sie wie Luft behandeln konnten. Zuweilen herrschte an einem Punkt der Erde ein sehr hoher und an einem andern ein sehr tiefer Luftdruck. Dann bewegten sich die Lüfte dazwischen in einer rasenden Geschwindigkeit. Der Orkan deckte Häuser ab und riß Bäume um. Zu viel Luft war die einzige Form von Luft, die meine Eltern zur Kenntnis nahmen. Vögel wurden über hunderte von Kilometern geschleudert. Es gab Vögel. Das war so um 1930 herum.

Ein ferner Verwandter von mir, ein Franzose, zog schon um 1877 auf eine Südseeinsel. Er malte dort viele Bilder und lebte mit einer Eingeborenen, obwohl er in Europa eine Frau und eine Tochter hatte. Die Südseefrau und er hatten auch eine Tochter, die Nâoum hieß, aber mein Verwandter sagte Mimi zu ihr. Beide d. h. später alle drei schrieben meinen Urgroßeltern Ansichtskarten mit von meinem Verwandten gemalten Ansichten, die immer seine Südseefrau, eine dicke braune Schönheit mit Mandelaugen und großen Brüsten, und das Kind, ein Mädchen mit sehr ernsten Augen, darstellten. Ich weiß nicht, was meinen Verwandten zur Flucht bewogen hat, die Luft war es jedenfalls nicht. Immer wieder rudert irgendein Wikinger in einem Einbaum nach Neufundland, oder ein einsamer Pinguin hält nach den Galapagos-Inseln Ausschau. Ich jedenfalls habe früher auch daran gedacht, auf und davon zu schwimmen. Wir alle haben das einmal gedacht. Wir haben aber auch alle gedacht, dazu ist es jetzt zu spät, wenn wir jetzt ankommen in Ozeanien, steht dort eine amerikanische Luftwaffenbasis oder ein Chemiewerk, das ohne Sicherheitsbestimmungen arbeitet, weil ringsherum nur Eingeborene leben. Diese dachten sich nichts dabei, als, so um 1965 herum, ein paar Amerikaner mit Meßlatten auf der Insel herumgingen. Später schossen sie zwei oder drei mit Giftpfeilen tot. Heute haben sie Kinder mit Bleibeinen, und damit sind sie noch gut bedient. Das alles ist unglaublich entsetzlich, die Banken und die Schnellstraßen und die lachenden jungen Familien auf den Plakatwänden. Andrerseits, vom Smog einmal abgesehen, leben wir hier gut. In der Kleinmarkthalle gibt es immer Trauben aus Sizilien und Avocados aus dem Libanon. Und auch die Luft ist besser als in Athen oder Teheran. Zum mindesten ist sie besser überwacht. Von meinem Fenster aus sehe ich die Windräder, Sonden und Meßtrichter des Amtes für Umweltschutz. Jeden Tag steigt ein Mann in einer weißen Arbeitsschürze auf das Gerüst mit den Instrumenten und liest sie ab. Später hängt er eine Tabelle in den Schaukasten vor dem Amt, auf der steht, was wir eingeatmet haben.

Kürzlich fuhr ich in den Taunus, aber als ich im Gipfelwind stand, spürte ich ein heftiges Reißen in der Lunge. Ich ertrug die Luft nicht. In der Nacht darauf träumte ich, daß mir ein Schaf und eine Katze in die Arme gesprungen seien. Sie preßten sich gegen mich. Sie waren beide abgehäutet. Ich spürte ihr Fleisch auf meinem.

Einmal, als ich noch zur Schule ging, so um

1945 herum, hatte ich versäumt, zum obligatorischen Röntgen der Lungen zum Schularzt zu gehen. Ich wurde deshalb als einziger Knabe mit den Mädchen mitgeschickt. In einem großen Umkleideraum zogen wir uns aus. Die Mädchen kicherten. Sie banden sich die langen Haare mit Tüchern hoch. Dann wickelten sie auch mir ein Tuch um den Kopf. Als ich in den Behandlungsraum kam, lachten der Arzt und die Krankenschwestern.

Eine Zeitlang tauschte ich meine Geschichten gegen die einer Schriftstellerin, die mir sympathisch war. Sie las sie dann an ihren Lesungen, und ich las ihre an meinen. Wir sahen uns eine Zeitlang Tag und Nacht. Ich liebte sie. Später bekam sie ein Kind und zog mit dem Vater des Kinds, einem Wirt, in den Spessart. Sie kochte für das Gasthaus. Ihr Kind, eine Tochter, wuchs heran. Als sie sie eines Morgens mit einem Mann aus der Scheune kommen sah, wußte sie, daß wieder eine Generation vorüber war. Der Mann war ein Lyriker, und alles fing wieder von vorne an. Er war einer, der immer auf die Empfindungen in seinem Innern horchte und sie dann sofort aufschrieb. Er erzählte mir damals, er habe eine Holunderallergie, ein einziges Holunderstäubchen genüge und er keuche wie eine Dampfpfeife. Die Tochter sagte, davon habe sie nie etwas bemerkt, sie seien tagelang in Holundergebüschen gelegen, und wenn ihr Freund gekeucht habe, dann nicht wegen des Holunders. Andrerseits habe sie eine Freundin, sie teilten im Büro zusammen einen Schreibtisch, sie erzählten sich alles und jedes, sie äßen zusammen, sie liebten sich, sie hätten fast zusammen eine Wohnung genommen, sie tauschten die Kleider aus, das zum Beispiel seien die Jeans von ihrer Freundin, die jetzt ihren roten Samtrock trage. Trotzdem sei ihr die Luft weggeblieben, als sie, nach einer Nacht, in der sie traumlos geschlafen hatte, hörte, daß ihre Freundin zum Abteilungsleiter, einem Herrn Hamburger, den sie beide immer für ein Riesenarschloch gehalten hatten, du und Günter sagte. Ich sagte, weil mich die Tochter der Schriftstellerin ansah, so sei das im Leben. Kaum stehe man auf einem Teppich, werde er einem unter den Füßen weggezogen. Zum Beispiel, ein irischer Mönch entwickelt ein kompliziertes Reimschema, und ein französischer Diplomat füllt es mit seinen Empfindungen und bekommt dafür den Nobelpreis. Man sagt, sagte ich zur Tochter der Schriftstellerin, daß, wer einmal gehört hat, wie seine Mutter unter seinem Vater keucht, später nie mehr ruhig atmen kann. Ich kannte einen, der sah im Fernsehen Laurel und Hardy, da wo sie das Auto eines cholerischen Herrn demontieren, der seinerseits ihres zertrümmert, und als Laurel, falls Laurel der dicke ist, gerade einen Kotflügel abfetzte, atmete der, den ich kannte, aus und nicht mehr ein und war tot. Das war 1968, während einer Retrospektive des anarchistischen Films. Es gibt Leute, sagte ich zur Tochter der Schriftstellerin, deren Muskeln wehren sich gegen unbekannte Gefahren. Man kann Kinder wie Holzscheite nach Hause tragen, wenn sie wütend sind, oder unglücklich, oder entsetzt, oder verzweifelt, oder einsam.

Als Kind stand ich zuweilen auch bolzstarr im Garten, oder in einer Zimmerecke. Oder wenn ich in einem fahrenden Eisenbahnzug saß, sah ich mich neben dem Zug einherrennen, draußen. Ich schnellte über Hütten und Hecken. Größere Hindernisse mußte ich umgehen, ich verlor mich dabei oft beinah aus den Augen, dann mußte ich hinter dem Zug herhetzen, bis ich wieder auf der Höhe meines Abteilfensters war. Wenn ich starr war, dachte ich an ein Land, mein Land. Ich war wie blöd. Mein Land in mir drin sah aus wie die wirkliche Welt. Es war voller Blumen, Straßen, Licht, Eisenbahnen, Frauen, Männer, Kinder. Ich war in ihm Lokführer, Mittelstürmer, Wirt und Staatschef. Ich hatte eine eigene Sprache, die in einer eigenen Schrift zu schreiben war. Ich zeichnete mein Land, das Bubien hieß, in Wachstuchhefte. Von jeder Seite zur andern führten Tunnels, die ich mit einem Taschenmesser ausschnitt, damit die Züge und die Menschen hindurchkonnten. Luft brauchten sie keine. Es gab mehr Schweine als Kühe, weil Schweine leichter zu zeichnen waren. Ein Freund von mir hatte ähnliche Hefte. Auch sein Land hieß Bubien. Unsre Hauptstädte hießen wie wir. Der Unterschied zwischen uns Staatchefs war, daß mein Freund sein Land nach der wirklichen Welt und ich die wirkliche Welt nach meinem Land formen wollte. Mein Freund hatte eine Zeitlang eine Atemtechnik, die darin bestand, daß er die Luft in einem wilden Ansauger in die Lungen holte und sie dann in kleinen Stößchen wieder ausatmete. Er hatte auch eine besondere Lauftechnik: eine halbe Stunde lang belastete er nur das linke Bein und eine halbe Stunde lang nur das rechte. So hatte er immer ein frisches Bein.

Meine Eltern erzählten mir, daß die Tenöre und Sopranistinnen, mit denen sie in den Zwanzigerjahren befreundet waren, Lungen wie Luftmatratzen hatten. Ich besitze zwei 78-Touren-Platten, aus denen ihr Atem weht. Damals ließen sich die Sänger noch nicht von Komponisten vorschreiben, was sie zu singen hatten. Das Ariensingen war ein Kampf, wer den langen Ton länger aushielt. Es gab Sänger, deren Stimmen noch

durch die Nacht hallten, wenn alle Opernbesu-
cher längst zu Hause waren. Heute könnte niemand mehr aus einem zugebundenen Kartoffel-
sack heraussingen, wie Gilda. Ich erinnere mich,
1960 mußte ich Kartoffelsäcke von Lastwagen
abladen, öffnen und auf eine Rutsche kippen. Der
Kartoffelstaub verstopfte mir jedes Körperloch.
Jede Nacht nieste ich zehn Taschentücher braun.
Es gab Männer, die das ein Leben lang taten, für
4,20 in der Stunde. Da war später die Arbeit im
Hauptpostamt viel besser. Ich war in der Brief-
verteilung, und ich hatte eine Liste mit Adressen,
wenn so ein Brief auftauchte, sortierte ich ihn
aus, und er kam in ein spezielles Büro, aus dem er
nach einer Weile wieder zurückkam. Proust. Alban
Berg. Hemingway. Keller. Mörike. Schiller. Miller.
Alle hatten Schwierigkeiten mit dem Atmen.

Ich erinnere mich auch, daß mein Vater einen
Revolver in der Nachttischschublade hatte. 1945
sah ein Dieb zum Fenster herein, und mein Vater
packte den Revolver und schoß in den Nachthimmel hinaus. Meine Mutter schrie. Ich war sehr erregt. Die Polizei kam mit Sirenengeheul, aber der
Dieb blieb verschwunden. Mein Vater stand unter der Tür, mit seiner rauchenden Pistole in der
Hand. Er hatte sich gewünscht, daß ich eine
Tochter werden würde. Meine Tochter, Irma, ist
jetzt neunzehn. Sie hat braune Augen, wie ihre

Mutter. Ihre Mutter war zart und zierlich. Sie heiratete einen Medizinstudenten, der jetzt Oberarzt ist. Sie zog mit ihm in den Bayrischen Wald ohne mir Adieu zu sagen, 1957. Irma besuchte mich nie, und ich sie nie. Ihre Mutter hatte gesagt, das ist meine Welt, und das deine. Einmal trank ich im Bayrischen Wald zwei drei Biere und sah allen jungen Mädchen mit braunen Augen in die Augen. Ich konnte mich für keine entscheiden. Vor einem Monat klingelte es, und Irma stand da, mit hennaroten Haaren, einem braunen Pulli und Jeans. Ich bin Irma, sagte sie. Ich sagte, komm herein, Irma. Wir gaben uns die Hand, und dann umarmten und küßten wir uns. Jetzt sitzt sie meistens vor dem Fernseher und wartet auf ihren Studienplatz.

Ich setze mich auch manchmal vor den Fernseher, neben Irma. Seit Jahren warte ich darauf, daß Warten auf Godot läuft. Einmal sah ich, sekundenlang, ohne Ton und durch einen heftigen Flimmerschnee, zwei Männer mit Hüten, die mit einem dritten, der einen vierten an einer Leine hielt, redeten. Dann war das Bild wieder weg, ein Irrläufer des algerischen Fernsehens oder sowas. Wie irr fummelte ich an meiner Zimmerantenne herum. Nur eine Sekunde lang tauchte noch einmal der an der Leine aus dem Nebel auf. Er tanzte wie ein Bär.

2

Gespräch mit meinem Kind
über das Treiben der Nazis im Wald

Heute sind wir im Urwald angekommen. Ich stehe unter dem Vordach unsrer Laubhütte und sehe über unsre Lichtung hin. Die Sonne geht langsam hinter uralten Bäumen unter, Mammutbäumen, Palmen, Lianen. Affen schreien. Unser Hund, ein weißer Pudel, streunt durch die Tomaten, die auf der Lichtung wachsen. Ich zerschneide eine Melone und winke mit meiner saftverschmierten Hand unserm Kind, das durch das hohe Gras getrottet kommt. Es trägt ein T-Shirt, auf dem University of Alabama steht, und eine Kapselpistole in der Hand.

Da, wo wir herkommen, lag eine gelbe Schwefelluft über der Stadt. Im Bürohaus, das unsrer Wohnung gegenüber war, gingen Männer auf und ab, mit Diktafonen in der Hand. Ihre Hände zitterten, sie telefonierten, und abends stürzten sie zur Klimaanlage und preßten ihre Münder gegen den Luftstrahl, bis sie dachten, jetzt sehen wir wieder so aus, daß wir nicht entlassen werden.

Früher ging ich zuweilen in alte Filme. Ich

49

starrte mit nassen Augen auf junge Frauen, die darin spielten. Sie waren blond, bleich, und hatten unglaubliche Leidenschaften. Heute, denke ich, wohnen sie in einer Einzimmerwohnung in Los Angeles und haben einen Hund, zu dem sie, wenn sie ihn auf die Terrasse hinaus lassen, sagen: Gell, wir haben uns lieb, Sam.

Ich denke, hier im Urwald werde ich Tomaten ernten, Schnaps brennen, einen Kamin bauen, ein Xylofon konstruieren, Pilze analysieren, Ratatouille kochen, den Wald erforschen, einen Brunnen graben, Leimruten auslegen, Susanne lieben. Das Kind steht vor mir und sieht mich an. Es steckt seine Kapselpistole in den Halfter am Gürtel und streckt die Hand aus. Ich gebe ihm ein Stück Melone.

»In Florida«, sage ich zu ihm, »reiten die Neger auf hohen Wellen, auf denen schwarzer Schaum schäumt. Die Weißen haben ihnen ihre Surfbretter verkauft und fahren jetzt im Himalaya Ski, auf 7000 Meter Höhe, in jungfräulichem Schnee.«

»Ich weiß«, sage ich, »wie der Tod riecht. Ich bebe, wenn mir sein Geruch in die Nase kommt. Mein Großvater setzte sich in die Badewanne und schnitt sich die Pulsadern auf. Er hatte Krebs, und die Pest wütet in Indien, wo die Menschen zu Millionen verhungern.«

Das Kind sieht mich an. Es streckt die Hand aus, und ich gebe ihm noch ein Stück Melone. Es beißt hinein. Saft läuft über sein Kinn und das T-Shirt. Ich sehe, daß seine Kapselpistole auf Einzelschuß gestellt ist.

»In San Francisco«, sage ich zu ihm, »ist ein Mann von einer großen Hängebrücke gesprungen. Die Reporter fragten ihn: Na, wie wars, der Tod? Noch nie in meinem Leben war ich so glücklich wie während den paar Sekunden Flug, sagte der Mann. Jetzt schauen ihn alle aus den Augenwinkeln an, ob er nochmals startet, er aber setzt seine Füße aufs Pflaster, als könnte er jeden Augenblick jeden Halt verlieren.«

»Nämlich, Martin Bormann trat vor drei Monaten am frühen Morgen aus dieser Laubhütte hier. Affen schrien, und in der Ferne brüllten Lamas. Martin Bormann witterte. Was für eine gute Luft, dachte er. Ab sofort stehe ich jeden Tag um 5 Uhr auf, das ist ein Befehl. Martin Bormann nahm Haltung an. Er ging auf und ab, glücklich, fast jung. Als seine Männer zum Morgenrapport kamen, sahen sie einen völlig veränderten Chef. Er strahlte. Er dampfte. Er glühte. Sie sahen ihn staunend an, dann sich. Sie grinsten. Sie hauten sich mit ihren Prothesen auf die Schultern. Sie rannten in ihre Hütten zurück und wichsten ihre

Stiefel, und der Wald hallte von ihren Marsch-
schritten wider. Ihre Peitschen knallten wie nie
zuvor. Das Leben ist ein Swinegelrennen, mur-
melte Martin Bormann, während er mit einer
Spritzkanne und braunem Bast in sein Tomaten-
feld ging. Jetzt aber, rief er in den Wald hinein,
stehe *ich* wieder am Ende der Ackerfurchen. Der,
der da rennt, wird an einem Herzschlag sterben.
Gute Zeiten kommen, ich spüre es, rief Martin
Bormann, Kind.«

»Dann, vor etwa zwei Monaten, fuhren wir auf
einem Schiff. Die Wellen waren meterhoch und
eisig. Ich stand tief im Unterdeck an der Bar der
billigen Klasse. Ich trank Bier. Ich hörte das
Dröhnen der Ladung, Kind, die sich aus ihrer
Halterung gelöst hatte und gegen die Schiffs-
wände schlug. Hörst du das? sagte ich zu Susanne. Sie nickte. Sie strich dir über den Kopf.
Wir tranken unsre Gläser leer. Dann lag das
Schiff plötzlich schräg. Die Gläser schlitterten
über den Boden. Wir rannten keuchend die Korridore hinauf, zu den schrägen Treppen. Überall
hasteten stumme Menschen. Verschlafene Köpfe
schauten aus Kabinentüren, wie aus Kanal-
deckeln, wegen der ungewohnten Lage des
Schiffs. Wasser schäumte die Treppen hinunter,
und wir schrien. Ich ließ die Hand Susannes los,

die dich festhielt. Blind wurde ich durch Korridore gespült, und ich weiß nicht, wie ich da herausgekommen bin.«

»Wenn es nach mir ginge«, sage ich zum Kind, »säße ich jetzt nicht auf dieser Lichtung in den Tomaten. Lieber ginge ich über eine unendliche Hochebene, unter einem Hut breit wie ein Wagenrad, in die untergehende Sonne hinein. Alte Frauen oder Männer gingen vor mir her, schwarze Schatten. Dann säße ich mit ihnen vor einer Hütte, wir tränken Wein und redeten wenig und leise, und ich könnte ihre Gesichter kaum erkennen. Wir äßen zusammen, und keiner von uns erwischte das bessere Ende der Wurst. Manchmal berührten sich unsre Hände.«

»Es ging aber nicht nach mir, Kind. Trotzdem dachte ich immer wieder an meinen Traum: daß Martin Bormann aus einer Laubhütte getreten sei, auf einer Lichtung mitten im Urwald, und daß er ausgesehen habe wie neugeboren. Stundenlang fuhren Susanne und ich mit den Zeigefingern über die Karte von Südamerika, bis wir eine Lichtung gefunden hatten, die genau so aussah wie die in meinem Traum. Wie im Fieber packten wir die Rucksäcke: Socken, Unterhosen, Bonbons für dich, Mückenspray, ein Netz, die Karte, ein

Ritterkreuz, ein Foto von Martin Bormann. Gespornt und gestiefelt gingen wir zum Bahnhof. Es wurde eine lange Reise, besonders wegen dem letzten Teil, den wir an ein Stück Reling geklammert zurücklegten. Naß und durchfroren kletterten wir eine Quaimauer des Hafens von Santa Cruz, das liegt in Argentinien, hinauf. Wir setzten uns auf eine Seilrolle und sahen aufs Meer hinaus. Ein Zollbeamter kam auf uns zu. Er blätterte in unsern Pässen und verglich unsre wirklichen Ohren mit denen auf den Fotos. Unschlüssig drehte er das Netz in seinen Händen hin und her. *Porchè utilizar usted esto filho,* sagte er, oder so ähnlich. Ich wollte ihm sagen, daß ich damit Martin Bormann fangen wolle, da aber sah ich, daß er das Ritterkreuz in meinem Rucksack entdeckt hatte. Seine Augen leuchteten. Er gab mir die Hand und lachte. Ich lachte auch. Dann gingen wir durch die Hafenanlagen, zwischen Kabelrollen und Lastwagen hindurch. Ich sah auf die Karte. Überall Urwald, Urwald, Urwald. Da war die Lichtung. Da mußte er sein.«

»Verstehst du«, sage ich zum Kind und wische ihm den Melonensaft vom Kinn, »niemals würde ich allein durch den Urwald gehen. Ich möchte keine Mandolinen töten und keine Türme mit den Fahnen meines Wahnsinns schmücken. Ich möchte nicht mit einem donnernden Schrei den Willen der andern auslöschen. Ohh«, sage ich zum Kind, das mich anstarrt, »ich schreie gern. Ich würde gern mit sieben Bällen jonglieren. Ich liebe das zarte Seufzen von Frauen, und wenn die geladenen Gäste ihre Handflächen gegeneinander schlagen. Ich möchte schon einmal auf einem hohen Seil über die Niagarafälle gehen, Kind. Ich sähe nach unten, in die tosende Gischt, nach oben, in den blauen Himmel, nach vorn, wo auf den Uferfelsen stumme Menschen stünden. Vielleicht nähme ich dich mit. Ich wippte auf dem Seil auf und ab, immer heftiger, unten werden meine Füße naß und oben verschwindet mein Kopf in den Wolken. Wenn wir Glück haben, können wir uns an die Füße eines vorbeirauschenden Kranichs krallen. Ein Sportflugzeug würde es auch tun, eines mit viel Benzin, damit wir nicht gleich wieder in Houston, Texas, oder Cleveland, Ohio, landen müssen. Dort steht dann nämlich ein zentnerschwerer Mann in einer Uniform. Er trägt ein graublaues Hemd, hat langsame Bewegungen und kaut mit einem vorgeschobenen Kinn. Hello, sagt er, Ausweise. Er spielt mit seinem Revolver, während er meinen Paß Seite für Seite durchliest. Als er zur Seite mit dem Foto kommt, dreht er den Paß um. Er spuckt den Kaugummi aus. Seine Lippen bewegen

sich. Ich halte dich auf meinem Arm, Kind, weil
du noch keinen eigenen Paß hast. Ihr Kind? sagt
der Beamte. Ja, sage ich. Schriftsteller? sagt er.
Ja, sage ich. Das muß, sagt der Beamte, ein wenn
auch faszinierendes so doch auch einsames Metier
sein, nicht wahr, Sir?«

»Einunddreißig Jahre lang ging Martin Bormann
jeden Morgen in seine Tomatenstauden, bis vor
einem Monat. Er stand aufrecht da und schaute
über die Lichtung, die er und seine Männer gero-
det hatten. Die Sonne brannte. Martin Bormann
nahm den Strohhut ab und wischte sich den
Schweiß von der Stirn. Er sah zum Himmel hinauf, immer wieder, jeden Tag, bis er eine kleine
schwarze Wolke sah, die hoch oben vorbeitrieb.
Er hatte von ihr geträumt. Er zitterte. Er hatte
den Anblick von Asche nie ertragen können.
Seufzend setzte er seinen Hut wieder auf und
streichelte seinen Hund. Vielleicht siehst du später einmal zum Himmel hinauf, sagte er leise zu
ihm, und dann siehst du zwei schwarze Wolken
von Horizont zu Horizont ziehen, die Aschen
von meinem Freund und mir, auf unsrer Umlauf-
bahn.«

»Tagelang kämpften wir uns durch den Urwald, du, Susanne, und ich. Mit Macheten schlugen wir Wege durch die Lianen, wir aßen Pilze und tranken Kokosnußmilch und saugten uns gegenseitig Schlangenbißwunden aus. Ich war unrasiert und stank, Susanne hatte ein rotes Gesicht und wirre Haare, und du warst voller Mückenstiche. Erschöpft brachen wir schließlich an einem Tümpel zusammen. Wir haben uns verirrt, wir werden hier sterben, flüsterte ich, wir können nicht mehr. Susanne nickte. Dann glotzten wir vor uns hin, Hand in Hand. Plötzlich fuhren wir wie auf Befehl in die Höhe. Ganz deutlich hörten wir das Singen von Männerstimmen, und wir kannten das Lied. Ich packte Susanne am Arm. Das ist er, flüsterte ich. Im Gänsemarsch schlichen wir durch Farnkräuter, auf Zehen- und Fingerspitzen, um keine Spuren zu hinterlassen.«

»In Nagasaki nämlich«, sage ich, während das Kind und ich zusehen, wie der Hund hinter einem Affen drein durch die Tomaten rennt, »in Nagasaki fuhr ein Mann an jenem Tag zweihundert Kilometer nach Norden, geschäftlich. Er hörte dort oben davon. Seine Frau, sein Kind, sein Vater, seine Mutter, seine Schwester, seine Freunde, tot. Er hatte von niemandem ein Foto. Die Fotos waren verglüht. Der Mann aus Nagasaki vergaß, wie seine Frau und seine Kinder aussahen. Er konnte sich nicht mehr an ihre Stimmen erinnern. Er versuchte es, stundenlang. Nur manchmal, wie ein Blitz, hörte er sie, deutlich, nah und heftig. Das ist alles wahr.« Das Kind sieht mich an. »Noch ein Stück Melone«, sagt es und richtet die Kapselpistole auf den Hund, der unter einer Palme steht und bellt. »Nein«, sage ich. Ich sehe, wie die Gesichtsmuskeln des Kinds zu zucken anfangen. »In Japan«, sage ich schnell, »werden jetzt schon Japaner gebaut, die haben ihren Fotoapparat nicht mehr über dem Bauch baumeln. Sie haben ihn in sich eingebaut. Wenn sie mit den Augen zwinkern, gibt es ein Foto. Jeden Abend ziehen sie sich den belichteten Film aus dem Arschloch und schauen, wie der Tag gewesen ist.«

»Oder werden wir doch einmal lange schmale Serpentinenpfade hinuntergehen, hoch über den bewohnten Gebieten, du, deine Mutter und ich? Früher, unsre Väter, als sie aus Spanien zurückkamen, wurden sie ins Gefängnis gesteckt. Sie hatten verloren. Dort oben in den Bergen, werden wir denken, da oben haben die Faschisten nichts zu sagen, wir können uns nicht vorstellen, daß die Bergbewohner auf ihre Parolen hören. Sie sind stur, aber sie haben eine gute Nase für verlogenen Firlefanz. Sie schneiden den Söhnen den Schwanz ab, wenn sie sie mit der Mutter im Heu erwischen, aber Ruhe und Ordnung und schwarze Uniformen mögen sie gar nicht. Im obersten Bergdorf werden die Bauern sofort merken, daß wir, trotz unsern Wanderschuhen und Geigenkästen, kein herumziehendes Orchester sind. Ein alter Jeep wird uns zur Bahnstation herunterfahren. Wir kommen zum Sammelpunkt, nicht weit vom Ort, wo der Führer des letzten Regimes aufgehängt worden ist. Wir wollen niemanden aufhängen, wir wollen nicht aufgehängt werden, wir wollen zusammen bleiben. Wir werden ein Foto von uns machen. Wir werden an die vielen Geschichten denken, in denen es endgültige Trennungen gab. Nie mehr sahen sich die Geliebten. Wir werden denken, einmal sind es dann plötzlich keine Geschichten mehr. Zum ersten Mal schauen wir uns an, wie noch nie.«

»In Wirklichkeit aber, Kind, lagen wir in den Farngebüschen am Rand der Lichtung. Fliegen surrten um unsre Köpfe. Ich bog die Kräuter auseinander und sah, daß die Männer Martin Bormanns, in zerfetzten, glänzenden Stiefeln und mit Holzprügeln auf den Schultern, in Zweierkolonne davon marschierten. Sie schleuderten beim Gehen die Beine von sich weg und wendeten ruckartig den Kopf, als sie vor Martin Bormann vorbeigingen. Dieser stand auf einer Kiste. Schau, der Mann dort, riefst du. Ich hielt dir die Hand auf den Mund und zischelte, du bekommst eine elektrische Eisenbahn, wenn du jetzt nur jetzt ein einziges Mal den Mund hältst. Ich löste mein Netz vom Rucksack. Der Urwald war jetzt völlig still. Ich sah, wie Martin Bormann, zusammen mit einem Hund, zu einem Tomatenbeet ging. Er blieb stehen, nahm den Strohhut vom Kopf, sah lange in den Himmel hinauf, seufzte und wischte sich mit der Hand über die Stirn. Auch der Hund sah nach oben. Ich warf das Netz. Mit einem Ruck zog ich es zu. Zu dritt zogen wir das zappelnde Bündel zu uns in die Farnbüsche, und dann lag Martin Bormann vor uns, zusammen mit seinem Hund und einigen Tomaten. Er stöhnte. Kein Laut, zischte ich auf deutsch, sonst setzt es was. Martin Bormann und sein Hund starrten uns mit offenen Mündern an.«

»Stundenlang gingen wir dann über sonnenglühende Ebenen, zwischen Kakteen und Felsen, unter denen Schlangen verschwanden. Ich ging vorn, dann ging Martin Bormann an einem Seil, dann, an einer Leine, der Hund, dann Susanne, dann du, mit deiner entsicherten Kapselpistole. Krächzende Vögel kreisten über uns. Wir schwitzten. Ich nestelte die Wasserflasche von meinem Gürtel los, trank und gab sie Martin Bormann. Dieser trank und steckte sie dem Hund in den Mund. Der Hund trank wie ein Irrer.

›Wie siehts denn jetzt in Europa aus?‹ sagte Martin Bormann plötzlich.

›So wie zu Ihrer Zeit ists nicht mehr‹, sagte ich.

›Hm‹, sagte Martin Bormann. ›Gibts denn niemanden mehr, der denkt, was wir denken?‹

›Also das sicher nicht‹, sagte ich. ›Sie sind der letzte von denen.‹

Martin Bormann schwieg. Langsam nahm er dem Hund die Flasche aus dem Mund. Er schraubte sie zu und gab sie mir. Er sah alt aus, verschwitzt und traurig.

›Was werden Sie mit mir tun?‹ sagte er leise.

›Ich bringe Sie nach Deutschland‹, sagte ich.

Martin Bormann seufzte. Er sah zum Himmel hinauf. Dann bückte er sich und kraulte seinen Hund hinter den Ohren. ›Was hab ich gesagt‹, sagte er.«

»Wir reisten im Laderaum eines Schiffs, das Rum transportierte. Es war stockdunkel. Die Luft war stickig. Um keine Angst voreinander zu haben, hielten wir uns an den Händen und sangen Lieder, zuerst meine, dann die Martin Bormanns.

Wir tranken. Wir legten die Arme umeinander. Dann hörte ich, daß du nicht mehr sangst, dann hörte Susanne mit dem Singen auf, dann war der Hund still. Als Martin Bormann aus meinen Armen wegsackte, nahm auch ich einen letzten Schluck und legte mich auf die Planken des schaukelnden Schiffs. Als ich aufwachte, schaukelte das Schiff nicht mehr, und Licht fiel durch eine offene Luke auf uns. Neben mir lag Martin Bormann, schnarchend, mit offenem Mund. Ich erhob mich. Mein Kopf dröhnte. ›Auf!‹ brüllte ich. Martin Bormann fuhr in die Höhe und preßte die Hände an die Hosennähte. Susanne, du und der Hund öffneten erstaunt die Augen. Ich sah euch an: Martin Bormann hatte einen wilden Bart, ein zerrissenes Hemd, rote Augen. Susanne hatte die Schuhe verloren, ihre Haare sahen wie Drahtgeflecht aus, und ihr Gesicht war verschmiert. Du warst von oben bis unten voller Rum. Der Hund war schwarz.

So betraten wir die nächstgelegene Polizeistation, vorne ich, dann, am Seil, Martin Bormann, dann, an der Leine, der Hund, dann Susanne, schließlich du mit deiner Waffe. Der diensthabende Beamte starrte uns an. ›Bitte?‹ sagte er.

›Ich habe Martin Bormann gefangen‹, sagte ich. ›Wen?‹ sagte der Beamte und sah zwischen mir und Martin Bormann hin und her.

›Martin Bormann‹, sagte ich.

›Bormann, Martin‹, sagte der Beamte und blätterte in einem dicken Buch. Er sah mich an. ›Haben wir nicht. Ausweis.‹ Ich gab ihm meinen Paß. Er blätterte darin, sah auf das Foto, dann auf mich. Dann blätterte er wieder im Buch. ›Ihren Namen haben wir auch nicht‹, sagte er. Er schaute uns an, auf das Seil zwischen uns, auf den Hund. Er schrieb meine Personalien auf einen Zettel und warf ihn nach hinten auf einen Tisch, wo ein Beamter in einem grünen Hemd vor dem Bildschirm eines Fahndungscomputers saß. Die beiden sahen sich an. Dann zuckte der Beamte mit den Schultern und gab mir den Paß zurück.

›Ich . . .‹ sagte ich.

›Das interessiert uns nicht‹, sagte der Beamte. ›Ich will jetzt für einmal ein Auge zudrücken, junger Mann. Sie gehen jetzt still hinaus mit ihrem Freund, und Sie lassen sich hier nie mehr blicken.‹

›Aber . . .‹ sagte ich.

›Und zwar heute noch‹, sagte der Beamte und richtete sich auf. Ich nickte und ging, mit Martin Bormann am Seil, der den Hund an der Leine hatte, durch die Tür des Polizeireviers. Ich hörte, wie du hinter uns das Magazin deiner Kapselpistole leerschossest. Draußen schien die Sonne. Wir standen auf dem Trottoir und sahen auf die Hochhäuser, die Autos, die Pizzerias.

›So sieht das also heute aus‹, sagte Martin Bormann und kratzte sich am Kopf.

›Tja‹, sagte ich, während ich das Seil losknüpfte. ›Also dann. Dann machen Sies gut.‹

Ich nickte Susanne und dir zu. Wir gingen los, an einer Selbstbedienungstankstelle vorbei. Du ludest deine Kapselpistole nach. Nach einiger Zeit wandte ich mich um und sah Martin Bormann mit seinem Hund vor der Polizeiwache stehen. Er kratzte sich am Kopf und sah in den Himmel hinauf. Schließlich trottete er in der entgegengesetzten Richtung davon.«

»Als wir zu Hause ankamen, stand ein Mann vor unsrer Wohnungstür.

›Ich bin von der Fremdenpolizei‹, sagte er und schlug sekundenschnell seinen Kragen nach oben. ›Kann ich mal Ihren Paß sehen?‹

›Aber sicher‹, sagte ich. Ich öffnete die Wohnungstür, nickte ihm zu und ging hinter ihm in die Wohnung. Eine dicke Staubluft hing im Korridor. Ich gab dem Beamten den Paß.

›Sie sind also Ausländer‹, sagte er und sah mich an.

›Ja‹, sagte ich.

›Und warum mischen Sie sich in die innern

Angelegenheiten der Bundesrepublik Deutschland?‹ sagte er.

›Ich?‹ sagte ich. ›Tue ich das?‹

›Allerdings‹, sagte er und holte einen Aktenordner aus seiner Tasche. ›Ich habe hier Ihr Dossier. Sie haben viermal unbefugt geparkt. Sie kennen einen Lehrer, der DKP-Mitglied ist. Sie haben einmal in einem portugiesischen Lokal gegessen. Sie schlafen zuweilen bis um neun Uhr früh.‹

›Verzeihung‹, sagte ich. ›Ich habe es nicht bös gemeint.‹

›Na schön‹, sagte er. ›Schon gut. Aber Ihre Aufenthaltsgenehmigung kann ich Ihnen unter diesen Umständen natürlich nicht verlängern, das werden Sie sicher verstehen.‹«

»Nachts um zwei, während wir die Koffer packten, klingelte es. Es war Martin Bormann. Er hatte sich gewaschen und war beim Frisör gewesen. Er trug eine graue Flanellhose, ein weißes Hemd, eine dunkelblaue Krawatte mit einem Wappen und einen blauen Blazer. Der Hund war blütensauber, ein Pudel.

›Entschuldigen Sie‹, sagte er, während er sich setzte und die Beine übereinanderschlug, ›daß ich Sie so spät noch störe.‹

›Aber das macht doch nichts‹, sagte ich.

›Ich habe jemanden gefunden, der sich um mich kümmert‹, sagte er. ›Ich werde im Schwarzwald wohnen.‹

›Wie schön‹, sagte ich.

›Und jetzt habe ich eine Bitte‹, sagte er. ›Könnten Sie nicht auf den Hund aufpassen? Ich möchte mir wieder einen größeren anschaffen.‹

›Nun ja‹, sagte ich. ›Ich reise sowieso morgen ab.‹

›Ah so?‹ sagte Martin Bormann. ›Gefällt es Ihnen nicht mehr bei uns?‹

Ich schwieg. Wir sahen uns an.

›Tja dann‹, sagte Martin Bormann und stand auf. Er streckte mir die Hand hin. Ich legte meine hinein, und er schüttelte sie. Dann ging er zur Tür hinaus. Ich hörte seine schweren sicheren Schritte, wie sie die Treppe hinabgingen. Ich stand da, starr, dann gab ich einem Koffer einen Fußtritt. Ich ging zum Hund und kraulte ihn hinter den Ohren, ein bißchen.«

»Es war ja schließlich sowieso nicht besonders schön da wo wir lebten«, sage ich also zum Kind, während wir Hand in Hand auf unsre Laubhütte zugehen, unter deren Tür jetzt Susanne steht, in einer roten Schürze und mit einer dampfenden Schüssel in der Hand. »Die gelben Schwefeldämpfe am Himmel. Die Autos. Das Arsen im

66

Trinkwasser. Das Strontium 90 im Teich, in dem deine Freunde und Freundinnen gebadet haben. Kürzlich hat man vergessen, daß in einer Aprikosenplantage, in der man Borkenkäfer vernichten wollte, ein Altersheim stand. Interessiert schauten die alten Leute, die heute alle blind sind, zu, wie ein Flugzeug mit einem feinen blauen Sprühregen hinter sich über sie hinwegflog.«

Das Kind bleibt stehen und schaut mich an. »Du hast mir eine elektrische Eisenbahn versprochen«, sagt es. Es richtet seine Pistole auf mich und zuckt mit den Gesichtsmuskeln.

»Ich weiß«, sage ich. »Ich kann nicht immer wie ich will.« Das Kind beginnt zu weinen. Ich beuge mich zu ihm nieder und streichle es. »Wir werden zusammen den Urwald roden«, sage ich. »Wir werden Schnaps brennen und einen Kamin bauen und ein Xylofon konstruieren und das Dach neu decken und einen Brunnen graben und Leimruten auslegen und Susanne lieben beziehungsweise du deine Mutter.«

Das Kind schaut mich mit roten Augen an. Es schluckt. Dann murmelt es: »Ich möchte General werden, oder Pfarrer.«

»Was?« sage ich.

»Da habe ich eine große Verantwortung«, sagt das Kind. »Ich kann einen Atomschlag auslösen, oder, wenn ich Pfarrer bin, bei einer Geiselnahme unangefochten durch den Kugelhagel schreiten und die armen Geiseln befreien.«

Ich nicke. »Aber natürlich kannst du General oder Pfarrer werden«, sage ich. Wir gehen in die Laubhütte und setzen uns an den Tisch, auf dem ein dampfender Maisbrei steht. Das Kind legt die Pistole neben den Teller. Stumm essen wir, ohne gebetet zu haben.

Die schreckliche Verwirrung
des Giuseppe Verdi

Giuseppe Verdi ist, sage ich zu Susanne, die die
Buchhaltung macht, schon ein Kerl gewesen, weiß
Gott. Er hat Arien geschrieben, Chöre, Ouvertü-
ren, die Tyrannen haben gezittert, wenn in ihrer
Landeshauptstadt eine Premiere angesagt war.
Sollen wir dieses Stück, das im fernen Babylon
spielt, verbieten oder nicht, haben sie zu ihren
Ratgebern gesagt. Stirnrunzelnd haben sie auf die
Leute geschaut, die, den Gefangenenchor singend,
aus der Oper gestürzt gekommen sind. Sie werden
uns und unsre Frauen an den Beinen in den
Schloßhof schleifen und auf uns herumtrampeln,
haben die Landesherren gesagt. Ich atme heftig.
Ich stiere auf mein Notenpapier, auf dem die
Ouvertüre zu meiner Oper steht. Ich nehme einen
Kugelschreiber und korrigiere eine Oberstimme.
Giuseppe Verdi, sage ich mit heißem Kopf, saß
auch als steinalter Mann mit seinem eisgrauen
Bart, seinem Vatermörder, seinem Gehrock und
seinen schwarzen Lackschuhen aufrecht in der
Loge der Scala, ohne darauf zu achten, was die
Beamten der Zensurbehörde in der Nebenloge

miteinander tuschelten. Er sah die bleichen Gesichter der Adeligen, denen das alles nicht ganz geheuer vorkam. In seinen Gedanken sah er Massen von Landarbeitern, die lachend auf den Brüstungen der Terrassen der Schlösser saßen und die Beine baumeln ließen. Ich, sage ich, wenn eine von meinen Opern gespielt wird, stehen allenfalls ein paar Leute vor dem Rundfunkgerät und dirigieren mit ihren Bierflaschen mit. Ja, Helmuth, sagt Susanne lächelnd zu mir. Im übrigen, Ricordi & Cie. hat deine letzte Auftragsoper wieder einmal nicht korrekt abgerechnet. Immer unterschlagen sie die Aufführungen mit Schülern, Laien und Invaliden.

Ich schreibe ununterbrochen an meiner Oper, ich stelle mir die Melodien genau vor, mit kräftigen Schlägen spiele ich sie auf dem Klavier nach. Ich schwitze. Ich esse nur noch wenig. Ich komponiere ein Crescendo an der Stelle, wo Giuseppe Verdi in meiner Oper sich ausdenkt, was alles werden könnte in Italien, aus den Äckern, den Weinen, dem Leben. Ich schnaufe. Ich schaue zum Fenster hinaus. Durch den Schleier vor meinen Augen sehe ich Hochhäuser, Autos, Baumaschinen, rauchende Kamine, Qualmschlieren am Himmel. Ich erinnere mich. Es sind dieselben Dinge wie gestern.

Zwar ist das ja gar nicht so schlecht, wenn ich die Abrechnungen von meinen alten Opern lese, schreie ich, aber. Wenn die Leute untergehakt aus den neuen Opern von Giuseppe Verdi kommen, dann weiß der Herzog von Mantua, daß seine Tage gezählt sind. Überall rumort es. Die Leute singen die neuen Lieder. Sie zwinkern sich zu, wenn die Kutsche des Herzogs vorbeifährt. Der Herzog wendet sich um, er sieht in die starren Augen der Untertanen. Er versteht nicht ganz, was das alles zu bedeuten hat, aber er spürt, wie eine kalte Gänsehaut seinen Rücken herabrinnt.

Jetzt, wo ich den zweiten Akt meiner Oper über Giuseppe Verdi fertig habe, kommt mir in den Sinn, daß wir Sankt Nikolaus vergessen haben in diesem Jahr. Wir müssen ihn nachholen, schreie ich Susanne an, in diesen Großstädten vergißt man sogar die ältesten Bräuche. Susanne nickt. Ich hole mir den Bart und nehme das Komponistenlexikon, ich steige die Treppe hinunter und klingle beim Hausbesitzer. Er öffnet. Ihr kömmt früh heuer, sagt er zu mir, aber er ist einverstanden, daß ich seinen Sohn durchwalke. Du Saubub, schreie ich mit tiefer Brummstimme, während ich auf ihn einschlage, daß du mir nie mehr Leim auf die Tasten von dem Klavier des Komponisten in der Wohnung oben dran tust. Merk dir das, du und dein Herr Vater haben zwar keine Ahnung davon, aber er ist ein Stern am Komponistenhimmel. Wenn dann die Welt einmal so aussieht, wie er sich das in seinen Opern vorstellt, dann ist es euch auch recht. Ja, lieber Nikolaus, sagt der Sohn des Hausbesitzers. Ich steige wieder zu Susanne hinauf, auf der Treppe ziehe ich den eisgrauen, würdigen Bart, den Vatermörder, den Bratenrock und die schwarzen Lackschuhe aus und lecke meine rotglühenden Hände. Dann, während Susanne die Kartoffelpuffer aus der Küche holt, will ich nochmals meine Introduktion zum Auftritt Giuseppe Verdis in meinem ersten Akt meiner Oper spielen. Zu spät merke ich, daß der Sohn des Hausbesitzers diesmal den schnellhaftenden Leim benützt hat, mit dem man auch Flugzeuge zusammenleimen kann. Fassungslos starre ich auf meine festgeklebten Hände, die immer denselben Akkord spielen, wild, wütend, heftig.

Der Inhalt meiner Oper ist, sage ich durch meine zusammengebissenen Zähne, als ich nachts mit Susanne im Bett liege: Giuseppe Verdi will eine Oper schreiben. Er denkt in meiner Oper, daß in seiner Oper ein toller wilder italienischer Landarbeiter vorkommt, der flammende Arien zu den andern unterdrückten Landarbeitern spricht. Er zeigt ihnen, daß es nicht geht, daß die Herzöge drei Viertel des Getreides bekommen, ohne es selber zu ernten. Meine Oper, denkt Giuseppe Verdi in meiner Oper, wird wie eine Sturmflut sein, die Tränen werden den Zuhörern aus den Augen schießen, ihre Herzen werden beben. Junge Mädchen werden wildfremden Männern um den Hals fallen, und die Gatten werden schluchzend die Gattinnen streicheln. Ja, sagt Susanne. Giuseppe Verdi, murmle ich, nennt sich in der Oper, die er in meiner Oper schreibt, Nabucco. Er hat ein Mädchen, Violetta. Er steht, im Licht der Blendlaterne, im Stall und spricht zu seinen Freunden. Verdi schreibt mit heftigem Schwung Arie um Arie. Er ist ein Genie, seine Tinte spritzt nur so übers Papier. Ja, sagt Susanne und gähnt. Ja, schreie ich wild und setze mich im Bett auf, im zweiten Akt tritt die Frau von Giuseppe Verdi auf. Sie merkt, daß ihr Geliebter nur noch Ohren für Violetta und Nabucco hat. Traurig geht sie hinaus. Violetta fängt in der Oper, die Giuseppe Verdi in meiner Oper komponiert, plötzlich zu husten an und Blut zu spucken, während Nabucco seine Freunde auf nächtlichen Schleichwegen zum herzöglichen Palast führt. Alle wissen, es ist das baldige Ende. Giuseppe Verdi weint, auf meiner Bühne, als er komponiert, wie Violetta stirbt, blaß und wie ein Engel. Er steht auf, er geht ins Schlafzimmer, und da sieht er, daß seine Frau tot ist. Ich atme heftig. Ich sehe den bebenden Rücken Susannes. Blitzschnell denke ich wieder an meine Oper, bald liege ich wieder glücklich da, ich denke, wie die Leute weinen werden in meinem Opernparkett, und wie der Dirigent sich tränenblind verneigen wird am Schluß. Ahh, das wäre schon etwas, ein ganzes schluchzendes Opernhaus, und ich bin schuld daran.

Jetzt ist meine Oper fertig. Ich lese sie immer wieder durch. Kein Zweifel, sie ist großartig. Mit klopfendem Herzen packe ich sie in meine Reisetasche aus Segeltuch. Ich küsse Susanne auf die Stirn, so wie ein Sohn seine Mutter, dann stürze ich die Treppe hinunter. Ich mache mich auf den Weg zur Erfindermesse von Mailand. Im Zug summe ich vor mich hin. Ich sehe nichts von der Landschaft. Nach stundenlangem Marsch betrete ich die riesenhafte Ausstellungshalle. Ich sehe die Erfinder in ihren Kojen stehen. Ich finde auch eine Box, wo ich meine beschriebenen Notenblätter ausbreiten kann. Ich singe, wenn jemand, der wie ein Impresario aussieht, stehenbleibt. Ich schlage dazu den Takt mit dem Fuß. Heute abend, sage ich zu mir, will ich mir, wenn ich meine neue Oper an den Mann gebracht habe oder wenigstens einen

Akt, mit dem verdienten Geld das Nachtleben von Milano ansehen, die Spezialitätenrestaurants, die Bars, die Stripteases. Ich lache vor mich hin. Während ich eine Postkarte an Susanne zu schreiben anfange, höre ich ein Gurren aus der Nebenbox. Es ist eine junge Frau. »Ich habe den Reißverschluß erfunden«, flüstert sie mir zu, »hier, ziehen Sie einmal.« Ich tue es, und erst viel später komme ich dazu, ihr zu erklären, daß ich ein Komponist auf dem aufsteigenden Ast bin. Ahh, sagt die Frau und dreht sich auf die Seite, ich heiße Violetta. Und du?

Jetzt, wo ich in Italien bin, spritzt meine Kompositionstusche nur so auf dem Papier herum. Das ist das furioseste Duett, das ich in den letzten Jahren geschrieben habe. Es birst förmlich vor Liebe, Leidenschaft und Glut. Mein Blick geht über die giebeligen Dächer, unter denen die Maiskolben hängen. Liebe Susanne, schreibe ich auf der angefangenen Postkarte, es geht mir gut bei meinem diesjährigen Erfindermessenbesuch. Meine Oper ist noch nicht verkauft, und ich glaube, ich muß sie ganz umändern. Ich arbeite viel. Ich wohne hier bei einer Bekannten, die jetzt im Nebenzimmer gerade bei der Arbeit ist. Es beunruhigt mich, schreibe ich, daß sich in das fröhliche Keuchen meiner Bekannten mehr und mehr ein heftiges Husten mischt. Die Tür öffnet sich. Violetta betritt den Raum. Sie ist totenweiß. Ich lege die Feder beiseite. Es ist, sage ich zu ihr, ein anstrengendes Metier, das du da hast. Ja, sagt sie leise, verdammt nochmal. Meine Oper, denke ich, wird ein graues Ende haben müssen.

Ich will dir, sage ich zu Violetta, als wir dann zusammen im Himmelbett liegen, die Geschichte von Giuseppe Verdi und Giovanni Battista Oberdan erzählen. Ja, sagt Violetta und schaut mich an. Allerdings, sage ich, ich habe das Gefühl, daß ich sie schon einmal irgendwo erzählt habe. Aber wo? Es ist die Geschichte, in der Giovanni Battista Oberdan, mit einem Damenstrumpf über dem Gesicht, durch die Straßen von Triest schleicht und dem Kaiser von Österreich einen Sprengsatz unter die Kutsche wirft. Darf man das? fragt Violetta. Nein, sage ich, da, wo ich die Geschichte schon einmal erzählt habe, erkläre ich auch lang und breit, warum Oberdan das tut, in der Hauptsache, weil der Kaiser von Österreich den Triestinern verbietet, Lieder von Giuseppe Verdi zu singen. Jedenfalls, die Bombe explodiert, die Pferde stürzen um, die Kutsche kippt, und dem Kaiser passiert nichts. Oberdan wird von österreichischen Geheimpolizisten gefaßt, in einem Brombeergesträuch hängend. Ohh, sagt Violetta und krallt

76

sich, mit vor Aufregung nassen Augen, in meinem Arm fest. Es kommt wie es kommen muß, sage ich. Oberdan, mein Freund, steht unter einem Holzbalken, und er spürt den Strick um seinen Hals. Ein Beamter prüft nochmals, wie stark er treten muß, damit die Kiste, auf der Oberdan steht, umkippt. Dann tritt er sie um, und Oberdan, unser Freund, hat nicht einmal Zeit gehabt zu sagen, Für Gott und Vaterland. Violetta schluchzt. Sie hustet. Ich streichle ihre Haare. Die ganze Geschichte ist länger und trauriger, murmle ich. Zum Beispiel hatte Oberdan eine Freundin, die sich nie mehr von dem Schock erholte. Sie lebte dann mit andern Männern zusammen, aber sie dachte immer nur an ihn. Als sie 28 war, sprengte sie ein Kaiserdenkmal in die Luft und wurde dafür zehn Jahre lang eingesperrt, bis zur Revolution. Violetta sieht mich an. Ich summe ihr eine Melodie von mir ins Ohr beziehungsweise eine von Giuseppe Verdi. Lächelnd, mit nassen Augen, schlafen wir ein.

Bei uns in den kalten Bergen ist das Wetter immer furchtbarer, schreibt Susanne in ihrem Telegramm, Hilfe. Sie hat einen Eiszapfen beigelegt. Ich nehme einen Schleck davon, er schmeckt bitter und ungewohnt. Ich gebe ihn Violetta, die mich bleich anschaut. Was tut dieses Fräulein Susanne dauernd in den eisigen Bergen, sagt Violetta, wer ist sie überhaupt? Weiß ichs, sage ich, einen Augenblick von meiner Partitur aufsehend.

Einen alten Dreck erlebt man heutzutage, schreie ich Violetta an, die sich den Schweiß von der Stirn tupft. Ich schreibe einen schrillen Ton. Ein Held sollte man sein, mit einem Roß und einem Spieß. Da komponiert man und komponiert man, und am Ersten steht der Hausbesitzer unter der Tür und will doppelt so viel Miete. Das war zu Giuseppe Verdis Zeiten, schreie ich, ganz ganz anders. Das Telefon klingelt. Das ist sicher einer von deinen sauberen Herren, schreie ich Violetta an, denen ich auch noch einmal die Gurgel umdrehen werde. Violetta nimmt den Hörer ab. Pronto, sagt sie. Sie wird rot. Es ist Susanne, sagt sie leise. Du hast mir noch gar nichts von ihr erzählt. Sie hustet. Was ist? schreie ich in den Hörer. Susannes Stimme klingt sehr fern. Es könnte sein, daß sie weint. Ich verstehe kein Wort, schreie ich, ich arbeite hier Tag und Nacht wie ein Stier, verstanden? Susanne sagt etwas aus der Ferne. Was soll das heißen, schreie ich. Ich haue den Hörer auf die Gabel. Violetta weint.

Wie ein Wahnsinniger arbeite ich jetzt am Schlußbild der zweiten Fassung meiner Oper, da, wo

Giuseppe Verdi sich, an einem Fastnachtsdienstag, ausdenkt, wie Nabucco die eben noch am Boden kauernden Landarbeiter mit sich reißt, auf und davon. Verdi weint, auf meiner Bühne. Im vierten Akt drängelt er sich einsam durch eine Menge jubelnder Masken, weil er einen Arzt holen will, der seine Frau rettet. Ich wische mir mit dem Jackenärmel die Tränen aus den Augen. Um mich auf andere Gedanken zu bringen, lege ich eine wilde Polka aufs Parkett. Ich gröhle. Ich springe und stampfe, bis Violetta, die im Nebenzimmer zu tun hat, an die Wand trommelt. »Du Hexe!« rufe ich. Ich weiß ganz genau, daß Violetta nachts aus dem Fenster steigt und sich, auf ihrem Besen hockend, davonmacht. Zischend verschwindet sie in der roten Qualmwolke, die über der Stadt liegt, und erst im Morgengrauen landet sie wieder auf meinem Fensterbrett und steigt in unser Bett. Tagsüber tut sie dann so, als könne sie kein Wässerchen trüben, aber mein Kaffee schmeckt auch hier im Süden immer mehr nach Chlor, Arsen, Farbe, Pech und Schwefel. Zornig streiche ich das strahlende hohe C der Frau von Giuseppe Verdi aus meiner Partitur, es geschieht ihr ganz recht.

Giuseppe Verdi schaut, sage ich, im letzten Akt meiner Oper zornschäumend auf den Brief, den ihm der Direktor der Scala geschrieben hat. Die neue Oper, schreibt der Direktor, sage ich zu Violetta, gefällt ihm sehr sehr gut, nur, er kann nicht einsehen, warum dieser Freiheitschor unbedingt von italienischen Landarbeitern gesungen werden muß. Hebräische Sklaven in Babylon wären doch auch etwas. Zwar hat die Zensurbehörde bis jetzt keinen Einwand erhoben, schreibt der Direktor, sage ich, aber man kann nie wissen, und dann hat er, der Direktor, die Schwierigkeiten, und nicht der Komponist. Wenn Sie, verehrter maestro, schreibt der Direktor, sage ich, zudem auf die vielen dem italienischen Ohr ungewohnten Quinten verzichten könnten, wäre ich auch außerordentlich dankbar. Er könne sich aber auch vorstellen, schreibt der Direktor, sage ich, daß auch das Theater von Modena sich freuen würde, einmal eine neue Oper des berühmten Komponisten zu bringen. Nur über meine Leiche, sagt Giuseppe Verdi heftig. Er macht einen weiten, langen Spaziergang. Dann setzt er sich an den Schreibtisch und streicht zornig den Landarbeiterchor durch. Er schreibt einige orientalische Töne. In der Zwischenzeit, sage ich zu Violetta, haben wir ja keine Zensur mehr. Ich darf in meinen Opern schreiben was immer ich will.

Ich bin noch immer zornig, aber heute ist Kaisers Geburtstag. Der Kaiser kommt zum Kaffee, das heißt, in Wirklichkeit ist er natürlich tot. Violetta und ich sitzen am Tisch, vor das Bild des Kaisers haben wir eine Tasse und eine Sachertorte gestellt. Er putzt sie tatsächlich weg wie nichts. Ich wische ihm mit einer Papierserviette seinen Mund unter dem gewaltigen Schnauz sauber. Trotzdem, sage ich dann lächelnd zu ihm, wir haben Eure Majestät und die Truppen Eurer Majestät damals ganz schön aus unserm Land hinausgeekelt, nicht wahr. Der Kaiser lächelt traurig, auf dem Bild. Ich erinnere auch an das beinahe geglückte Attentat von meinem Freund Oberdan in Triest, mit Verlaub, sage ich. Ich darf mir schmeicheln, Majestät, mit meiner revolutionären Musik auch einiges dazu beigetragen zu haben, nicht wahr, Violetta. Violetta lächelt. Jaja, Giuseppel, sagt sie. Schluchzend bricht sie zusammen, sie sinkt von ihrem Stuhl und liegt totenweiß auf dem Teppich, auf dem Rücken, mit weit ausgebreiteten Armen.

Endlich wache ich mit dem Gedanken auf, daß ich Giuseppe Verdi bin. Ich schreite, mit auf dem Rücken verschränkten Händen, im Zimmer auf und ab, dann beschließe ich, das Beste aus der ungewohnten Situation zu machen. Ich fahre zu Gioacchino Rossini. Ich steige die breite Freitreppe hoch, von der ich aus dem Reiseführer weiß, daß sie zu Rossinis Alterssitz führt. Ich öffne die im Reiseführer angegebene Tür. Ein Mann fährt aus dem Bett hoch. Guten Morgen, Herr Rossini, sage ich zu Rossini. Ich heiße Herr Verdi. Rossini starrt mich an. Er ist viel schlanker, als ich ihn mir vorgestellt habe, er ist beinahe hager. Er richtet sich auf in seinem Bett, das in einem palazzoartigen Zimmer fast ohne Möbel steht. Was wollen Sie? fragt er mich mit einer gewissen Schärfe in der Stimme. Na, maestro, sage ich, ich bin sicher, daß Sie, allen Gerüchten zum Trotz, hin und wieder heimlich ein paar Nötlein schreiben, oder? Rossini bekommt einen roten Kopf. Ich schreibe überhaupt keine Noten, sagt er laut, spinnen Sie? Das nicht, das nicht, sage ich, ich wollte Ihnen nur meine neue Oper zeigen, hier. Rossini blättert in meiner Partitur. Hören Sie, junger Mann, sagt er dann leise, erstens kann ich überhaupt nicht Noten lesen, und zweitens. Ich habe es ja gedacht, murmle ich und fange an zu weinen, immer trampeln die von der älteren Generation auf einem herum. Überhaupt ist Ihr *Barbiere* auch ein ziemliches Scheißstück, merken Sie sich das, Meister. Ich gehe mit energischen Schritten zur Ausgangstür, und als ich mich nochmals umdrehe, sehe ich Rossini, der lang und hager und eigentlich noch ziemlich jung auf seinem Bettrand sitzt und mir nachsieht. Ich schlage die Tür hinter mir zu. Dem habe ich es aber gegeben, brummle ich vor mich hin.

Ahh, sage ich zu mir selber, während ich mit heißem Kopf durch die Parkanlage gehe, manchmal möchte ich schon gern eine Frau sein. Ich hätte zierliche kleine Füßchen, schwarze Stöckelschuhe, einen Rüschenrock, kleine Apfelbrüstchen, ich hätte einen weißen Sonnenschirm und ginge mit zierlichen Schritten über die knirschenden Gartenwege, bis auf die Terrasse vor dem städtischen Pavillon, in dem die Jubiläumsfeier zu Ehren des Komponisten Rossini stattfände. Sinnend stünde ich, im letzten Abendlicht, an der Balustrade, bis ich die leisen Schritte hinter mir hörte, die ich erwartet hätte. Ich drehte mich nicht um. Ich zitterte. Ich legte die Hand auf den heißen Busen. Gioacchino Rossini wäre einige Meter hinter mir stehengeblieben, im Dunkeln, ich hörte seinen Atem, vor Aufregung und weil er so dick ist. Treten Sie ruhig näher, maestro, sagte ich. Sie sind das mitreißendste Geschöpf dieser Erde, sagte Gioacchino Rossini, sich vor mir auf die Knie werfend. Er ergriffe meine Hand und bedeckte sie mit Küssen. Ich überließe sie ihm widerstrebend. Siedendheiß stiege ein Gefühl in mir auf, und als ich nun den Mund Gioacchino Rossinis auf meiner nackten Haut höher klettern fühlte, die Hand hoch, den Arm, die Schultern, bis zum Hals, da seufzte ich tief. Ich wendete mein tränenüberströmtes Gesicht dem Komponisten zu. Endlich, stammelte ich, endlich. Ich liebe Sie, Giuseppe, sagte Rossini. Er täte seine zarte weiße Hand auf meine Brust. Sie wäre eiskalt. Ich bebte. Stumm stünden wir so eine Weile, und Rossini summte mir eine Melodie ins Ohr, die weder von ihm noch von mir, sondern von uns beiden wäre. Dann zöge er mich mit sich fort, ich sähe seine tapsige Bärengestalt vor mir, wie sie in die nachtschwarzen Gebüsche des Parks eindränge. Was dann käme, wäre kaum vorstellbar. Ich läge auf dem Rücken. Ich hustete. Gioacchino Rossini löste brummelnd meine Brosche von meiner Seidenbluse, ja, und stundenlang hörten wir aus der Ferne die Musik des Festes. Schließlich, als wir die Stimmen der ausschwärmenden Gäste hörten und die Suchlaternen sähen, sagte ich errötend, wir sollten hineingehen, man könnte Sie vermissen. Ja, sagte Rossini, Sie sind ein vernünftiges Geschöpf. Ich liebe Ihre Art, Musik zu machen. Hand in Hand gingen wir über die Kieswege, Rossini und ich, die Freitreppe hoch, wo, bei unserm Anblick, ein dröhnender Applaus losbräche.

Auf dem Heimweg, im finstern Hausgang, schaue ich in den Briefkasten. Ich sehe eine Postkarte von

Susanne. Die Tränen schießen mir in die Augen, und plötzlich weiß ich, daß ich nicht mehr in die Wohnung Violettas hoch will, weil es da so süßlich riecht seit einigen Tagen. Ich stürze zum Haustor hinaus. Ich renne zum Bahnhof. Ich breche in einem Abteil zweiter Klasse zusammen. Ich lese, durch die tanzenden Sterne vor meinen Augen, die Postkarte Susannes, aber ihre Schrift ist so zittrig, daß ich nichts entziffern kann. Oder zittern meine Hände so? Ich singe laut. Ich gehe vom Bahnhof nach Hause, durch die Straßen mit den Hochhäusern, den Autos, den Baumaschinen, an den rauchenden Kaminen vorbei. Durch den Nebel vor meinen Augen erkenne ich einen Beerdigungszug. Die schwarzgekleideten Leute starren mich an. Ich singe. Zu Hause stürze ich die Treppe hoch, in die leere Wohnung. Ich rufe. Ich schreie. Die Tür geht auf, und die Nachbarsfrau starrt mich entgeistert an. Ja, Herr Helmuth, stammelt sie, sind Sie nicht beim Trauerzug, haben Sie den Trauerzug denn nicht gesehen? Ich, sage ich, nein, wen? Sie hat immer mehr gehustet in den letzten Tagen, sagt die Nachbarsfrau, und sie wurde bleich und bleicher. So, sage ich, aha. Ich singe. Wie sehen Sie denn aus? ruft die Nachbarsfrau. Ich stürze zum Spiegel, und da sehe ich selber, wie ich aussehe. Ich sehe, daß ich tatsächlich einen würdigen eisgrauen Bart, einen Zylinder, einen Vatermörder, einen Gehrock, eine Uhrkette, einen Stock mit einem Elefenbeinknauf und schwarze Lackschuhe trage. Ich sehe meinen offenen Mund, der singt. Singend schreite ich die Treppe hinunter, den Spuren des Begräbniszugs meiner Geliebten nach. Ich stehe am offenen Grab. Der Pfarrer sieht mich an. In meinem Kopf bildet sich langsam der Plan zu einer neuen Oper.

Der unbekannte Duft
der fremden Frauen

Es soll Frauen geben, die wie manche Blumen des tropischen Urwalds sind: bei Tag ein blasses Nichts, einmal im Jahr aber blühen sie, nachts, im blauen Licht des Vollmonds, drei Minuten lang. Dann verstummen die Spatzen und Papageienvögel in den Bäumen, wenn sie endlich ihre Spangen aufmachen, langsam die Seidenröcke fallen lassen, mit einem blinkenden Mund und glühenden Augen. Der Mann, der dann dabei ist, starrt in sie hinein wie in einen Vulkankrater, in dessen kochende Lava er sich stürzen muß. Langsam sinkt die Frau zwischen Orchideenblüten. Sie lächelt und öffnet die Arme. Später sitzt der Mann dann auf der Bank vor seinem Haus, wackelt mit dem Kopf und erzählt seinen Enkelkindern, was Schönheit ist. Die Enkel spüren, daß es für solche Schönheit keine Worte gibt. Sie ahnen plötzlich, daß ihre Freundinnen, denen sie beim Doktorspielen zwischen den Hinterbacken herumfingern, auch in einem blauen Mondschein nicht wie Vulkane glühen.

Das Rolltreppenfahren ist der Osterwunsch des verklemmten Lüstlings. Da steht er dann, mit seinem Osterhasen, den er als Alibi gekauft hat, und schaut den Frauen unter die Röcke. Er macht in seinem Kopf Striche für die Farben der Slips, einen roten für einen roten, einen blauen für einen blauen, einen schwarzen für einen weißen, und einen goldenen für keinen.

Schwitzend vor Erregung steht der unbefriedigte Ehemann am Guckloch des Massagesalons. Seine linke Hand hat er zwischen seinen eigenen Beinen, mit seiner rechten Hand stützt er sich an der Wand ab, an die er sein Auge preßt. Im andern Zimmer geht es wild zu. Er sieht, keuchend vor Lust, den auf und nieder wippenden Hintern des Kunden und die schneeweißen schönen Beine der jungen Masseuse. Jetzt schließt sie sie wie eine Schere über dem Rücken des tobenden Liebhabers. Leider ist die Lautsprecheranlage kaputt, so daß der Ehemann die Geräusche diesmal nicht hören kann. Statt dessen spielt der Salonbesitzer eine Nummer von James Last. Jetzt steht der Kunde auf. Er hat Schweiß auf der Stirn. Wer aber beschreibt den Schweiß am Körper des unbefriedigten Ehemanns, als er sieht, daß die junge Masseuse, die strahlend vor Glück auf dem Bett liegt, Gisela, seine Frau, ist?

Der ältere Mann träumt vom Becken der noch nicht Siebzehnjährigen. Entweder, er wird Lehrer an einer Mädchenschule, oder er wird Maler und besucht so lange die Aktklasse, bis die Frau, die immer Modell steht, die Grippe bekommt und von ihrer Tochter vertreten wird. Der ältere Mann wird das Mädchen ansprechen. Er kann es nach der Malstunde versuchen, wenn sie von ihren Freundinnen umgeben ist, eher aber tut er es, wenn sie einen Freund neben sich sitzen hat. Sie will ihm zeigen, daß sie keine Angst hat. Der ältere Mann hat eine Kröte im Hals. Er hustet. Sein Herz klopft, als er sagt, daß er nur zufällig Steuerbeamter, im Grunde seines Herzens aber Feuerschlucker, Weltkriegsteilnehmer, Diplomat oder Gärtner ist. Schwer zu sagen, was das junge Mädchen mit dem schmalen Becken mehr schätzt. Dann, wenn das Mädchen neben ihm auf dem Bett liegt, zieht durch das Herz des älteren Mannes ein Jubel, der einer tiefblauen Trauer gleicht.

Viele Männer schlitzen die Unterleibe der Frauen mit großen Messern auf. Das geschieht in Unterhölzern, im Schilf, in dunklen, reifüberzogenen Parks, am Rand von Autobahnen. Diese Männer dringen in Dienstmädchenzimmer ein, es nützt nichts, wenn die Frau schreit – der Mann hat sich Watte in die Ohren getan, und seine Seele ist taub. Er sticht auf sie ein. Blut spritzt, und in höchster Erregung schreibt der Mann seine Telefonnummer auf den Spiegel, mit dem Blut der toten Geliebten.

Wenn alle Frauen immer überall mit jedem, dann gäbe es keine Intimität mehr. In den Bois de Boulogne gerieten die Kavaliere in Erregung, wenn sie sekundenschnell den weißen Knöchel einer Dame sahen. Dennoch ist auch eine Orgie etwas Schönes. Weiße Körper wälzen sich im Licht einer Lampe, die mit einem Seidendessous verhängt ist. Man hört Lachen und Stöhnen. Die besten Freunde verlieren den Überblick darüber, wer es ist, der sie am Hintern leckt. Nachher essen alle eine Gulaschsuppe. Wer hätte gedacht, daß Judith, der alle scharfe Zähne zugetraut hätten, gefesselt, ausgepeitscht und angebrannt werden will?

Auch ein einsamer Junggeselle hat eine Putzfrau, eine Zimmerwirtin und eine Nachbarin. Warum traut er sich nicht zu sagen: Darf ich Ihnen meine Sammlung von Bismarcktürmen zeigen? Oft ist dann die scheinbar putzigste Frau die wildeste Geliebte. Sonst muß der Junggeselle halt krank werden. Krankenschwestern sehnen sich nach Liebe, am heftigsten die Hebammen. Sie haben

Tag und Nacht mit dem menschlichen Elend zu tun. Der Junggeselle hält sie in seinen Armen. Er hört ihr Schluchzen und küßt ihre Tränen weg. Am nächsten Morgen wird er seine Nachbarin, Zimmerwirtin und Putzfrau in einem neuen Licht sehen, diese werden sich wundern, daß der eigenbrötlerische Mieter beim Gurgeln Arien aus Carmen singt.

Leck mich am Arsch, jahrelang kann ich von Frauen reden ohne zu stocken, sagt der Matrose, der aus der Südsee zurückkommt. Wir starren alle auf seinen steifen Schwanz. Ja, sagt er und schaut uns in die Augen, in China haben sie das, was bei unsern Frauen gerade ist, quer, und in Malaysia singen sie mit gurrenden Lauten, wenn sie lieben. Es ist furchtbar, ganz allein in einem Mastkorb zu sitzen und auf das unendliche Wasser zu blicken. Man hat dann nur die Wolken, die über einem wechselnde Formen bilden: Brüste, Bäuche, Beine. Unser Kapitän duldet keine Frauen an Bord. Er sitzt in seiner Kajüte und schaut sich Zeitschriften mit nackten Knaben an, die er in Honolulu, Tanger oder Panama kauft. Kennt ihr Stenka Rasin? Er war ein Wolgaschiffer, und ihm passierte es, daß, als er im Mastkorb saß, eine Frau angeschwemmt wurde. Er nahm sie in seine Kajüte, gab ihr Grog und wärmte sie. Die eifersüchtige

Crew warf sie beide über Bord. Eng umschlungen, Brust an Brust, Mund an Mund, gingen die beiden im eiskalten Wasser unter. Seither sitze ich, murmelt der Matrose und starrt vor sich hin, da oben und glotze ins Wasser. Aber ich sehe nur hie und da einen hungrigen Tigerhai, mit dem ich lieber nicht Brust an Brust und Mund auf Mund im Wasser versinken möchte, oder doch?

Man kann der Vater eines kleinen Mädchens sein, man kann der Vater eines kleinen Jungen sein. Man kann beides sein, und die Mütter können Susi und Inge heißen. Mit Inges Sohn gehe ich in Wirtschaften. Wir rauchen und hauen die Faust auf den Tisch und lachen laut. Ich habe ein großes Bier, er einen kleinen Apfelsaft, aber er macht dasselbe Gesicht wie ich. Wenn er nach Hause kommt, kann er so viele neue Flüche, daß Inge gar nicht versucht, sie ihm abzugewöhnen. Mit Susis Tochter gehe ich in ein gepflegtes Kaffeehaus. Wir sitzen auf den Vorderkanten der Stühle, essen Eis und sprechen leise. Susis Tochter erzählt mir, wie ihre Puppen heißen. Ich zeige ihr, wie man Tee trinkt, und daß man den kleinen Finger nicht spreizt, wenn man vornehm aussehen will. Auch furzt man nicht, wenn man will, sondern drückt den Furz in sich zurück. Susis Tochter und ich gehen dann über die Rheinbrücke, sie hat ein kleines weißes Sonnenschirmchen, und ich lockere ein bißchen den Knoten von meinem Schlips. Aber, keine Frage, es war schön, so ein Kaffeeschlürfen aus Silberkannen und feinstem Porzellan.

Der Unterschied zwischen einem Mann und einer Frau ist, daß die Frauen einen Spiegel nehmen müssen, um sich anzuschauen. Nonnen, Frauen von Frauenärzten und Handarbeitslehrerinnen schauen nie zwischen ihre Beine, sie phantasieren deshalb das wildeste Zeug, wie es da unten aussieht: wie im Urwald bei Sonnenuntergang, wie der Mund eines durstigen Walfischs, wie ein süßes Versinken im Schlaf, wie ein lohend brennendes Dorf. Sie verlangen von ihren Männern, daß sie ihnen erzählen, wie ihre Expeditionen nach da unten verlaufen sind und was sie gesehen haben. Aber nie sind sie ganz zufrieden mit dem Bericht. Die Nonnen haben es am schwersten. Ihr Bräutigam ist stumm, und seine Hände und Füße sind ihm gebunden. Die Nonnen baden nur nachts, und zwischen ihnen und ihrer unkeuschen Hand ist immer ein großes Stück Sandseife. Nach dem Bad, vor dem Insbettgehen, trinken die Nonnen einen großen Schluck Schnaps, einen, den irgendwelche Brüder im fernen Südfrankreich gebrannt

haben. Er rinnt brennend heiß durch ihre
Gedärme.

Immer wieder, wenn ich am frühen Nachmittag
schläfrig in einem fremden Gasthof liege, höre ich
ein Quietschen durch die dünne Holzwand, die
mich vom Nebenzimmer trennt. Herrgott, zische
ich, hetzen mich die Dämonen denn unbarmherzig
um den ganzen Erdball?! Das Quietschen ist
rhythmisch, es ist das Quietschen der Matratze
eines Betts, es ist immer heftiger. Ich bin hellwach,
ich liege mit gespitzten Ohren da, ich knirsche mit
den Zähnen. Immer die andern, brumme ich,
immer die Ausländer, die Juden und die Tüchti-
gen. Endlich ist es still im Nebenzimmer. Ich stehe
auf von meinem keuschen Bett, wasche mein heißes Gesicht und gehe in die Gaststube hinunter.
Ich sortiere meine Rechnungsbelege. Ich trinke so
lange einen Rotwein, bis ein Mann und eine Frau
die Treppe hinunterkommen und sich an den
Nebentisch setzen. Ich schaue sie lange an. Ich
wundere mich, daß man weder der Frau noch dem
Mann ansieht, daß sie grad eben ein wildes Liebe-
stoben miteinander hatten. Sie bestellen einen
Tee mit Zitrone. Ich finde, die Frau sieht aus wie
eine schlechtgelaunte Papierwarenverkäuferin
und der Mann wie ein von Terminen gehetzter
Reisender. In Wirklichkeit aber haben sie Ferien,

sie sind glücklich wie noch nie, und ich bin neidisch wie eine Sau.

Wenn ich in gewissen Büchern lese, durchschauert mich plötzlich eine Ahnung von einem besseren schöneren tolleren Leben. Weiße Kraniche fliegen durch die Wohnküche, und die Luft, die durchs Fenster strömt, riecht nach auslaufenden Schiffen, liebenden Frauen, schwitzenden Matrosen. Eine Frau in einer dämmrigen Abendstunde, ist sie nicht wie so ein gewisses Buch? Sie hat himmelblaue Augen und ein Lachen, das uns an Shanghai, wo wir noch nie gewesen sind, erinnert. Ich glaube, ich liebe sie. Jetzt aber spricht sie der schwitzende Matrose an, sie nickt lachend und hängt sich an seinen Arm. Mir bleibt das gewisse Buch übrig. Ich könnte es auffressen vor Wut. Ha, wenn jedes meiner Bücher eine Frau wäre, dann wäre etwas los bei mir! Es ginge zu wie bei Sultans persönlich. Ich hätte ein alfabetisch geordnetes Harem, und die großformatigen Frauen stünden neben dem Plattenspieler. Ein Eunuche würde mir die Frauen bewachen. Das einzige Buch, das ich nicht in eine Frau verwandelt hätte, wäre die Mutzenbacher. Sie wäre die Lektüre meiner Frauen, die dadurch gut vorbereitet in meinem Zimmer auftauchen würden. Ich würde nie mehr als drei gleichzeitig nehmen, ich lese auch nie mehr als drei Bücher gleichzeitig, besonders wenn sie zu den gewissen Büchern gehören, aus denen rote Flamingos hervorsteigen und mit heftigen Flügelschlägen durch die Straßen davonfliegen.

Eine dicke Frau ist ein Lachen in einer heißen Augustnacht. Eine dünne ist ein Schrei in einer düsteren Vorstadtstraße. Eine kleine ist die Arie eines Boten in einer Oper von Cimarosa. Eine große ist der Atem einer Giraffe, die, über die grünen Blätter hinweg, zum Kilimandscharo aufblickt.

Werbedirektorinnen, Pilotinnen, Aufsichtsrätinnen haben einen makellosen Teint und reden laut. In ihr Lachen mischt sich zuweilen ein scharfer Ton. Sie fahren einen BMW. Aber noch gibt es Berufe, die den Frauen verschlossen sind: Bassist, Papst, Boxer. In China aber geht Tag für Tag die Sonne auf. Der lehmige Jangtsekiang überschwemmt die Ufer. Geduldig schaufeln die Männer und Frauen ihre Keller frei. Mit verschmierten Gesichtern setzen sie sich an den Abendessentisch. Es gibt, wie jeden Tag, einen Fisch. Heute knirscht er ihnen zwischen den Zähnen. Die Frau lächelt den Mann an, der zurücklächelt.

Seit Dutzenden von Jahren sind die schönsten

Frauen mit guten Männern verheiratet. Sie lieben sie. Aber wenn die Frühlingsvögel vor den Fenstern lärmen, denken sie, wie herrlich ein stürmisches Abenteuer wäre. Eine heftige Liebe im Sand eines Kiesgrubensees. Ein Herunterfetzen der Kleider im Park. Ein plötzliches Lecken eines unbekannten Munds. Ein starker Griff im dunklen Kino. Die schönen Frauen baden in ihrer Sehnsucht wie in einem traurigen Film. Was bedeutet das Lärmen der Vögel? Die Spatzen wollen eine Amsel, die Amseln eine Elster, die Elstern einen Geier. Die Geier sitzen mit Tränen in den Augen vor Papageien, die mit Ketten im Park angeschmiedet sind. Sie üben das Wort Lora, immer wieder, aber das, was sie dann vor der Angebeteten hervorstoßen, ist weder ein Wort der Geier- noch der Papageiensprache, sondern es fällt in den Dreck und verdorrt. Dann kommt der Sommer, und der lachende Spatz sitzt mit der fröhlichen Spätzin auf dem Kirschbaum, der Amsler mit der Amsel, der Geier mit der Geierin. Es ist gut, daß sie nicht wissen, daß, im verflossenen Frühling, die Kohlmeise zu einer jungen Drossel ins Nest gekrochen ist und daß die Federn so geflogen sind, daß die Kohlmeise es im nächsten Frühling mit einer Wiedehöpfin versuchen will.

Die Bücher von früher
oder Ein Beweis, daß der Schnupfen
der Vater aller Dichtung ist,
ein Essay

Ich hatte einmal ein Buch, in dem der eine Held lang und dürr, der andere dick und dumm war. Ich aß und aß, aber ich wurde nicht dick und nicht dumm. Bei uns gab es keine Windmühlen, nicht einmal Bachmühlen. Der Schularzt hielt mich für ein Mädchen, der Vikar für einen Mörder. Stundenlang lagerte ich an den Rinnsalen der Sierra Morena, aber nie tat sich die Erde auf, nie traten der Hagere und der Dicke aus den Farnsträuchern hervor und hauten mich auf die Schulter.

In einem andern Buch hatte Methusalem eine blaue Nase vom vielen Reisweintrinken, ein rotes Gesicht von den Monsunen, und er war uralt. Er schlurfte durch die heißen Straßen Pekings. Er glaubte sich daran zu erinnern, daß ihm einmal heiße Taifune um den Hintern gebraust waren.

Als die Mörder der Indianer, die mir in einem dritten Buch begegnet waren, in den Himmel kamen, rechnete ihnen der heilige Petrus alle ihre Morde vor. Es nützte ihnen nichts, daß sie sagten, sie hätten es im Dienst einer guten Sache getan. Im Himmel weht der Wind aus einer andern Richtung. Die Mörder der Indianer wurden auf eine kleine Wolke gesetzt. Sie klammerten sich aneinander, weil ihre Beine in der freien Luft hingen. Sie trieben an riesenhaften Wolken vorbei, auf denen johlende Engel saßen. Sie starrten nach unten, auf den tiefblauen Pazifik, auf die Fidjiinseln. Als sie über Nordamerika waren, sahen sie, daß ihre Wolke immer schwärzer wurde. Dann fielen die ersten Regentropfen unter ihnen weg. Sie rückten näher zusammen. Ihre Hintern wurden naß. Dann stürzten sie, pi mal 9,8, auf die Erde hinunter, auf der sie, tot oder nicht tot, zerschellten, umtanzt von schreienden Indianern.

Andere Völker lösen sich in Luft auf, wenn ihre Zeit vorbei ist: die Hunnen, die Westgoten, die Phoenizier. Ein Engländer aber steht Schlange, auch wenn er allein ist. Das hat Robinson gerettet. Mit einem eingebildeten Regenschirm und einem imaginären Bowler ging er jeden Tag auf die Hasenjagd. Pünktlich bei Sonnenaufgang machte er seine Liegestütze. Immer schnitt er seine Kerben in den Kalenderbaum. Immer spürte er, über die weiten Meere hin, die Nabelschnur, die ihn mit seiner Königin verband. Es war auch damals schon eine schwere Aufgabe, Königin zu sein. Von ihrem Nabel gingen Millionen von Nabelschnüren aus. Jeden Morgen rupfte sie pauschal an ihnen, um die verzweifelten Untertanen für einen Tag zu beruhigen. Dann stand sie auf und ging Tennisspielen, Polospielen, Dominospielen. Dann und wann sah sie sich in Filmen an, was ihre Untertanen taten. Sie sah, daß sie Kohlensäcke herumtrugen oder röchelnd in Rinnsteinen lagen. Die Königin dachte, von mir aus können sie machen was sie wollen, *ich* allerdings würde nie einen Kohlensack tragen oder im Rinnstein röcheln. In ihren Filmen kam Robinson nicht vor. Er hatte jetzt einen Freitag, dem er beibrachte, wie man einen unsichtbaren Zylinder aufsetzt und einen Spazierstock aus Luft durch die Luft schwingt, kurz, heftig, fröhlich, selbstsicher. Freitag versuchte es. Dann spazierten die beiden Gentlemen einen langen weiten Sandstrand hinunter, mit gemessenen Schritten, in kluge Gespräche vertieft. Sie schwangen ihre Stöcke. Dann und wann zogen sie vor einem vorbeihuschenden Kaninchen ihre Hüte.

Was haben die Dichter immer mit den Farben? Vielleicht wären sie lieber Maler geworden? Mir sind die Töne das heiligste. Ich hätte gern eine Schreibmaschine, die, statt zu rattern wie ein Banküberfall, holde Töne von sich gäbe. Der Beistrich wäre ein fis, die 9 ein cis, der § ein zweigestrichenes c. Während ich für meine Leser einen Essay über den Schnupfen schriebe, spielte die Maschine für mich eine Sonate von irrer Schönheit. Bald würde ich meine Argumente nach den Tönen meiner Maschine wählen. Meine Leser wären überrascht, sicher aber fände sich dann ein Germanist, der ihnen alles erklärte. Ich schriebe inzwischen vierhändig zusammen mit meiner Frau, wir schrieben mit gespitzten Ohren, weil meine Maschine nur die leisesten Töne von sich gibt, wie das Hauchen eines Grashalms, wenn der Mond über ihn hinwegrauscht.

Der Schnupfen ist deshalb der Vater aller Dichtung, weil er die Sperren der Selbstzensur auf Null reduziert. Schriftsteller wie Thomas Mann, Siegfried Lenz und Günter Herburger legen sich immer dann ins Bett, wenn ihnen allzu heiße Gedanken im Kopf herumzischen. Wenn ihr Puls wieder ruhig ist, schreiben sie weiter. Natürlich müßten sie es umgekehrt machen. Dann würde die deutsche Literatur heute anders aussehen. Ein großer Schnupfer war Arthur Rimbaud, obwohl er später in ein Klima zog, das die Dichtung nicht begünstigt. Warum hat er uns nie eine schwarze Sklavin geschickt? Wir hätten seinen verzweifelten Brief gelesen, wir hätten die Sklavin gut behandelt, gegen unser Lebensende, das auch ihr Lebensende gewesen wäre, hätten wir ihr die Freiheit geschenkt. Frei wäre sie durch die Innenstadt von Frankfurt geschlendert, nackt, schwarz. Mit offenen Mäulern hätten die Innenstädter das Bild der schwarzen Freiheit angestarrt. Niemand hätte gewagt, sie anzusprechen.

Warum, junger Mann, machen Sie nie Reime? schrie mein Poesielehrer. Ich mache welche, antwortete ich verlegen, für die Elche. Der Lehrer sah mich an. Na schön, sagte er, ich gebe Ihnen eine Zwei plus. Zufrieden ging ich mit meinem Zeugnis nach Hause, zu meiner Mutter. Sie saß in einem Schaukelstuhl und häkelte. Sie sah auf mein Zeugnis, streichelte mich und sagte: Und jetzt putz deinen Tafelrahmen. Ein Liebesgedicht, das einen schmutzigen Rahmen hat, ist wie ein Vanilleeis, über das man heißes Petroleum gegossen hat.

In einem fünften Buch saß ein hölzerner Kasper auf einer Burgzinne im Abendwind und kicherte auf die Schildknappen hinunter, die schwitzend die Zugbrücke hochzogen. Er konnte gehen und sprechen. Tagsüber schlief er in einer Holzkiste, und nachts zupfte er Prinzessinnen die Nachthemdchen hoch. Die alten Könige glaubten nicht an ihn, für sie war er ein Holzkopf und ein bißchen Stoff. Der Unglaube der Häuptlinge war seine beste Tarnung. Er war es, der immer wieder in die Verliese schlich und die Gefangenen befreite, die an nasse Mauern angeschmiedet waren, weil sie über die neuen Kleider des Kaisers gelacht oder unter die alten der Kaiserin geblickt hatten.

Lustig ist ein Exil nie. Aber warum gehen wir nicht alle zusammen nach England: alle deutschen Dichter? Die zu Hause werden schön schauen, wenn kein einziges Lied mehr aus den deutschen Wäldern aufquillt. Wenn es keinen einzigen Protest mehr gibt, weil der Bundeskanzler einen Physiker, der eine Irrlehre verbreitet hat, öffentlich auspeitschen läßt. Wenn die Sonntagszeitungen ohne ein einziges Sonett von mir oder Max von der Grün erscheinen. Wir aber werden alle auf einer Farm in Cornwall leben. Carl Améry kümmert sich um die Artischocken, Peter Bamm um die Bohnen, Elias Canetti um die Chicorée, Heike Doutiné um den Dünger, Helmut Eisendle um die Erdäpfel, Günter Bruno Fuchs um die

Fische, Martin Gregor-Dellin um das Goulasch, Hans Habe um die Heilkräuter, und ich mich um den Weinbau. Auch in unserer neuen Heimat werden wir still durch den Nebelglanz tappen, auch hier werden wir die Büsche im Tal kaum erkennen können.

Wenn ich bedenke, daß mein Vater aus dem gleichen Dorf wie die Habsburger stammt: welch verschiedenartige Entwicklung unsrer Häuser. Vom Geburtshaus meines Vaters sieht man auf die Mauern der Habsburg, deren Zinnen, hoch über uns, im Nebel verschwinden. Ich habe zwar keine hängende Unterlippe, aber auch in meinem Reich geht die Sonne nie unter. Der Vater meines Vaters hatte den Stier des Dorfs. Ein Leben lang hegte und pflegte er ihn, um ihn einmal auf einen Habsburger hetzen zu können. Die aber reisten nur in gepanzerten Kutschen oder mit seltsamen Flugmaschinen. Sie segelten an großen Drachen hängend davon, mit dem Wind. Schließlich war ja überall ihr Reich. Sie landeten in Sizilien oder Spanien und taten so, als sei ihr Erscheinen ein geplanter Staatsbesuch. Die Untertanen jubelten. Sie wußten nicht wie wir im Dorf, daß die Habsburger Säue waren, auf die wir unsern Stier nur deshalb nicht losließen, weil sie Flugmaschinen und gepanzerte Karossen hatten.

Überhaupt die Familie: Vater lustig, im Alter ernst geworden. Mutter ernst, im Alter lustig geworden. Schwester selbstbewußt, mit heimlichen Tränen. Großvater Aufsteiger. Der andere Violinist und Schulmeister. Die eine Großmutter schön und jung gestorben, die andre mit vorwurfsvollem Kinn und uralt geworden. Die Urgroßeltern: einerseits Malzfabrik, andrerseits Weinbauern, dritterseits Apfelbauern, vierterseits Stierhalter. Napoleon setzte jahrelang meinem liebsten Vorfahren nach, über Berg und Tal, er erwischte ihn aber nicht, obwohl mein liebster Vorfahre Tonnen von Gewehren und Pistolen in die Cisalpinische Republik schmuggelte, die damals von allen braven Leuten Veltlin genannt wurde. Mein liebster Vorfahre trank seinen Wein aus Fünfzigliterfässern, die er einhändig hochhob. Meine Mutter hat Tränen in den Augen, wenn sie von ihm spricht. Welcher Sohn kennt die Sehnsüchte der Mütter? Wir denken, die Mütter sind unmusikalisch und lieben den Haushalt. Nachts aber spielen sie heute noch auf Blockflöten und drehen sich in imaginären Ballkleidern um den Küchentisch, mit unserm liebsten Vorfahren im Arm, der ihretwegen sogar das Weintrinken vergißt.

Wie alles läuft: das Wasser, die Sportler, die Hasen, die Hunde, das Schreiben, die Zeit.

Auch außen sind überall Ghettos: Studenten studieren in hügeligen Landschaften mit Studenten. Alte Männer sitzen in großen kahlen Hallen mit alten Männern. Leitende Angestellte sitzen, hinter einem tadellos eingeschenkten Pils, in Pubs, mit leitenden Angestellten. Dichter fallen, in christlichen Hospizen, Dichtern um den Hals, bestenfalls Dichterinnen. Arbeiter trauen sich kaum in die Kinos der Innenstadt. Nur die Juden verstreut man sorgfältig über die ganze Stadt, ins Westend einen, ins Ostend einen, einen ins Nordend und einen ins Südend.

Andere Väter der Dichtung sind: eine unglückliche Kindheit. Eine sehr glückliche Kindheit. Schnaps. Ein älterer Freund, der auch dichtet. Eine heftige Abneigung, jeden Morgen um sechs Uhr früh aufzustehen. Der Glaube, daß man ein Wort aussprechen kann, und Bäume zerbersten. Rheuma. Liebe. Bedrohte Freiheit. Eine junge Mutter, die sagt, wenn du nicht Anwalt, Offizier oder Chirurg wirst, springe ich vom Wasserturm. Eine alte Mutter, die im Schaukelstuhl sitzt und häkelt und sagt: Genau das habe ich ein Leben lang erhofft, Sohn.

Leise stirbt der alte Dichter, weil er sich plötzlich beim Dichten langweilt. Immer deutlicher scheinen durch die neuen Wörter die alten Gedanken hindurch. Hätte er, vor zehn Jahren, eine neue Sprache lernen sollen, like Mr. Beckett who writes in french now? Oder hätte er neue Gedanken suchen müssen, aber wo?

Jedes Element hat sein eigenes Buch: das Wasser den Moby-Dick, das Feuer das Alte Testament, die Erde den Don Quixote – aber welches Buch ist so, daß wir es einatmen können ohne es lesen zu müssen?

Berufe!

Bundesligaspieler!

Wie um Slalomstangen flitzt du um deine Gegenspieler herum, und dein Herz lacht, wenn sie Spiel- und Standbein verwechseln. Du schießt mit dem Innenrist, und die Stehplatzzuschauer stöhnen auf. Die Kameraden küssen dich. Dein Körper ist aus Muskeln, dein Herz ist aus Sehnen. Lieber als die Küsse der zehn Kumpels wäre dir die Umarmung einer Frau, einer ganz bestimmten Frau, aber bei ihr hast du, vor Monaten schon, das Stand- und das Spielbein verwechselt. Tja. Als du ein Kind warst, hatten die Torhüter eine Bierflasche im Toreck, und sie verwechselten nie das Spiel- und das Standbein, denn sie hatten zwei Standbeine. Auf denen standen sie, auf zwei Stützen für ihr schweres einfaches Herz, das sie abends seelenruhig nach Hause trugen, trotz dem 0:2, das sie, dank der Bierflasche im Toreck, nicht so tragisch nahmen.

Bäcker!

Jeden Morgen stehst du um drei Uhr auf und eilst in die Backstube, das heißt, das Gesetz über das Verbot der Nachtarbeit verbietet dir das. So tust du am Abend ein Pulver in den Teig, damit er frisch bleibt. Montag bis Freitag gehst du in die Fabrik. Dein Job ist es, das Programm des elektrischen Holzkohlenofens nach Bauernart zu überwachen. Leuchtet eine rote Lampe auf, mußt du die Temperatur nachregeln. Bäcker! Am Sonntag ziehst du mit deiner Braut durch Feld und Wald, ihr küßt euch, und dann geht ihr in einen Gasthof und eßt Speck und Brot, einen fetten guten Speck und ein duftiges Bauernbrot, und deine Braut sagt, dieses Brot schmeckt unvergleichlich, hast du es gebacken, Geliebter, und du sagst, ja, und dieser Speck ist auch Spitze. Ihr eßt schweigend. Am liebsten würdest du von Luft und Liebe leben. Hier im Wald ist die Luft sehr gut, und die Liebe auch. Du denkst, Brot kann man aufwärmen, wenn es nicht mehr ganz frisch ist, Liebe nicht. Nachdenklich gehst du mit deiner Bäckersbraut zur Omnibusstation, und zu Hause bist du besonders stürmisch, weil du ein paar Gedanken in dir verscheuchen willst, die Zukunft betreffend.

Buchhändler!

Du kletterst auf Leitern und Stühle, um unsre Werke in die Hände der Kunden zu legen. In deinem Büro hängt ein Poster, auf dem steht, was der moderne Buchhändler von heute nicht tun darf, wenn er am Ball bleiben will. Du aber stolperst über jeden Ball, Buchhändler! Du liebst deine Leitern und Stühle. Da sitzt du und liest unsre langsam vergilbenden Erstlinge. Für dich wollen wir ein Buch schreiben, das, statt fast niemand, gar niemand kauft, das kannst du am Lager behalten ein Leben lang. Wir kommen dich jede Woche besuchen, du kochst einen Tee, wir bringen einen Schnaps mit, und dann erzählst du uns, wie du einmal, 1933, ein Buch schreiben wolltest, das die Welt von damals auf einen Schlag verändert hätte.

Paukist!

Deine Einsätze sind selten, aber eine ruhige Kugel schiebst du nur im Opernorchester, da sehen nur die billigen Zuschauer in den Orchestergraben hinab und bemerken deine Auf- und Abtritte. Sie ahnen, daß du hinter der Bühne sitzt und mit dem Feuerwehrmann Feuerwasser trinkst. Du hast alle Opern von Wagner und Humperdinck im Ohr und bist immer zehn Sekunden vor deinem Paukenschlag am Pult. Einmal fiel ein Gastdirigent, als er dir den Einsatz geben wollte mit einem innigen Blick und dein leeres Pult sah, in Ohnmacht und in deine Pauke, und sein Paukenschlag war genau richtig. Ratlos standst du neben Pauke und Furtwängler, und das Orchester brachte den Rest des letzten Akts allein über die Runden, d. h. ein junger Cellist sprang ans Pult und dirigierte wie ein Gott. Du lagst die ganze Nacht wach im Bett und dachtest, warum bin nicht *ich* ans Pult gesprungen, Mann, so eine Schangs kriegst du nie mehr, und so war es dann auch.

Manager!

Ich weiß, welche Verantwortung auf dir lastet, und du weißt es auch. Wir wollen beide zusehen, daß es nicht auskommt. Du gleitest jeden Morgen als erster in die Arbeitszeit hinein, in deinem Kammgarnanzug und deinem Schlips mit dem Firmenaufdruck. Du brüllst deine Briefe ins Diktiergerät. Manchmal schaust du minutenlang deine Diners-Club-Karte an, deinen Namen darauf. Zweimal im Jahr fährst du zu den Negern, um ihnen eine Software zu verkaufen. Sie stinken, aber sie stellen schöne Stoffe und Schnitzereien her, und sie haben etwas Urtümliches. Nächtelang sitzt du in der Bar des Hilton von Nairobi und genießt die Vitalität des fremden Kontinents. Dein Magen schmerzt, wenn du scherzt mit deinem Boss, weil du nie weißt, sagt er jetzt gleich *You are fired.* Hired in Düsseldorf, fired in Kapstadt, das sind deine Highs und Downs. Dein Boss, neben dir auf dem Barhocker, trägt einen feschen Jeansanzug, er raucht eine Havanna und bläst den Rauch einer braungebrannten jungen Frau in den Busenausschnitt, und du weißt plötzlich, so weit wirst du nie kommen in diesem deinem Leben.

Hausfrau!

Du putzt die klebengebliebene Scheiße des Hausherrn weg und kochst wie eine Göttin. Dein Hausherr hat einen Stellenwert in der Gesellschaft, und du bist seine Frau, Hausfrau! Ihr habt getrennte Schlafzimmer, du schnarchst und er schnarcht. Du stehst früh auf, weil du Kinder hast, und er spät, weil er Professor ist. Er bringt das Geld und du nicht. Abends sitzt er vor dem Fernseher. Hausfrau, tu ab deinen hären Gewand und zieh deine durchsichtige Bluse an, die du ja tatsächlich besitzt, und stürme ins heiße Leben der Hauptstadt und bestell dir ein Schnitzel mit Bratkartoffeln. Dazu ein

Bier oder einen Beaujolais. Jetzt mußt du das essen und trinken, und dann trinkst du noch ein Bier oder einen Beaujolais, und dann tritt ein junger Mann an deinen Tisch und fragt, ob er dir seine Sammlung von Hitlerbriefmarken zeigen dürfe zuhause, und jetzt sagst du, nein danke, und gehst durch die Sommernacht nach Hause, zum Professor, dem du über die Glatze streichst und ins Ohr flüsterst, er soll seine Scheiße selber wegputzen in Zukunft.

Polizist!

Tief in deinem Herzen drin bist du wie ich, aber irgendwie hat es dich in deine grüne Uniform hineingeschlagen. Polizist! Tief in meinem Herzen drin bin ich auch wie du, aber auch mich hat es in meine Uniform hineingeschlagen. Zufall oder schicksalhafte Fügung? Du willst auch nicht, daß dein Haus abgerissen wird und daß an deinem Himmel Giftgaswolken hängen, aber plötzlich stehst du dann in Reih und Glied vor einer Giftgasfabrik, mit einem Plexiglasschild in der einen Hand und Tränengasbomben in der andern. Polizist! Schöner grüner Polizist! Nimm diese Rose aus meinem Rosengarten und steck sie an deine Jacke, so daß man deine Dienstnummer nicht mehr sehen kann, und dann zeig es mir mal tüchtig.

Bruder Pförtner!

Du verbringst dein Leben an der Klosterpforte und wehrst die Besucherinnen ab, die zu deinen Brüdern in die Zellen wollen, Bürgerstöchter mit bebenden Busen, auf denen kleine Kreuze aus Silber liegen. Du weißt, sie können kein Latein, und schweigen können sie auch nicht. Du schaust ihnen lange in die Augen und schüttelst ernst den Kopf. Besser brennen denn Pförtner sein, aber du brennst nicht, zu dir kommen die Besucherinnen ja, du bist ja der Pförtner, Bruder Pförtner! Du bittest die Besucherinnen von Pater Anselm, Pater Hans und Pater Detlev in deine Loge. Du blickst auf ihr bebendes Silberkreuz. Ihr trinkt Benediktiner, lange und schweigend und zitternd, bis ihr spürt, jetzt halten wir dem Anblick der nackten Wahrheit stand.

Sachbearbeiterin!

Seit 26 Jahren bist du für Ausländerfragen zuständig, für Bu bis Czkor. Wie viele Millionen Schnäuze hast du an dir vorbeiziehen sehen! Glühende Augen! Knorrige Hände! Breitschultrige Jacketts! Gegerbte Häute! Singende Stimmen! Haben Sie in dir Träume ausgelöst, oder ist dir das Träumen dabei vergangen? Du gehen Kasse, du zahlen zwanzig Mark, sagst du, dann du kommen zurück, alles klar? Am Wochenende steigst du in den Schießstand in deinem Keller hinunter, du und deine Freundinnen, ihr schießt auf Pappuppen, daß die Fetzen fliegen. Dann grillt ihr im Garten ein Steak, von dem die Argentinier nur träumen könnten, denn die Argentinier haben längst keine Steaks mehr. Sie haben nur noch ihre Tangos, und auch die nicht mehr, seitdem die Miliz einen neuen Rhythmus propagiert.

Prostituierte!

Jeden Tag sehe ich dich vor der Pension Luxor stehen, und ich denke dann, wenn ich dann einmal zerschossen, zerhauen und allein bin, das gibt es, was tue ich dann ohne dich. Ich werde großzügig sein, denn ich bin scheu, ich bin noch nie bei dir gewesen. Von dir denke ich, daß du eine Trink-halle haben möchtest, für wenn *du* zerschossen, zerhauen und allein sein wirst. Ich werde ganz einfache Dinge von dir wollen, Luft und Liebe, schwierige Dinge. Ich werde nie zu dir sagen, sag mal du, wieso hast du diesen Beruf ergriffen? Du sagst das ja auch nicht zu mir, wenn ich sage, ich bin ein Schriftsteller auf einem abgesägten Ast, und jetzt trinken wir noch einen Schluck von diesem Asti. Nennen wir ihn Champagner. Ich trinke ihn aus deinem Schuh, wie mein Großvater es schon nicht getan hat, mein Großvater war Volksschullehrer und saß abends in einem Apfelweinlokal und sprach darüber, daß die Blutwürste früher blutiger gewesen seien.

Lokomotivführer!

Du sitzt im Führerstand deiner E-Lok, du tippst die Brems- und Beschleunigungsprogramme in den Fahrtencomputer, du hast alle Hände voll zu tun, aber später, wenn du pensioniert bist, wirst du am Fenster deines Hauses die Stellung einnehmen, die vor dir alle Lokführer aller Generationen schon in der Lokomotive hatten: Fenster offen, Ellbogen draußen, Augen zusammengekniffen. Du wirst die Autos unten auf der Straße beobachten, wie sie einspuren und überholen, und bei besonderen Gefahrenlagen wird es in deinem Kopf pfeifen. Jedesmal hast du dir in jedem Tunnel gesagt, Paul, alle Züge fahren immer auf dem richtigen Geleis. Ein Freund von dir ist verunglückt, weil er Durchfall hatte und sich nicht traute, seinen Zug auf freiem Feld anzuhalten, auszusteigen und sich vor den Augen der Fahrgäste ins Gras zu hocken. So fuhr er wie von Furien gehetzt in die letzte Kurve vor dem Bahnhof von Bever, und der Zug entgleiste. Als du ein Kind warst, träumtest du davon, Lokführer zu werden, Lokführer! Dein Sohn träumt davon, Pilot zu werden. Für ihn wird es, wenn er dann einmal Durchfall hat, noch schwieriger sein, aus seinem Flugzeug auszusteigen und sich in die weißen weichen Wolken zu hocken, vor den Augen aller Fluggäste.

Filmemacherin!

Du hast einen Blick wie Mimi und herrschst Produktionsbosse an am Telefon, daß sie zittern. In dir zittern das Herz und das Gefäß, in dem die Erinnerungen aufbewahrt sind. Sie wirbeln herum, Bild für Bild, vielleicht ergeben sie einmal einen Film, in dem ich weinend versinken werde. Vorläufig sagen deine Filme, daß die Welt schlecht ist, und warum. Du bist hübsch. Du machst Witze, nur deiner Stimme merkt man an, daß du der Zukunft nicht traust. Du traust überhaupt wenigen. Heimlich denkst du, Charlie Chaplin war schon ganz o.k., der rettete immer so Mädchen wie ich eines bin. Aber was taugt Charly, wenn er seine Melone, seinen Frack und das Oberhemd auszieht, da bin ich mir geradewegs unsicher darüber.

Skirennfahrer!

Wie bescheiden du bist! Der Holzhacker, der du im Grund deines Herzens bist, spritzt dir aus allen Ohren, und daß du Kneissl fährst, steht eher zufällig auf deinem Overall. Morgens holst du 20 Weltcuppunkte, und mittags stehst du im Kuhstall und gehst dem Vatter zur Hand. Auch der hatte schon eine ansehnliche Faßdaubentechnik! Die Zeiten stürmen vorwärts, wer hat noch Zeit, dem Wandern der Gletscher zuzuschauen? Manchmal telefonierst du mit Niki Lauda, aber in deinem Beruf gibt es nur den Weißen Tod. Du weißt, daß die Strecken gut gesichert sind, aber dein Freund Roland, genannt die Taube, hat auch einmal einen Waldweg übersehen mit 120. Sein Schicksal will dir nicht aus dem Kopf. Andrerseits, man ist nur einmal jung. Man ist auch nur einmal alt, Skirennfahrer, und manchmal keinmal! Soll ich dir verraten, daß Niki Lauda säuft? Er weiß, daß es selten vorkommt, daß ein Formel-1-Pilot mit 240 auf die Seite gewinkt wird und in eine Tüte blasen muß. Ungerechte Welt! Wenn meine Frau und ich eine Piste hinunterwedeln, filmt uns niemand, obwohl wir lustiger als du aussehen. Zuweilen trinken wir einen Liter Roten oben in der Hütte, ich weiß nicht, ob du das auch tust vor einem Start, wir jedenfalls rasen dann wie die Kamikazes tal-

wärts. Die Stürme brausen uns um die Ohren, die
Bretter knallen über Querrinnen, der Schnee stiebt,
die Herzen toben, und in uns sagt eine Stimme,
Franz, wenn du uns *jetzt* sehen könntest.

Arzt!

Du sitzt an deinem Schreibtisch, diagnostizierst
mich fernblicklich, füllst einen Rezeptzettel aus,
und der nächste bitte. Du spielst mit dem Gedanken, einige Kassettenrecorder zu installieren, aus
denen die Patienten ihre Diagnosen abrufen können, sowieso ist es immer dasselbe, Stress, Wut,
Unglück. Was aber tue ich armer Asthmatiker?
Geh ich zu dir, vergeß ich die Peitsche. Verschüch-
tert sitze ich auf meinem Stühlchen, in meinen
Unterhosen, die Hosenträger hängen rechts und
links herunter, und ich habe vergessen, was mein
Leiden ist. So merkst du, daß für mich Kassette
Nr. 3 am Platz ist. Ich höre mir deine knarrende
Stimme an und kaufe die Pillen, die du mir ver-
schreibst. Schon geht es mir besser. Ich werfe die
Pillen in den Müll. Arzt, ich will nicht, daß du
dies liest. Sicher brauche ich deine Freundschaft
einmal. Zudem liebst du die Dichtung. Du zitierst
Goethe, wer weiß, eines Tages wirst du Bukowsky
zitieren, wenn du auf ein ungutes Geschwür stößt.

Du und ich, wir haben beide mit dem Verfall des Menschen zu tun. Wir wollen ihn beide aufhalten. Beiden gelingt es nicht.

Verfassungsschützer!

Früher dachte ich, du schleichst vor meinem Haus herum, mit deinen Wanzen, aber du schleichst nicht, einen Schleicher würde ich auch sofort enttarnen. Du gehst aufrecht, denn du schützt einen Rechtsstaat. Abends, nach deinem Tagewerk, triffst du dich mit deinen Kollegen in einem Pub, ihr habt schwarze Balken über den Augen und erzählt euch Witze. Jeder erzählt einen Artikel des Grundgesetzes. In meiner Wohnung richte ich oft das Wort an dich, weißt du, ich bin der mit dem alemannischen Akzent. Du antwortest mir nie. Im Taxi zum Beispiel antwortet die Zentrale, wenn der Fahrer was sagt in seine Wanze. Aber eine Wohnung ist ja auch kein Taxi. Eher könnte man diesen unsern Rechtsstaat als ein Taxi ansehen, wir sind angeschnallt auf unsern Sitzen, die Zentrale hört mit, und der Zähler läuft, ich will den Vergleich nicht zu weit treiben. Manchmal denke ich, das macht ja nichts, daß du ein bißchen an meinem Leben teilnimmst, sicher ist es angenehmer bei mir als bei dir, und vielleicht kennst du auch nicht alle meine Platten. Kürzlich erzählte ein Freund von mir den uralten Witz, wie Beethoven nichts einfällt, und er sagt zu seiner Haushälterin, lachen Sie doch bitte einmal, das inspiriert mich immer so, und die Haushälterin, eine saure Gurke, lacht, hahahahaaa. Hast du lachen müssen? Oder hast du gedacht, Beethoven, ist das auch wieder so einer?

Bundeskanzler!

Im Fernsehen sehe ich dich immer nur von vorn, wie du dastehst und die Zügel in der Hand hältst. Einmal, vor Monaten, schwenkte die Kamera plötzlich um dich herum, und da sah ich, daß du auch hinten Zügel hast. Sie kamen aus deinen Schulterblättern und verloren sich am Bildschirmrand. Einmal rupfte jemand daran, da erschrakst du und riefst Arbeitsplätze sichern oder sowas, und dann wurden die Zügel hinter dir wieder lockerer. Auch du gabst uns wieder etwas mehr Leine. Bundeskanzler! Nicht traurig sein! Als ich ein Kind war, bekam ich von meinem Papi, einem jetzt toten Kommunisten, einen Staat aus Karton geschenkt. Ich konnte in ihm herumregieren, bis alles gerecht war und überall die Sonne gleichmäßig schien. Ich gebe ja zu, daß ich in dem Teil des Pappkartonstaats, in dem ich und mein Papi und meine Mami und meine Schwester wohnten, ein paar Blumen mehr pflanzte als da, wo die andern Leute waren. Mein Papi konnte da lange die Stirne runzeln, und zudem hatte er den Glauben an die Welt verloren. Ich glaube, er glaubte, daß die Menschen immer überall auf Teufel komm raus all das tun, was zu tun ihnen möglich ist, und ich fange auch an, das zu glauben.

Programmierer!

Du beherrschst eine Maschine, die zu Gutem und Bösem gleichermaßen fähig ist. Du tippst Daten in eine Tastatur und schaust, wie lange Fahnen aus weißem Papier durch einen Schlitz kommen. In einer Tasche deiner weißen Arbeitsschürze steckt ein Ding, das piepst, dann mußt du auf einen Knopf drücken, und der Chef weiß, daß du an deinem Arbeitsplatz bist und noch lebst. Was genau ausgerechnet wird in der Maschine, weißt du nicht, etwas Wichtiges jedenfalls. Immer wieder werden Gruppen von Japanern an dir vorbeigeführt. Dann stehst du stolz und verlegen da, deinetwegen sind sie über den Pol geflogen, 10 000 Meter über den Eisbären. Sie fotografieren dich nicht, es ist verboten. Seit Jahren liebst du deine Cousine. Sie hat ein Programm, das du nicht verstehst. Einmal bist du vor ihr in die Knie gesunken und hast geweint, aber die Cousine sagte nur, Hubert, laß das, und stand auf und ging weg.

Uhrmacher!

Du bist der letzte in Europa, der eine Uhr auseinandernehmen und wieder zusammensetzen kann, eine Zahnräderuhr. Die neuen Quarzuhren verachtest du, weil ein dressierter Schimpanse sie montieren kann. Du hast Angst, wenn du am frühen Morgen in die Zenith gehst, auch hier geht es schon zu wie bei Opel. Jeder hat seinen Handgriff. Du sitzt an deinem Tisch und siehst auf die Lupen, Zahnräder und Pinzetten und Saridontabletten und denkst, die Zeit selber ist verrutscht, man sollte einmal nachsehen, ob sich Sonne und Erde noch drehen. Vielleicht ist jetzt 12 Uhr 03 und nicht 11 Uhr 55. Du beginnst in deiner Freizeit Uhren zu konstruieren, die nur laufen, wenn die Zeit, die du lebst, sich lohnt. Fast immer stehen die Uhren, sagen wir, oft. Dabei tust du alles, um sie zum Gehen zu bringen, du machst Witze und kaufst ein Steak an einem Dienstag. Die Uhren lassen sich nicht betrügen. Sie stehen und stehen, und machmal denkst du, sie haben recht. Zuweilen, wenn du gar nicht an sie gedacht hast, bemerkst du, daß sie zehn Minuten vorgerückt sind. Dann zerbrichst du dir den Kopf, welche zehn Minuten das nun gewesen waren an diesem Tag.

Papst!

Ich habe dir viele, viele Postkarten geschrieben, Papst! Warum hast du nie geantwortet? Hast du Postpriester, die meine Grüße verschwinden lassen? Du weißt vielleicht gar nicht, wie nett ich dir schreibe? Ich wollte dich meiner Hochachtung versichern, auf lateinisch, denn einer in dieser Welt muß der Vater sein und reich und ungerecht. Gerecht sind schon so viele, arm auch, kinderlos sowieso. Schau mich an. Ich bin Tag und Nacht gerecht und kinderlos, allerdings empfinde ich mich zur Zeit als beinahe reich. Aber, ich glaube, du bist doch reicher. Jedenfalls, Papst, bitte, lies meine nächste Postkarte, wer weiß, wie viele du noch kriegst in deinem Leben. Du bist schon der dritte Papst, an den ich schreibe.

Senn!

Beim ersten Sonnenstrahl springst du von der Sennerin deiner Träume und trittst in die eisige Alpen-luft hinaus. Die Gipfel färben sich golden, und die Masten des Kabinenlifts ragen schwarz in die Morgennebel. Du jodelst. Du hörst die Antwortjodler der Arbeiter, die die Skipiste für den nächsten Winter freisprengen, und jetzt hörst du auch das Donnern des Trax. Er schiebt ganze Wälder beiseite. Du gehst in den Stall. Strahl um Strahl schießt in die Milchbrente. Während du auf die verdreckten Hinterbeine der Kuh starrst, überdenkst du noch einmal das Angebot der Holdinggesellschaft aus dem Tal, das aus dir einen reichen Mann machen würde, einen Senn ohne Alp. Du seufzt und stehst auf. Du stellst den Stand mit den geschnitzten Bären und den Ansichtskarten an den Wanderweg hinaus, dann zündest du dir eine Pfeife an. Du siehst, wie, durch eine helle Morgensonne tief unter dir, die ersten Wanderer den Weg hinaufkeuchen, mit weißen Wolken vor dem Mund. Du stößt einen zweiten Jodler aus. Die Touristen gehen schneller.

3

Bildnisse von Dichtern

Wolfgang Bauer

Wenn er einen Wienerwalzer tanzt, zieht er tiefe
Furchen durchs Parkett. Er hat einen knallroten
Kopf, er zischt und raucht, er juchzt. Damen in
Ballroben drehen sich nach ihm um. Seine Leber
möchte ich persönlich nicht kennenlernen. Ich bin
allerdings ein Hypochonder, er nicht, er schlägt
mit seiner Faust zu, bevor sich der Todesgedanke
in seiner Seele auch nur bilden kann. Das kann er
nun wirklich nicht ausstehen, dieses beständige
An-den-Tod-Denken, da stemmt er schon lieber
einen Wirtshaustisch hoch und läßt ihn einem
Gast, einem Studiendirektor aus Kärnten, auf die
Füße fallen. Wenn er zu Hause weinen muß,
steckt er schnell den Kopf ins Abwaschbecken, so
daß man Dusch- und Tränenwasser nicht mehr
unterscheiden kann. Über seinem Schreibtisch
hängt ein Punchingball aus getarntem Blei, damit
seine Freunde, wenn sie ihm beim Schreiben über
die Schulter schauen und probeweise ein bißchen
auf den Ball klopfen, sich die Finger brechen.

Aber Herrgott, was ihm im Lauf eines Tages alles einfällt, zum Herrgott und zu anderen Themen. Wie er nur schon angezogen ist! Etwa so, als säße ich am Karfreitag mit einem Alphorn in der Hand in meiner Dorfkirche. Aus Frauen macht er sich nicht so furchtbar viel, aber er läßt es sich nicht anmerken. Darum fallen die walzertanzenden Damen in Ohnmacht, wenn er zu ihnen herübergrinst. Wir platzen fast vor Neid, wenn wir zusehen, wie er einen Fuß auf das Opfer stellt und sich fotografieren läßt, mit einer doppelläufigen Flinte in der Hand. Über der Mündung retouchiert der Fotograf dann später ein Räuchlein hinein. Böse Menschen mag er nicht. Andrerseits muß ja irgendjemand diese Welt erfunden haben. Er versucht, genau aufzupassen, wie sie es machen, aber es ist nicht ganz einfach, sich ihre Technik anzueignen.

Barbara Frischmuth

Ihre Stimme ist wie ein türkisches Öl, sie sieht auch aus wie so ein Lukumia. Nach jedem Ausritt duscht sie in einem Zuber voll Mandarinensaft. Möglicherweise denkt sie, daß das Pferd des Menschen bester Kamerad ist, aber sie sagt es nicht. Hunde mag sie auch, und, um das Maß vollzumachen, auch Katzen. Für sie müßte es ein Tier geben, das galoppieren und wie eine Nachtigall singen kann. Klettern müßte es auch können, wie eine Gemse, denn mindestens theoretisch liebt sie hohe Gipfel. Von dort aus schaut sie auf die Wichtel und Waldfrauen hinunter, mit denen sie sich früher herumgeplagt hat und die sich jetzt mit ihren sadistischen Späßen an die Touristen halten müssen. Nachts, auch bei Vollmond, geht sie noch immer nicht durch einen Föhren- oder Arvenwald. Sie wohnt jetzt in einer Ebene, weil man da die Gnomen gleich sieht, wenn sie durch den Staub geschlichen kommen. Zudem kann man sich mit ihnen in der Fremde besser anfreunden, sie merken, daß man einen Akzent hat und sich auskennt in der Welt. Echte Wichtel greifen nur Eingeborene an, da lohnt es sich, die gehen nie weg, auch wenn sie schon acht Liter Blut verloren haben. Sie kann Zauberformeln. Sie sagt sie manchmal, im Bad, vor sich hin, und wenn dann der Badezimmerspiegel zerspringt, erschrickt sie wahnsinnig. Dann muß man sie unter Holunderbüschen hervorzerren und sie ins Bett tragen, ihr viel Schnaps geben und sie streicheln. Stundenlang tritt sie mit den Beinen die Bettdecke weg, dann fällt sie in wilde Träume und schreit. Am nächsten Morgen steht sie auf wie frisch gebadet und kocht das irrsinnigste Gulasch, das man sich denken kann.

Wenn wir von der Galerie des Gastraums aus auf ihn herunterschauen, dann sieht er nicht wie ein Großvogel aus, wie er so am Tisch kauert, über seinem Bierkrug. Als wir aber an unserm Feldstecher drehen und ihn besser ins Bild bekommen, sehen wir, daß er gewaltige Schwingen hat, sie bestehen aus langen schwarzen Federn und sind mit dicken Muskelpaketen am Rücken befestigt. Er hat die Pranken eines Mörders. Jetzt hebt er den Kopf, er sieht uns und winkt. Er lächelt. Wir setzen den Feldstecher ab und werden rot, wie nur hat er gemerkt, daß wir ihn beobachten? Verlegen gehen wir zu seinem Tisch und setzen uns auf den Stuhl, auf den er deutet. Er kritzelt etwas auf eine Papierserviette, eine Geschichte oder ein Gedicht oder ein Testament. Warum, schreiben wir auf unsre Serviette, kreist du nicht um die höchsten Berggipfel mit deinen Schwingen? Wir wollen ihm das hinüberschieben, da sehen wir, daß am rechten Flügel die Federn irgendwie verwachsen sind, ein Hautlappen ist über sie gewuchert, und darum kann er sie nicht richtig bewegen. Oder sind sie mit Heizöl verdreckt? Jedenfalls, jetzt knallt der Wirt ein neues Bier vor uns hin, der Schaum schwappt hin und her, immer langsamer, jetzt ist er still. Wir lächeln uns an und trinken. Sein Glas ist leer, während wir noch am ersten Schluck schlucken. Zusammen glotzen wir auf den Wirt, der jetzt an seinen unerklärlichen Zapfröhren steht und mit einem Holzstück Schaum von den zu vollen Krügen wischt. Die Augen, diese Augen. Wenn er nicht aufpaßt, schießt so viel Wasser aus ihnen, daß die Gäste in Sekundenschnelle ersaufen. Aber daß er aussieht wie ein nasser Hund, das ist seine Tarnung. Wie ist er wohl, wenn er sich auszieht, seine Kleider, seine Haut? Dann sind seine Hände zärtlich, dann streicheln sie über die Tischplatte, daß das Holz zu glühen anfängt. Dann verstummen die Gäste. Sie wissen nicht warum, aber sie hören auf das Schlagen ihrer Herzen, bis der Wirt, der als einziger von all dem nichts merkt, auf unsern Tisch zustampft und uns zwei neue Biere daraufdonnert. Der Tisch zuckt zusammen, obwohl er jetzt schon zwanzig Jahre in diesem Lokal steht. Wir singen. Die andern Gäste singen mit. Später dann gehen wir, aber wir können uns, wenn wir ehrlich sind, nicht erinnern, ob wir, höflich den Hut lüftend, gegangen sind, oder ob uns der Wirt am Kragen hatte.

H. C. Artmann

Ist es sein Fehler, daß er wie ein Adler in unsern Gefiederkäfig einbricht? Wir schwirren schnatternd in die Ecken. Erst nach Minuten recken wir die Köpfe. Da sehen wir, daß die Heftigkeit seines Auftritts die Liebe des Zugroßgewachsenen ist. Er schaut uns traurig an. Fast läßt er den Kopf hängen, für einen Augenblick. Wenn er die Laterna-magica-Bilder vor seinen Augen wegschiebt, sieht er eine Welt voller Mörder und Grundstücksmakler. Wir trauen uns langsam wieder hinter unsern Biedermeiermöbeln hervor. Wir sagen ihm, daß er wie vom Salzatlantik gegerbt aussieht. Er haut uns lachend auf die Schultern. Jetzt taut er auf. Er erzählt uns vom Nordkap, vom Südkap, vom Kap der Guten Hoffnung, von den Frauen von Feuerland. Ich habe, sagt er uns ins Ohr, eine mitgebracht. Komm herein! Wir staunen sie an. Einer von uns flüstert, sie sieht ähnlich aus wie die letzte. Auch die da ist in durchsichtige Kleider gehüllt. Wir applaudieren alle. Plötzlich sehen wir, daß er jetzt keinen Jägeranzug mehr trägt, sondern einen Frack und den Hosenbandorden. Er lacht und trinkt einen Schluck. Nicht alle haben das gleiche Gefieder, sagt er, aber jeder hat ein paar schöne Lieder. Wir brummeln ein paar Töne vor uns hin. Dann hören wir ihm zu, wie er etwas in einer uns unbekannten Sprache singt.

Gert Jonke

Wo bin ich, wie heiße ich, was soll das, schreit er und tobt durch das leere Zimmer. Er hat eine Nadel in einem seiner Organe, in welchem, das ist nicht ganz klar, jedenfalls sticht sie und das soll aufhören. In seinen Kinderhänden hält er einen Vorschlaghammer. Er wirbelt ihn durch die Luft, er wird, weil er den Hammerstiel nicht rechtzeitig losläßt, von ihm mitgezogen und kracht gegen die Zimmermauer. Sie fällt in Trümmer, und er steht im Freien. Er blinzelt. Es ist wunderbares Wetter draußen. Gleich schreitet er rüstig aus, schade, daß er, bevor er den Hammer zu schwingen angefangen hat, kein Wämslein angezogen und sich kein Felleisen umgeschnallt hat. Er geht zwischen Kirschen- und Apfelbäumen, er denkt darüber nach, was man aus diesen köstlichen Früchten alles machen kann, Mus, Kuchen, Konfitüre und anderes. Er hört eine Musik. Er lauscht, aber dann ist es doch die Musik in ihm drin. Er setzt sich an einen Waldrand und singt mit, und leck mich, wenn es halt sonst niemand hört. Abends kommt er in ein Dorf, er will sich eine Arbeit suchen für einige Zeit, bei einem Schmied oder einem Wagner. Weil er aber das A so gut vom B unterscheiden kann, heuert er dann doch bei einem Klavierstimmer an. Während der Arbeit lernt er Fräuleins der guten Gesellschaft kennen, er zieht an ihren Saiten und küßt ihre Füße, während sie die Pedale drücken. Während ihrer Konzerte sitzt er versteckt unter dem Flügel und stimmt blitzschnell die Töne nach, wenn sie daneben hauen. Dann, wenn der Applaus verrauscht und Fräuleins und Zuhörer weg sind, setzt *er* sich auf den Klavierstuhl und spielt Mazurken, die die Fräuleins zu Tränen rühren würden, säßen sie nicht schon längst in einem Schaumbad und wüschen sich für einen andern, einen jungen Assistenzarzt oder einen Diplomkaufmann. Am nächsten Morgen jedenfalls hat er das Klavierstimmen bis hier, er wandert weiter, ohne Kompaß. Hätte er einen, würde er doch nur der Nadel nachgehen, wie einem Befehl, es würde immer heißer, und er käme nie in den Wald mit der Lichtung mit dem Dorf mit dem Haus mit der jungen Frau mit den Rosenwangen, die ihm jetzt ein Glas Milch und einen Schnaps anbietet und ein Lager an ihrer Seite.

Ernst Jandl

Das muß man gesehen haben, wenn ihm die blauen Zornäderchen an der Schläfe anschwellen. Dann stammelt sein Mund, aus seiner Kehle kommt Staub und seine Augen verdrehen sich. Die, die ihn kennen, tun die Finger in die Ohren. Dann schreit er. Niemand schreit so wie er. Wenn wir einmal einen Krieg auszufechten haben werden, spannen wir ihn vor unsern Karren und er schreit uns eine Schneise in die Feinde hinein. Mit dieser Technik haben die Schweizer schon einmal die Österreicher besiegt, bei Sempach. Er spricht ein Englisch wie ein Berserker. Wie er wohl ißt, und was? Er donnert die Gabel, die er mit der Faust hält, in den Rehrücken und säbelt mit einem Tranchiermesser ellenbogenlange Stücke herunter. Er frißt sie rasend schnell. Man meint, jetzt platzt er, aber nein, er lacht plötzlich ganz laut. Wir sehen uns an, dann ihn, und jetzt lachen wir auch. Sein Gesicht glänzt, er sieht jetzt aus wie ein Mond, und wir denken, schade, daß er nicht unser Vater ist oder wenigstens unser Onkel. Dann setzen wir uns zusammen an einen Tisch und spielen eine Partie Schach. Ich ruckle an meinen Bauern herum, er aber kracht gleich mit seinen Türmen übers Brett, und daß er dabei ein paar Rösser verliert, ist ihm wurscht. Sowieso hupfen die so unvorhersehbar. Auch den König mag er eigentlich nicht. Ihm sind die Figuren am liebsten, die wie Kegelkugeln dahinfegen können. Ich schaue auf das Chaos, das er auf dem Brett angerichtet hat und denke, wie er wohl Schnipp-schnapp spielt, mein Lieblingsspiel, früher, vor jetzt dreiunddreißig Jahren.

Michael Krüger

Sein Auge möchte leuchten, aber er spürt, daß jemand auf seiner Augenleitung steht. In seine Augen kommt ein Zucken, und sein Blitz, der sei-nem Gegner in die Gedärme hätte fahren sollen, fährt nach innen.

Er schaut einer Dame nach, sie hat blonde Haare und einen Blick, der sich in seine Seele einbrennt. Wo sind die Moose, auf denen er liegen möchte? Aus welchem Urwald hört er die Stimme, deren machtvoller Klang ihn um-haut?

Er geht mit der Dame einen See entlang. Das Schilf rauscht. Wasservögel krächzen. Mondlicht flimmert auf der Seeoberfläche. Die Dame bleibt stehen. Sie schaut ihn an aus schwarzen Augen. Langsam öffnet sich ihr Mund. Er weiß, was jetzt kommt. Soll er schnell einen Witz machen, oder soll er in weiten Sätzen über den Acker fliehen? Weinend liegt er in seinem Bett, der Morgen dämmert schon, er nimmt ein Buch und blättert darin. Er feuert es in eine Ecke. Endlich schläft er ein. Er träumt, daß er auf einer Matratze liegt, mitten in einem leeren, weiß gekalkten Zimmer.

Alfred Kolleritsch

Nein, schreit er, nein, nicht schon wieder Wein trinken. Aber gnadenlos schenkt ihm der Dämon, der heute wie einer seiner besten Freunde aussieht, das Glas voll, er führt es ihm an den Mund, und schon gluckt das tödliche Naß in ihn hinein. Hilflos stiert er vor sich hin. Was soll er nur machen? Soll er den Koffer packen und nach Indien? Er reißt sich zusammen, das heißt, er hängt an der Landschaft, in der er wohnt, an den Häusern, den Bäumen, den Schlössern und sogar den Rebbergen. Es ist ja auch schön hier, in diesem uralten Trinkgewölbe, mit diesen schreienden Burschen. Während der Rauch immer dichter wird, stellt er sich eine Küche vor, mit einer mutterartigen Frau drin, nicht freiwillig, das passiert ihm so, mit Pfannen, in denen Truthähne brutzeln. Dickärschige Dienstmägde huschen um die Ecken. Sein Herzschlag geht unregelmäßig. Er versucht, den Mägden unter die Röcke zu schauen, wenn sie auf den Leitern oben stehen und nach dem Zimt suchen. Dann schreckt er hoch und sieht seinen besten Freund, wie er in der linken Hand ein Bier, in der rechten einen Schnaps hält und beides zum Mund führt. Vor ihm steht ein Teller mit Spaghettis und Kartoffelpüree drauf. Das kann doch nicht möglich sein, denkt er, aber es *ist* möglich.

Klaus Hoffer

Wenn Napoleon einen wie ihn gehabt hätte, hätte er ihn in die erste Reihe von denen, die nach Moskau marschierten, gestellt, obwohl ihm das gar nicht gepaßt hätte. Mit seinen dicken Schritten hätte er durch die Russenkugeln schreiten müssen, bis ihm das Lachen vergangen wäre. Aber wäre er zu jener Zeit geboren worden, hätte er einem andern Kaiser dienen müssen, und allenfalls bei der Völkerschlacht zu Leipzig wäre dem *Empereur* sein Lachen zu Ohren gekommen. *Mon Général*, hätte Napoleon dann durch seine Zelttür gerufen, wessen ist dieses ferne Lachen, das da vom Schlachtfeld zu mir dringt? *Sire*, hätte der Chef des Generalstabs geantwortet und die Zelttür ein bißchen zurückgeschlagen, es ist ein Feind, er steht seit Schlachtbeginn in der ersten Reihe, unsere tapferen Pariser, Bretagner, Schweizer und Baden-Württemberger fallen zu Dutzenden unter seinen Streichen. Man fange ihn mir, sagt Napoleon. Gottseidank aber kommt es anders, denn er hat zu Hause eine junge Frau, von der er befürchtet, sie könnte während seiner Abwesenheit einem Briefträger, einem Hirten, einem Deserteur erliegen.

Wie der rasende Roland rennt er, überhaupt nicht lachend, über die Berge. Jetzt spürt er auch die vielen Wunden, deren Schmerzen er vorhin zugelacht hat. Er beißt auf die Zähne. Zu Hause findet er seine Frau, im aufgewühlten Bett liegend. Wie schön sie ist! Er reißt Türen und Schränke auf, er schaut unters Bett und unter die Kommode. Dann sieht er, daß seine Sorge unnütz war, oder sein Nebenbuhler schneller. Er findet sein Lachen wieder, er bestellt eine Fischplatte und ein großes Bier und erzählt vom kleinen Kaiser, wie er in der Ferne vor seinem Zelt gestanden und herübergestarrt hat. Gott weiß, was es da zu sehen gab.

Sie ist nie am blauen Nil gewesen, nie in hängenden Gärten spazierengegangen, jedenfalls hat man keine Spuren von ihr gefunden. Allerdings hinterläßt sie auch keine Spuren. In Paris aber war sie, das wissen wir. Sie war Platzanweiserin in einem Kino, mein Großvater, der damals einen Zylinder trug, hat sie gesehen. Sie trug ein kurzes, wippendes Röckchen und knickste, falls wir die krakelige Schrift meines Großvaters richtig entziffern. Sie sah sich das Programm durch den Spalt des Vorhangs an. Manchmal stieß sie kleine Schreckensschreie aus. Am besten gefiel ihr, daß der Klavierspieler so schön spielte. Sie sang dann leise mit. Mein Großvater kniff sie einmal in die Wange und sagte *Charmant, très charmant*, aber dann wurde doch nichts daraus. Später, als wir dann selber ins Kino durften, haben wir sie in einem Film gesehen, sie ritt zusammen mit Rodolfo Valentino auf einem Elefanten durch Indien und stürzte in eine mit Bambusstäben getarnte Falle. Der Film ist inzwischen unauffindbar. Sie wurde auf dem Sklavenmarkt verkauft. Man weiß nicht, was aus ihr geworden ist. Wir haben hunderte von Stummfilmen angesehen und tausende von Asienforschern befragt. Manche erinnern sich dunkel an ihre Stimme. Es gibt eine alte Platte von ihr. Man muß sie ganz laut abspielen, dann hört man ein fernes Zwitschern darauf. Es ist unendlich süß, ein großes Sehnen packt einen. Schnüffelnd steht man auf und gibt seinen trockenen Topfpflanzen Wasser. Auf der Plattenhülle sieht man sie, auf einem Foto, in weißen Kleidern in einer Hängematte liegend. Sie ist ganz jung, sie trinkt einen glühenden Kaffee und schaut in die Kamera. Jünglinge, die sonst nur Bilder von Sportlern sammeln, starren minutenlang auf das Bild, stumm. Wie die unbekannte Frau auf dem Bild machen sie mit der Hand eine Muschel und halten sie ans Ohr. Sie hören, durch eine ferne Brandung hindurch, einen Gesang, den sie aus einem sehr viel früheren Leben kennen, einem, in dem sie auf Mammuts sitzend durch Lianen ritten.

Gerhard Rühm

In unsrer Agententarnung schleichen wir die Treppe zu seinem Ausguck hinauf. Wir haben alles Nötige bei uns, Folien für Fingerabdrücke, Ausweise und alles. Auf Zehenspitzen gehen wir die letzten Meter, wir pressen das Auge aufs Schlüsselloch, und wirklich überraschen wir ihn in einem Augenblick, wo er überhaupt nicht gut gelaunt ist. Ich richte mich auf und grinse meine Mitarbeiter an. Wir haben es ja gedacht. Quengelnd sitzt er vor seinem Teller. Er macht schnalzende Laute mit seinem Mund und verdreht seine Augen, bis sie schielen. Und ich fresse meine Suppe nicht, schreit er jemanden an, der außerhalb unsres Schlüssellochausschnitts ist. Er ißt sie nicht. Wir filmen das Ganze, vielleicht können wir das Dokument später einmal gebrauchen. Jetzt geht er im Zimmer auf und ab, redend. Wir spitzen die Ohren, wir verstehen ihn nicht ganz. Unser Tonmann dreht verzweifelt an der Aussteuerung. Seine Stimme schlägt dauernd in den roten Bereich, flüstert er. Ich tippe mit dem Zeigefinger an die Stirn, dann schaue ich wieder ins Zimmer. Ich begreife plötzlich, daß er wahnsinnig glücklich ist. Er geht immer schneller, er räumt seine Freundin, die jetzt ins Bild kommt, aus dem Weg. Er rennt jetzt beinahe, in seinem Kopf scheinen Gedanken hin und her zu sausen, er stürzt an den Schreibtisch, und ich denke, jetzt dichtet er. Aber nein. Er ist völlig unberechenbar, flüstere ich meinen Mitagenten zu, da kommt er schon auf die Tür zugestürzt. Ich kann mich gerade noch aufrichten und ein Gesicht wie ein unangemeldeter Besuch machen und nach dem Ausweis vom Telefonamt greifen. Er aber stürzt an mir vorbei ohne mich zu erkennen, die Treppe

hinunter, in einem Affentempo. Wir pappen
schnell einen Wanzensender an seinen Teekessel,
dann schleichen wir ihm im Galopp durch den
Novembernebel nach, mit unserer lange geübten
Beschattungstechnik, zwei links zwei rechts, damit
er nicht auf uns aufmerksam wird. Er ist aber
überhaupt nicht aufmerksam, er schaut lange in
Schaufenster von Schustern hinein und lacht ganz
für sich allein, dann liest er aufmerksam ein
Schild an einem Haus, auf dem wir nichts Beson-
deres erkennen können. Wir notieren den Text,
für die Akten. Dabei hätten wir ihn fast verloren.
Wie ein Gnom ist er durch die Nebelschwaden
gezischt. Wir sehen ihn gerade noch in einer Wirt-
schaft verschwinden. Ich und mein fähigster Mit-
spitzel setzen die Schnurrbärte auf, die wir für
Gasthausüberwachungen bei uns haben, und treten ein. Es ist ein anrüchiges Lokal. Er sitzt am
Tisch des Wirts, der ihn auch noch zuvorkom-
mend behandelt. Die Wirtin geht in die Küche
und kocht eigens für ihn etwas mit Fleisch und
Zwiebeln drin. Wir fotografieren alles mit unsrer
Streichholzschachtelkamera. Na, ihr Sauertöpfe,
ruft er, und erst da merken wir, daß wir gemeint
sind. Wir lächeln verkrampft hinüber und heben
den Humpen, in den wir heimlich Mineralwasser
geschüttet haben. Das sind die Spitzel, die mir
den ganzen Tag schon nachlaufen, sagt er gar

nicht leise zum Wirt. Er lacht wie ein Irrer, so daß wir schließlich mitlachen, vielleicht hat er nur einen Witz gemacht. Die Nacht wird sehr lang. Er trinkt viel und wir, um nicht aufzufallen, auch. Um vier Uhr früh zeigt es sich, daß er mehr erträgt als wir, trotz unsern Vorsichtsmaßnahmen, und wir müssen die Fahndung abbrechen. Auch die Kollegen, die seine Wohnung durchwühlt und die Freundin gefoltert haben, sind nicht weiter gekommen. Irgendwie ist er ein Mensch wie du und ich, aber eigentlich doch wieder nicht. Denn wieso kann er durch geschlossene Türen gehen und wir nicht?

Oswald Wiener

Mit offenem Mund und großen Augen steht er hinter den Gittern. Er hat einen schweren Gegenstand in der Hand, er geht hin und her, wie ein Tiger, wie einer, der sich über seine Bewegungen Gedanken macht. Warum trägt er eine weiße Schürze? Er schaut zum Himmel hinauf, an dem sich glutrote Wolken auftürmen. Ein heißer Wind weht, und er preßt das Blut mit aller Kraft in den Kopf, um den Gang der Gestirne zu beeinflussen. Warum scheucht er eine Gruppe Frauen vor sich her, wie Hühner? Jetzt beginnen wir zu begrei-

fen, vielleicht ist er kein Patient hier, vielleicht ist
er der Oberarzt. In der Zwischenzeit hat er sich in
den Sand gesetzt. Er redet mit präziser, lauter
Stimme, und die Besucher starren auf die Zeichen,
die er in den Sand kritzelt. Mit einer Geste ent-
läßt er sie. Kopfschüttelnd, als hätten sie Fieber,
wanken sie zum Ausgang. Er steht indessen in der
Mitte des Hofs, allein, im Treibsand, den der
immer heftiger werdende Wind vor sich hertreibt.
Unbeweglich steht er da, den Blick auf den Horizont gerichtet. Der Sand staut sich an seinen
Füßen, dann geht er ihm bis an die Waden, dann
bis zu den Knien. Er schaut um sich herum. Der
Wind heult, und der Sand wächst höher. Die Fen-
sterscheiben, hinter denen die andern Häftlinge
wimmernd stehen, klirren. Sie schauen auf ihn
heraus, wie er mitten im Sturm steht, bis zur
Brust im Sand, bis zum Hals. Sein Mund sagt
etwas, eine Formel, eine Lösung. Aber niemand
kann sie ihm von den Lippen lesen. Die Sand-
schlieren peitschen wild über die Ebene dahin. Es
herrscht ein Wetter, gegen das auch keine Arche
Noah mehr hilft.

Wenn Autoreifen rot wären, sähe er aus wie ein Autoreifen. Er sitzt hinter einer Weinflasche. Er hat eine Stimme wie ein Russe und ein Herz wie ein Russe. Er singt wie ein Orkan. Nasse Konfetti liegen herum, faule Bierdeckel, ein Hund. Er liegt, das Gesicht zwischen seinen Armen begraben, auf einem Tisch. Die frühe Morgensonne bescheint ihn, und die Wirtin, die schwankt zwischen heftigem Abscheu und heftigster Liebe, weiß nicht, soll sie die Polizei holen oder zusperren für einen Tag. Sie sieht ihn an. Er hebt den Kopf, er hat Augen wie ein Bernhardiner. Komm, sagt er leise zur Wirtin, wir fahren in den Süden, ich will ein Porträt von dir malen, unter einem Kastanienbaum. Seine Pranken umfassen ihre Taille. Er drückt sie, und beide hören, wie die Knochen knacken. Die Wirtin stöhnt. Seit Jahrzehnten hat sie auf so einen Augenblick gewartet. Sie schreit. Jetzt lacht er, er nickt im Spiegel seinem blauroten Gesicht zu, dann singen sie zusammen ein Lied, dessen Bedeutung nur sie kennen. Mindestens bedeutet es, daß sie heute nichts arbeiten wollen und daß die andern ihnen können. Es bedeutet aber noch mehr. Lachend, mit ihren gebrochenen Herzen, Knochen, Gedanken schleppen sie sich zum Schlafzimmer der Wirtin hinauf.

Sie ist eine junge Witwe, das heißt, sie wird es gleich werden, falls in ihrer Kammer ein brummliger Wirt liegt, dem der Besuch am Arm seiner Frau nicht paßt. Aber dieser Gedanke ist ihm eigentlich zu blutrünstig. Sie legen sich in der Küche auf den Boden, auf seinen Purpurmantel. Sie decken sich mit der Schürze der Wirtin zu. Erst um Mittag fällt ihnen die im Zenith stehende Sonne ins Gesicht und weckt sie auf.

Päuli Zwigli

Wenn er eine Bierflasche sieht, muß er hineinbeißen. Er kann nicht reden wie die andern. Er platzt, wenn er hört, daß andere ganz ähnliche Sätze bilden wie er. Schon schreit er los. Schon daß alle Menschen zwei Füße haben und mindestens er nicht drei, ist kaum verständlich. Wenn er eine Frau sieht, will er sie haben, jetzt, nicht in fünf Minuten. Dasselbe gilt für Taschenmesser, Weißwein, Angelruten, Kompasse, Lackfarben, Hüte. Ströme aus glühender Lava stürzen durch ihn hindurch, aber er ist ganz sicher, daß man sie von außen nicht sieht. Wenn er seine Hände um den Hals von jemandem gelegt hat, weiß er selber nicht, wird er jetzt zudrücken oder das verschüchterte Opfer so streicheln, daß es sich jahrelang nach seinen Handklammern sehnen wird. Er haßt Leute, die aus schwarzen Autos mit getönten Scheiben steigen, mit Pudeln in der Handtasche. Er kocht wie Krösus, er braucht viel Knoblauch, er braucht von allem viel. Er reist gern. Er sieht aus wie einer, der sich auskennt, aber er hat gern einen bei sich, der ihm sagt, wo es durchgeht und dem er dann widersprechen kann. Er wird nie altern, und wenn, schrecklich. Er wird nie sterben. Wenn er stirbt, dann stimmen die Naturgesetze nicht mehr, und es wird in Strömen regnen aus einem Himmel ohne Sonne.

Günter Brus

Er steht in seinen kleinen Unterhosen auf den Zehenspitzen am Fenster und sieht ins Schneegestöber hinaus, er glaubt zu sehen, wie seine Mutter in einem schwarzen Mantel auf und davon geht, für immer. Aber seine Mutter ist schon lange tot. Er hustet, er schreit: Scheißmutter, und als er wieder in den tötenden Schnee hinaussieht, sieht er wirkliche Tappen darin. Er erschrickt. Soll ich hintendreinhasten und meine Mutter einholen und sie unter eine Fichte werfen und sie küssen? Jetzt, wo ich erwachsen bin, könnte ich. Er wischt sich mit der Hand über die Stirn. Er kippt den

Kühlschrank um und trampelt in den Bierflaschen herum, schreiend, er reißt sich die Haare aus. Stundenlang sitzt er auf einem Küchenhocker und starrt auf das Desaster, und wie sich die Milch mit dem Blut aus seinen Füßen langsam vermischt. Dann bindet er die Schlagader endlich ab und räumt die Scherben beiseite. Mit der nackten Zeh schreibt er einen Abschied in das schmierige Übriggebliebene am Boden. Er macht ein kleines Herz dazu. Dann rennt er aus dem Haus. Bei der Bushaltestelle merkt er, daß er einen Mantel hätte nehmen können bei der Kälte, und Geld. Er rennt neben dem fahrenden Bus her. Mit geschlossenen Augen rennt er durch den Winterwald, mit zusammengebissenen Zähnen. Er sieht die vielen Spuren nicht, oder doch? Er blinzelt. An manchen Bäumen hängen Frauen und Männer, aber viele Bäume sind noch frei. Er lächelt den Verurteilten zu, die sich im Winde wiegen. Er weiß nicht, wie diese Nacht vorbeigegangen ist, jedenfalls starrt er dann von einem Waldrand aus in eine rote, aufgehende Sonne. Vor ihm liegt eine Stadt. Er nickt einem Eichhörnchen zu. Immer schneller geht er auf die Häuser zu, es ist schön, daß auch heute morgen junge Frauen die Rolläden der Bäckereien hochschieben. Er lächelt sie an. Die Frauen lächeln zurück. Dann aber, weil es kalt ist, gehen sie schnell in den Laden zurück. Lange schauen sie dem fast unbekleideten Mann nach, der dicke weiße Dampfwolken vor dem Mund hat, während er rennt. Friert er nicht? sagen sie, Mensch, mich hätte es längst mit einer Brustfellentzündung hingehauen. Jetzt spürt auch er sein Brustfell oder so etwas, aber mit festen Schritten betritt er sein Daheim und stellt die Morgenmilch für seine Kinder auf den Tisch.

Gerald Bisinger

Man mag ihn mit einem Glas in der Hand ertappen, soll man daraus aber Schlüsse ziehen? Rimbaud handelte mit Sklaven, und Mozart starb im Bordell. Er allerdings schmuggelt allenfalls kaisertreue Traktate ins Veneto. Die Welt ist nicht nach seinem Rhythmus gebaut, ach, gäbe es einen Gott, der den Fuß an die Achse halten und den Lauf der Welt so bremsen könnte, daß er mit ihm übereinstimmte. Dann würde er sich mit staunenerregender Sicherheit bewegen, ginge blind über Drahtseile und spräche alle Sprachen der Welt. Es gibt Kulturen, in denen die Menschen sich so bewegen wie die Blumen wachsen, aus so einer kommt er. Wir andre, wir zucken herum wie die Irren, mit der linken Hand drehen wir am Fernseher, mit der rechten blättern wir die Zeitung um, mit dem Mund tasten wir nach dem Bierglas. Er ist eher wie Cäsar, der auch nur eine Sache aufs Mal machte, die aber richtig. Er wohnt an einem Ort, den er haßt, vielleicht haßt er auch die Orte, an denen er nicht wohnt. Glücklich ist er, wenn er einen Risotto ißt. Er erzählt manchmal davon. In Italien schlendert er durch die Rebberge wie ein König im Exil. Er kommt immer rechtzeitig zum Abflug der Maschine nach Berlin, weil er eigentlich die vorhergehende erwischen wollte. Wenn nachts um vier das Telefon klingelt, ist er es, und eine warme Luft aus polnischem Wodka strömt ins Zimmer. Wir atmen tief ein, während wir ihm zuhören, langsam vergessen wir, wo und wie wir leben, schon atmen wir in seinem Tempo, und jetzt ist auch für uns ein Tag eine Minute und eine Minute ein Tag.

Gerhard Roth

Viele sind stolz auf ihn, denn er spielt Fußball wie ein steirischer Uwe Seeler. Er ist eine geborene Sturmspitze und ein Kopfballspezialist. Wie Rommel bei El Alamein tankt er sich durch die gegnerische Abwehr, Brennholz hinterlassend. Ja, wir durften ihm auch schon halbhohe Flanken in den Strafraum schlagen. Lässig nickte er sie ins

Tor, und auch uns tat der donnernde Applaus der Tribünengäste gut. Wir wissen, daß er für ein Heimspiel von Sturm Graz jedes Gastspiel der Rolling Stones sausen läßt. Er kann jeden Spielzug des 5:3 gegen die Schweiz, 1954 in Lausanne, auswendig, genau wie wir.

Die österreichischen Uhren haben zwar in den übrigen Alpenländern nicht den besten Ruf, aber sein Vater muß doch so etwas wie ein Uhrmacher gewesen sein. Oder war er Lokomotivführer? Er jedenfalls sitzt mit einer unfaßbaren Disziplin an seinem weißlackierten Schreibtisch. Sein Haus steht auf einem hohen Berg. Winde umbrausen es. Wenn er auf seinen Balkon tritt und auf die schlafende Stadt hinuntersieht, heulen die Stürme auf und die Wolkendecke zerreißt vor einem fahlen Mond. Allerdings tritt er nie auf den Balkon bevor er nicht 2500 Silben geschrieben hat. Das macht in der Woche 17 500, das macht im Jahr 910 000 Silben. Wie zählt er sie wohl? Zählt er, wie Thomas Mann, während des Schreibens mit, oder hat er, wie Hemingway, plötzlich das Gefühl, jetzt ists so weit? Sicher ist, daß er sich erst danach einen Whisky einschenkt und, die Eiswürfel umrührend, auf den Balkon tritt. Totenkäuzchen rufen.

Eine natürliche Scheu hindert ihn daran, von seinen Erfolgen in der weiten Welt zu sprechen.

Er freut sich aber, wenn andere, etwa ausländische Zeitungen, es tun. Dann rahmt er die Zeitungsausschnitte mit kleinen Goldrähmchen ein und hängt sie ins Goldrähmchenzimmer, in das er nur auserlesene Freunde, Freundinnen vor allem, hineinläßt. Er ist mit Günter Netzer befreundet, aber er findet, es ist doch besser, wenn sie in verschiedenen Mannschaften spielen.

Wenn er in Mexiko oder in Hongkong ist, notiert er sich alles, was er sieht, in kleine Wachstuchhefte. Noch Jahre später kann er die Preise für Tequila und Reiswein auswendig. Nach Sonnenuntergang allerdings vergißt er alles. Dann spricht er mit schnauzbärtigen Männern und schlitzäugigen Frauen. Sie staunen, was ihm alles einfällt. Er steht unter etwa 1000 Volt. Er ist nicht zu bremsen, niemand auch will ihn bremsen. Die Mexikaner und Chinesinnen umarmen ihn vor Begeisterung und schenken ihm Hüte und Liebesglöckchen. Auch wir, die wir hinter einem Kaktus liegen, biegen uns vor Lachen. Woher hat er das alles? Gewiß haben wir zuweilen den Verdacht, daß, wenn wir ihn mit einem seiner Klappmesser aufschnitten, ein Gewirr von Drähten aus ihm herausschaute. Wenn das aber stimmt, dann ist er außerordentlich differenziert programmiert. Vielleicht, denken wir, vielleicht, weil er ja etwas davon versteht, hat er sich selber ausgedacht? Und während wir das denken, tasten wir über unsre Armsehnen und spüren, nicht deutlich aber immerhin, die Anoden und Kathoden in uns. Ein eiskalter Schrecken fährt uns ins Herz. Wir fürchten, daß, wenn man *uns* aufschlitzte, unsre Wicklungen ziemlich einfach gewickelt wären. Entsetzt trinken wir ein Bier.

Er aber ist weder entsetzt noch trinkt er. Das Leben ist so kurz. Wenn er ihm ein paar Dutzend Romane abringen will, muß er mindestens das Rauchen, die Frauen und den Alkohol aufgeben. Auch wir rauchen ja nicht. Wir wollen ihn, um zu erfahren, wie er dieses Problem löst, anrufen, aber es meldet sich nur sein automatischer Auftragsbeantworter. Dieser hat eine ähnliche Stimme wie er. Er sagt, etwas schnarrend, daß sein Herr jetzt nicht zu sprechen sei, und um was für einen Auftrag es sich denn handle? Wir stottern und sagen: Hm, öhh, herzliche Grüße jedenfalls. Wir hängen auf. Viel später, in der Nacht, sehen wir ihn, wie er auf seinen Balkon tritt. Der Mond bescheint ihn. Er öffnet die Arme und atmet wie ein Genesender. Er blickt über das Land unter sich. Wir winken ihm, aber er sieht uns nicht, da müßte er sich zu weit vorbeugen. Schließlich zotteln wir halt weiter, mit unsern Füßen, die uns wehtun vom vielen Gehen.

$$\overline{\quad 4 \quad}$$

Erinnerung an Schneewittchen

Nachts reißt der Sturmwind Fenster und Balkon-
türen auf. Alte Männer sitzen im Dunkeln im
Bett und erdrosseln Frauen im Schlaf. Andere
Frauen, alte, tanzen in glühenden Schuhen durch
die Küchen. Atemlos rennen Kinder durch Wälder, um die herum Männer mit großen Knüppeln
in der Hand stehen.

Mädchen stürzen von Wassertürmen.

Vom Wasserturm aus herrscht eine schöne Aus-
sicht über die Stadt, man sieht bis weit in die
Rheinebene hinein. Aber wenn man den Blick
senkt, sieht man einen verwaschenen Blutfleck auf
den Steinfliesen.

Es gibt Nächte, in denen Männer metergroß
vor den schwarzen Fenstern stehen. Dann sprechen die Toten aus den Zimmerecken. Ich muß
mir dann ein heißes Bad machen oder im Fernsehen eine Beethovensinfonie ansehen, mit einem
gutgekämmten Dirigenten.

Schneewittchen war ein Mädchen, wie ich nicht,
es wohnte in einem Schloß, ich nicht, es hatte eine
Mutter, ich auch, und irgendwo gab es einen

Vater, wie bei mir. Ich kann mich an ihn erinnern. Er saß früh am Morgen hinter einer Kaffeetasse und las in einer Zeitung. Er rauchte wie ein Schlot und hatte immer ein in Pergament gebundenes Buch in der Tasche. Angestellte Musiker, die er sich eigentlich gar nicht leisten konnte, spielten Gavotten, während er seufzend die Staatspost von Forstministern prüfte und sie dann irgendwohin auf seinen Schreibtisch legte. Er streichelte Schneewittchen über die Haare, während er den nächsten Brief las.

Manchmal warf er chinesische Vasen an die Wand und brüllte. Schneewittchens Stiefmutter schluchzte dann, hämmerte mit den Fäusten gegen die Wand und schrie, sie halte das nicht länger aus. Schneewittchen stand starr in einer Ecke und sah die rasenden Eltern an.

Es ging am liebsten in Bubenhosen. Es beobachtete die Eltern, wenn sie sich ins Ohr tuschelten. Beim Fangenspiel ließ es sich nie fangen. Es wollte einmal jemandem ein schönes Geschenk machen, aber es wußte nicht, wem. Es wollte Geschichten erzählen, aber wem? Es spielte mit den Kindern des Gesindes Völkerball und wurde, weil es so rasend schnell dem Ball auswich, als letztes getroffen. Dann war es stolz und hatte ein glühendes Gesicht. Es mußte allein nach Hause gehen, weil die lustigen Gesindekinder woanders aßen, im Gemeinschaftssaal, in dem Prinzessinnen nicht zugelassen waren, und wenn, dann verstummte jedes Gespräch. Schweigend ging es an der Hand des Kindermädchens durch den Park.

Es machte Witze, erzählte aus der Schule, brachte Blumen mit nach Hause und aß alles, was die Stiefmutter kochte. Es beobachtete aus den Augenwinkeln heraus, wie die Stiefmutter im Ofen herumstocherte. Es ahnte, daß man es in ein Kinderheim abschieben wollte, auf einem Opferstein schlachten, in einem Weidenkorb aussetzen, in eine Schlucht werfen. Es erinnerte sich dunkel, jemand hatte schon einmal seine Wiege in die eiskalte Winternacht gestellt, dann aber war gerade rechtzeitig noch der Frühling gekommen.

Ich werde ganz anders werden, sagte Schneewittchen zu sich selber, so wie mein Vater, und wie der auch nicht. Einmal sah sie den Vater in der Badewanne. Sie starrte ihn an. Ihr Mund war offen. Nie mehr dachte sie daran.

Der Vater war nicht viel kleiner als die Stiefmutter, aber wenn *er* dem Kindermädchen einen Befehl gab, sagte dieses: Jaja, Herr König. Der König bekam einen roten Kopf. Vielleicht traf sich seine Frau mit einem Hofmarschall in den Tomaten, wenn er auf der Jagd war oder Jerusalem belagerte? Er saß hinter seinen Pergamenten und hörte zu, wie die Musiker ihre Drehleiern stimmten. Schneewittchen hätte gern auf seinen Knien gesessen, aber er hatte einen Stapel Bücher drauf.

Eigentlich war die Stiefmutter nicht sehr schön, wenn sie mit ihren Kontrollisten in der Hand durch das Schloß fegte. Aber wenn sie ausging, zu einem Maskenball oder zum Einkaufen oder wenn sie Schneewittchen an den Haaren in die Schule schleifte, dann verschwand sie im Badezimmer, cremte sich ein, malte die Lippen zu knallroten Kurven, spritzte sich die Haare voll bis sie starr und steif wie Gebirge waren und zog sich ein Tailleurkleid und ein Gesichtsnetz an. Der König, in Hut und Mantel, mit einer Zigarette im Mund, stand dann ungeduldig im Flur und rief: Also sag mal, kommst du heute noch oder erst morgen? Schneewittchen, das vielleicht noch einen kleinen Bruder hatte, stand daneben. Es dachte, diese Geschichte werde ich später einmal erzählen als Geschenk für jemanden, den ich gern haben werde, dann werden mein Vater und meine Stiefmutter tot sein, tot, und ich und mein Geliebter werden weinen. Schneewittchen sah den kleinen Bruder an. Er patschte im Wasser der Blumenvase herum. Schneewittchen gab ihm einen Tritt. Man hat gehört, dachte es, daß ganz kleine Mädchen jemanden vom Wasserturm herunterstoßen können, oder wie sonst ist es erklärbar, daß manchmal zerschmetterte Frauen auf den Steinfliesen vor dem Turm liegen?

Die Königin, im Badezimmer, schaute derweil in ihren riesenhaften Wandspiegel. Sie war nackt. Sie sagte aus vollstem Herzen ihr Sprüchlein und schaute sich jede Faser ihres eiskalten, aber wirklich schönen Körpers an. Draußen im Flur hörte sie die Schritte ihres Mannes. Sie lächelte. Sie war jetzt 36 und besser im Schwung denn je. Sie hob mit beiden Händen ihre Brüste und ließ sie wieder fallen. Sie waren fest und schön, und wenn sie sich umdrehte, sah sie ihren schönen Frauenhintern. Sie spritzte sich Spray zwischen die Beine, zog Slips aus lachsiger Seide an und rief: Jaja, ich komm ja schon.

Wenn sie durch die Flure ging, konnte man ein leises Klirren hören, wie von Glas.

Dann bekam auch Schneewittchen Brüste, kleine, und wenn sie sich in ihrem kleinen Spiegel anschaute, vor dem sie in ihrem Dachzimmer auf einen Stuhl steigen mußte, sah sie, daß sie eine Pfirsichhaut hatte. Sie zitterte vor Aufregung. Dann zog sie sich ihre Hosen an.

Wenn die Königin jetzt den Spiegel fragte, zögerte dieser. Die Königin merkte am Klang seiner Stimme, daß etwas anders geworden war. Sie fragte ihn immer seltener. Manchmal, wenn die Königin etwas gesoffen hatte oder wenn sie aus den Tomaten zurückkam, hatte der Spiegel eine Stimme wie früher. Dann freute sich die Königin, sprang ins Bett und auf den schnarchenden Monarchen drauf und ließ ihm keine Ruhe, bis er sich zu regen begann. Schneewittchen, die ihr Ohr an die Wand preßte, erschauerte.

Dann aber kam der Tag, wo die Königin zum Fenster hinaussah, und sie sah tatsächlich Schneewittchen, das kleine, lächerliche Schneewittchen, wie es Hand in Hand mit einem Jüngling mit Bluejeans und einem Kindervollbart durch den Park ging. Er mußte der Sohn des Kutschers sein, oder so einer. Die Königin schäumte. Sie stürzte zum Spiegel, und dieser sagte ihr die Wahrheit.

Schneewittchen spürte sogleich, daß das Klima umgeschlagen hatte, als sie zum Nachtessen nach Hause kam. Sie war noch ganz heiß von den ersten Küssen ihres Lebens. Sie putzte sich die Zähne. Die Stiefmutter sagte kein Wort. Der Vater löffelte die Suppe, machte zwei drei Witze und verschwand in seinem Lesezimmer. Schneewittchen ging früh ins Bett. Sie dachte mit glühendem Herzen an ihren Geliebten. Sie behielt die Schuhe an, um schneller fliehen zu können.

Aber am nächsten Morgen, als sie in die Schule schleichen wollte, wurde sie von den Palastwachen gefesselt und in den Wald geschleppt. Sie blickte zu den leeren Fenstern des Palasts zurück, bis sie hinter der hohen Gartenmauer verschwanden. Ein schrecklicher Jäger mit Bartstoppeln im Gesicht hatte das Kommando. Sie ritten stundenlang. Es war kalt. Ferne Wölfe heulten. Dann, an einem reifüberzogenen Waldrand, hob der Jäger die Hand, die Pferde blieben stehen, weißer Dampf kam aus ihren Nüstern. Ich werde das notwendige Werk allein verrichten, sagte er zu den Palastwachen, abtreten, marsch. Die Palastwachen sprengten davon. Vor sich sah Schneewittchen Berge, Berge, Berge. Wenn es dahinter Menschen gibt, dachte sie, vielleicht sind sie glücklicher als wir es sind in dieser Erdenwelt.

Dann drehte sich der Jäger um. Er lächelte jetzt merkwürdig. Er riß an seinem Bart herum, und als er ihn abhatte, erkannte Schneewittchen ihren Vater. Papi, juchzte sie, ohh, ich hatte solche Angst. Schluchzend sank sie in seine Arme. Der Vater streichelte sie über die schwarzen Haare, und ich glaube, er weinte jetzt auch, wie ich jetzt auch.

»Was soll ich denn machen, Schneewittchen«, sagte er dann. »Es ist doch schon ein Glück, daß mir diese Verkleiderei gelungen ist. Ich habe gesagt, ich muß an einen Kongreß. Renn du jetzt in den Wald hinein. Meine Frau verlangt von mir deine Zunge als Beweis, aber mach dir keine Sorgen. Ich werde mir schon irgendwie aus der Patsche helfen.«

Schneewittchen starrte ihren Vater an. Dann nickte sie. »Du bist nicht sehr mächtig«, sagte sie leise.

Der Vater schüttelte den Kopf. »Geh jetzt, Kind«, sagte er. »Da hast du ein bißchen Geld. Machs gut.«

Er drehte sich um und ging den Weg zurück, ohne auch nur einmal zu winken. Schneewittchen stand da und sah ihm nach, wie einem Toten. Er verschwand hinter Brombeergebüschen in der Ferne. Wenn sie lauschte, hörte sie seine immer ferner raschelnden Schritte. Dann war es still. Äste knackten, der Wind rauschte, und Häher schrien. Schneewittchen drehte sich um und ging in den Wald hinein, die ersten Hügel hinauf.

Nach Tagen, an denen sie sich von Beeren und Wurzeln ernährte, sah sie einen Rauch am Horizont. Sie begann zu rennen. Vielleicht, dachte sie, vielleicht schaffe ich es, den Ring, der sich um meine Brust geschmiedet hat, zu sprengen. In einem Waldsee schaute sie, wie es aussah, wenn sie lächelte, lachte und grinste.

Auf dem Waldweg, auf dem sie jetzt ging, wuchsen rote Pilze mit weißen Flecken. Hasen saßen mit spitzen Ohren im Unterholz und bewegten ihre Nasenmünder. Die Sonne schien schräg durch die Blätter. Es duftete. Der Weg ging über einen umgestürzten Baumstamm, der an einer Seite ein Geländer hatte, ein ganz niederes. Holzstere standen im Wald aufgeschichtet. Als der Weg abwärts ging, hatte er Steinstufen. Vögel sangen. Dann kam sie an eine Lichtung. Sie rannte los, auf ein kleines Holzhaus mit roten Läden zu. Aufgeregt ging sie darum herum. Sie bückte sich und sah zum Fenster hinein. Holla, rief sie, heda.

Als sich nichts rührte, drückte sie die Türklinke hinunter. Die Tür ging auf. Hier schließt man die Türen nicht ab, dachte sie, natürlich nicht, daß ich das vergessen konnte. Sie sah sich im Zimmer um. Es war genau so wie sie es schon einmal geträumt hatte: rotweißkarierte Vorhänge, kleine Bettchen, winzige Gläser neben großen Rotweinflaschen. Was sind denn das für merkwürdige Liliputaner, dachte Schneewittchen. Keinen Augenblick lang dachte sie, daß das die schrecklichen grausamen Waldmänner sein könnten, von denen man im Schloß immer wieder einmal gemunkelt hatte und daß man sie gelegentlich einmal ausrotten müsse. Zollbeamte standen mit großen Ferngläsern auf den Höhenzügen und suchten die Wälder nach den bärtigen Männern ab, die keine Steuern zahlten und zum Königsgeburtstag keine Salutbotschaften schickten.

Dann kamen die Zwerge in einer Einerkolonne zurück, fanden das eingeschlafene Schneewittchen, fütterten es mit Suppe und hörten sich seine

Geschichte an. Jaja, sagten sie, so sind die Menschen da drüben. Uns erstaunt da gar nichts mehr. Du wirst vielleicht einmal werden wie sie.

Jahrelang ging alles gut. Die Zwerge gingen ins Bergwerk, und Schneewittchen kümmerte sich um den Salat hinter dem Haus. Die Sonne schien fast die ganze Zeit. Manchmal stand Schneewittchen vor dem Haus und starrte auf den siebenten Berg vor seiner Nase. Dann weinte es.

Dann klopfte die alte Frau an die Tür. Schneewittchen war wie elektrisiert, die Frau erinnerte sie an eine fast schon vergessene Welt. Wie geht es dem König hinter dem ersten Berg, fragte sie die alte Frau. Dem König, dem König, feixte diese, was für einem König? Wir haben eine Königin, und die ist irrsinnig schön, mein Kind. Der Kamm kostet einszwanzig, und da lege ich noch drauf.

Schneewittchen lernte nichts aus dem vergifteten Kamm. Es war geradezu wild auf den giftigen Apfel. Es wollte in den gläsernen Sarg hinein. Es stieg, als die alte Frau wieder weg war, mit dem Apfel in der rechten Hand auf den Stuhl und sah in seinen Taschenspiegel hinein. Da sah es, daß die Zwerge ihm nicht gesagt hatten, daß seine kleine Brust inzwischen groß geworden war, und daß es, wenn es sich umdrehte, einen Frauenhintern hatte. Es erschrak. Es biß in den Apfel. Die Zwerge legten es in den Glassarg. Sie ist nicht

wie wir, sagten sie traurig, sie ist eigen, eigensüch-
tig und eigentümlich. Sie schweigt immer. Sie will,
daß man sie liebt, aber sie will niemanden lieben.
Schade. Dann gingen die Zwerge ins Haus zurück
und spielten eine Runde Schafskopf.

Schneewittchen lag auf dem Rücken im Glassarg und sah in den Himmel hinauf. Es litt so
sehr, daß es dabei sehr glücklich war. Immer
dachte es an den Prinzen, der ja sicher einmal
kommen mußte. Es bewegte keine Zehe die ganze
Zeit. Es hörte undeutlich die Zwerge, wenn sie
frühmorgens, wenn Schneewittchen noch schlief,
zur Arbeit gingen. Es dachte dann, daß diese
Trottel ja auch im Bett bleiben könnten statt so
penetrant fleißig zu sein. Die Zwerge schauten
zuweilen in den Sarg hinein. Nachdenklich und
traurig standen sie davor, aber dann stellte
Schneewittchen sich tot, bis sie wieder weggingen,
traurig und nachdenklich.

Jetzt mußte wieder einer von den Zwergen auf
den Markt, der fehlte dann im Bergwerk. Auch
beunruhigten sie sich darüber, daß immer mehr
Patrouillen des Königs durch ihre Wälder ritten.
Zwischen dem fünften und dem sechsten Berg
wurde eine Autobahn gebaut. Wir sollten unterir-
dische Gänge anlegen, sagten die Zwerge zueinander, aber wer kann schon so pessimistisch sein.
Seit Urzeiten wohnen wir so wie wir wohnen,

diese Königin ist zwar wohl eine ziemliche Sau, aber so schlimm wird es schon nicht werden.

Dann kam der Prinz über die Lichtung geritten. Die Zwerge waren gerade dabei, ihr Haus neu zu streichen, kaisergelb. Sie hatten die Pinsel an Besenstiele gebunden, um bis in die Giebel hinaufzukommen. Jeder hatte eine Bierflasche neben sich stehen. Stumm sahen sie zu, wie der Prinz von seinem Pferd stieg und zu dem Glassarg ging, der mitten auf der Lichtung stand. Er trug einen blauen Blazer, weiße Freizeithosen, ein hautenges Hemd, eine Studentenverbindungskrawatte und schnürsenkellose Lackstiefel. Mit offenem Mund stand er am Sarg und staunte Schneewittchen an, das ihn gebannt anblickte, denn es wußte, das ist mein Prinz. Wenn er jetzt nicht das rechte Wort findet, tue ich den ersten Schritt. Sie stieg aus dem Sarg.

Die Zwerge standen mit ihren Pinseln in der Hand da. Schneewittchen wendete sich nicht um, als es mit dem Prinzen, engumschlungen, über die Lichtung davonging. »Es wird uns noch nicht einmal eine Postkarte schicken«, sagte der älteste Zwerg leise. Schneewittchen lag inzwischen mit dem Prinzen im Moos, es herzte ihn, bis der Prinz dachte, diese Frau ist einfach irre und ich werde alles tun, um sie zu erobern. Schneewittchen stöhnte vor Glück.

Dann sahen die Zwerge, wie der Prinz das Pferd holte, Schneewittchen vorne auflud und mit ihm davonritt, auf den siebenten Berg zu. Er sagte Schneewittchen mit einem glühenden Kopf, daß sie einen wunderbaren Körper habe, daß sie heiraten würden, daß sie mit dem Geld seines Vaters eine Firma gründen könnten, und daß die Konkurrenz in zwei, drei Jahren mit dem Rücken gegen die Wand stehen müsse, denn sein Vater habe Beziehungen wie niemand sonst. Sein Vater sei ein König, und er sei ein Erbprinz. Schneewittchen küßte ihn.

Im Schloß warf sie ihre Zwergenkleider aus Karomuster weg und kleidete sich standesgemäß ein. Sie gab große Bälle. Der Prinz fand seine Frau toll. Wenn er auf der Jagd war oder Jerusalem belagerte, lag sie mit einem Grafen im Bett, der 56 war und weite Reisen gemacht hatte. Er ist so reif, dachte sie, fast wie mein Papi. Sie bekam ein Kind, eine Tochter. Sie liebte sie. Dann gab sie das Fest, an dem die Stiefmutter die glühenden Eisenschuhe bekam. Ungerührt sah Schneewittchen zu, wie sie herumsprang, schreiend, verzweifelt. Sie ließ die ohnmächtige Tote von den Palastwachen wegschleppen. Dann saß sie am Fenster und sah über die Ebene hinweg, in die Richtung, wo ihr Kinderschloß gewesen war und wo, vielleicht, ihr Vater jetzt Witwer war, wenn er nicht gestorben war. Dann wischte sie sich mit der Hand über die Stirn und ging einkaufen. Die Türen öffneten sich vor ihr, ohne daß sie die Klinken berühren mußte.

Beim Abendessen zeigte ihr Mann ihr auf einer Karte, wie der Feldzug gegen die kleinen heimtückischen Revolutionäre hinter den Bergen vorankam. Das Gebiet bis zum sechsten Berg ist fest in unsrer Hand, sagte er. Wir haben es entlaubt, und schließlich führt ja auch die Autobahn bis dahin, also haben wir mit dem Nachschub keine Probleme. Wir sind auch schon über den siebenten Berg vorgestoßen. Ich habe Fotos vom Hauptquartier bekommen, hier. Stumm schauten sie die Bilder an, auf denen ein zerschossenes, abgebranntes Blockhaus zu sehen war. Davor lagen sieben tote Männer, auf dem Bauch, so daß man ihre Gesichter nicht sehen konnte. Neben ihnen lagen Spitzhacken. Schneewittchen schluckte heftig. Tu das weg, sagte sie, ich kann das nicht sehen. Dann brach sie zusammen. Der König und der ältere Graf, sein Ratgeber, trugen sie zu ihrem Bett. Der König sagte: Frauen sind so sensibel, besonders in unsern Kreisen. Jaja, antwortete der Graf, und darf ich fragen, wann Sie wieder auf die Jagd reiten wollen oder zu einer Belagerung? Ich möchte mich, wie immer, um die Stallungen kümmern. Morgen, sagte der König, ich muß den

Feldzug jetzt persönlich leiten, die hinter dem letzten Berg scheinen die zähesten zu sein. Stellen Sie sich vor, sie haben ganze Labyrinthe unter der Erde angelegt, um fliehen zu können, wenn unsre Panzer ihre Hütten zusammenkartätschen. Der Graf sagte: Unglaublich, was die sich alles erlauben.

Jahre vergingen. Schneewittchens Kind wurde größer und groß, und eines Morgens hatte Schneewittchens Spiegel einen neuen Klang, als Schneewittchen in ihn hineinschaute. Am Frühstück sahen sich die beiden Frauen in die Augen, die alte und die junge. Die junge Frau dachte an glühende Schuhe, die alte an herausgeschnittene Zungen. Wie alt bist du jetzt eigentlich? fragte Schneewittchen sein Kind. Vierzehn, sagte dieses. Darf ich heute nacht bei einer Freundin schlafen, nur eine Nacht lang? Na schön, sagte Schneewittchen, zu meiner Zeit gab es sowas zwar nicht, aber bitte. Das Kind ging hinaus. Schneewittchen schaltete das Fernsehen ein. Ihr Mann stand in der Tagesschau vor abgebrannten Hütten, er wies empört auf Spitzhacken mit verkohlten Stielen und sagte: Und mit *solchen* Waffen haben diese, ich kann es nicht anders sagen, Unmenschen auf unsere tapferen Soldaten eingeschlagen! Schneewittchen schaltete aufs zweite Programm. Sie glotzte einen Schlagersänger an. Das Geschenk, das sie einmal jemandem machen wollte, hatte sie vergessen. Ihr machte auch niemand ein Geschenk.

Sie lag schon im Bett, als ihr Mann zurückkam, spät in der Nacht. Er hatte ein bißchen den Sieg gefeiert mit seinen Funktionären. Weißt du was, sagte er kichernd, als er neben Schneewittchen lag, da hinter den sieben Bergen sind eigentlich nur Wälder und Schluchten und Seen und Flüsse. Die Braunkohle liegt an der Erdoberfläche. Der Abbau kostet ein Butterbrot. Der Prinz mußte sich im Bett aufsetzen, weil er einen Hustenanfall bekam. Schneewittchen sah ihn mit großen Augen an. Ja aber, sagte es dann leise, im Fernsehen hast du doch gesagt, daß dort böse Leute wohnen. Der Prinz bekam jetzt wieder Luft und nahm eine Tablette mit Wasser. Er schluckte. Er strich Schneewittchen über die Haare. Jaja, sagte er. Beide lächelten. Der Prinz löschte das Licht und kuschelte sich an seine Frau, die noch immer Haare wie Ebenholz, Lippen wie Blut und eine Haut wie Schnee hatte.

Rinaldo Rinaldini

Rinaldo Rinaldini ist edel, hilfreich und gut. Er trägt einen roten Hut. Unter seinem Hut sind Geheimnisse verborgen.

Rinaldo lebt in einer tiefen warmen Höhle, in den Bergen Siziliens, zusammen mit vierzig andern Räubern, seinen Freunden. Wenn sie wieder einmal eine Filiale der Banco dello Santo Spirito ausgeplündert und das Geld an die Landarbeiter verteilt haben, reiten sie singend durch die Olivenhaine bis zu ihrem Untergrund zurück, zu ihren Frauen, die, in Baby Dolls, auf Laubbetten auf sie gewartet haben. Rinaldos Freundin heißt Rosalie. Sie hat eine rosa Haut, himmelblaue Augen, warme Hände. Sie ist wie Pfeffer. Rinaldo liebt sie. Sie liegen in der dunklen Höhle beieinander, sie lecken sich in den Ohren, von überall her hören sie das Lachen und Ächzen der andern Räuber und Mädchen, tausendfach verstärkt durch die Reflektion der Höhlenwände. Nur der wachhabende Räuber sitzt einsam in seiner Pinie, er friert und kratzt sich am Hintern.

Stunden später wärmt die Sonne die Nase des Räubers im Ausguck. Er erwacht. Benommen reibt er sich die Augen. Gott im Himmel, ruft er dann, noch zehn Minuten, bis die Postkutsche kommt, die bis zum Halszäpfchen mit Gold angefüllt sein wird. Wie ein Tobsüchtiger reißt er an der Liane, deren Ende an den Deckbetten der schlafenden Räuber und Räuberinnen befestigt ist. Schon liegen alle frierend da. Sie setzen sich auf. Dann begreifen sie. Die Räuber sausen wie die Feuerwehrleute in die Hosen, Hemden und Stiefel, während die Mädchen lachend die Arme in die Höhe recken und sich dann noch einmal aufs Ohr legen. Rinaldo küßt Rosa, die ganz verschlafene Augen hat. Dann schwingt er sich von Pinie zu Pinie, zum geplanten Kampfplatz hin.

Die Räuber haben einen Baum umgesägt und halten ihn mit den Schultern im labilen Gleichgewicht. Sie sehen eine ferne Staubwolke, die schnell näher kommt. Ein Rauchsignal ihres Vorpostens sagt Rinaldo, daß das Goldfahrzeug wie vorgesehen nur einen dicken Spekulanten, seine Sekretärin sowie zwei bullige Polizisten enthält, dazu den Kutscher. Den Kutscher werde ich ungeschoren lassen, denkt Rinaldo, nicht aber die Sekretärin, die für ihre lieblosen Liebesnächte im Hotel Hilton ruhig ein bißen büßen kann. Oder schläft meine Rosa auch nur mit mir, weil ich der Chef bin?

Da donnert der gepanzerte Ford Transit um die Kurve. Rinaldo Rinaldini gibt das Zeichen. Der Baum fällt auf die Straße. Die Räuber hören die Reifen quietschen, dann kracht es. Lachend stürzen sie zum Wrack hinunter. Sie schneiden es mit Schneidbrennern auf. Das Gold wird auf Maultiere geladen. Es sind Züchtungen, die Rinaldo von Großvater zu Vater zu Sohn geerbt hat und die geradeaus wie Windhunde, bergauf wie Gemsen und bergab wie uralte Bergführer laufen. Der Spekulant und seine Geliebte müssen ihre Kleider ausziehen. Rinaldo signiert ihre Hinterbacken, dann schickt er sie los. Er schaut ihnen nach, wie sie, mit seinen wabbelnden Unterschriften, über die spitzen Steine stelzen. Die Polizisten werden an einen Affenbrotbaum gebunden. Der Kutscher bekommt einen Klumpen Gold, der ihm einen schönen Lebensabend garantiert. Glücklich verschwindet er im Olivenhain. Dann schwingen sich die Räuber auf ihre Gäule und rasen, mit den Maultieren im Schlepp, davon. Kilometerweit hören die Bauern in ihren Lehmhütten das Donnern der Hufe. Sie wissen, daß die Gerechtigkeit in Italien wieder einige Zentimeter weiter vorangekommen ist.

Staunend blicken die Mädchen auf das viele Gold. Rinaldo, sagt Rosa leise: nur einmal in unserm Leben wollen wir zusammen auf den Jahrmarkt von Palermo gehen, wie alle Leute. Bitte, bitte. Rinaldo nickt nachdenklich. Seit Jahren hat er keinen Film mehr gesehen, kein Eis mehr gegessen, keine Gartenwirtschaft mehr betreten, auf keine Papierrose mehr geschossen. Er ist so ernst geworden. Er seufzt. Räubergenossen, ruft er dann heiser, ich verlasse euch für 48 Stunden. Kümmert euch um die gerechte Verteilung des Goldes an die Armen. Seid wachsam. Wir bringen euch dafür Lebkuchen und Teddybären mit, die wir beim Lottospielen gewinnen werden.

Rinaldo und Rosa fahren mit ihrem Fiat Topolino über die holprigen Wege Siziliens. Sie küssen sich. Sie zeigen sich die Sonne über dem blauen Meer. Sie singen. Am Straßenrand stehen zwei Gestalten, die winken. Rinaldo lächelt. Er bremst. Wir haben leider nur einen Zweiplätzer, meine Herren, sagt er. Aber Sie können auf den Trittbrettern mitfahren. Die beiden nicken. Sie sind verdreckt und voller Mückenstiche. Warum sind Sie nackt, fragt Rosa schließlich den, der auf ihrer Seite steht, und was steht auf Ihrem Hintern? Wenn Sie wüßten, wenn Sie wüßten, sagt dieser. Ich bin ein ehrbarer Bürger Siziliens, aber das ist

die Höhe! Ich werde diese Banditen zu Tode hetzen lassen! Der Gendarmerieoberst von Palermo
gehorcht mir aufs Wort! So? sagt Rinaldo und
erhöht die Geschwindigkeit auf 160. Die Brüste
der Sekretärin werden vom Fahrtwind nach hinten gedrückt.

Rinaldo und Rosa gehen Zuckerwatte essend über
den Jahrmarkt. Sie lachen. Sie gehen in ein
Kaspertheater, wo Rinaldo Rinaldinis Taten
gezeigt werden. Alle Leute klatschen wie wild.
Rosa klatscht mit leuchtenden Augen, länger als
alle andern. Dann essen sie ein Eis. Dann legen sie
sich, abseits, in der schon tiefer stehenden Sonne,
unter einen Olivenbaum. Rinaldo kitzelt die
Nase Rosas mit einem Grashalm. Er sieht ihre
atmende Brust. Er legt seine Hand darauf, dann
aber seufzt er und sagt: Jetzt müssen wir, sonst
reißen uns die Räuber die Höhle über dem Kopf
ein.

Heiß und staubig ist die Straße, über die sie zum
Grottensystem zurückfahren. Rosa und Rinaldo
sprechen kein Wort. Der wachhabende Räuber
im äußersten Ausguck ist nicht da. Wenn die Katz
aus dem Haus ist, sagt Rinaldo Rinaldini, dann
tanzen die Mäuse, und Gott weiß, mit wem, und
was.

Zu Fuß gehen sie dann den vertrauten Geheimpfad hoch. Auch der Räuber vom inneren Ausguck ist zum Tanz gegangen. Endlich tritt ihnen einer der Räuber entgegen, mit seinem Schnauzbart, seinem Hut, seiner Indianerdecke. Aber was ist mit ihm? Er geht anders, und er ist dicker geworden.

Verrat, ruft Rosa als erste. Sie hat den verkleideten Gendarmerieoberst von Palermo erkannt. Rinaldo zieht die Pistole. Jetzt sieht er auch die Leichen der toten Kameraden. Er wirft sich hinter einen Felsen. Flieh, ruft er Rosa zu, flieh! Leb wohl! Weinend schießt er alle Magazine leer, während Rosa den Waldhang hinunterstürzt. Ich werde sie nie wieder sehen, denkt Rinaldo, während er auf die Schatten schießt, die er nun in allen Baumwipfeln erkennt. Als sie verschwunden ist, wirft er die Pistole weg und steht auf. Hocherhobenen Hauptes geht er auf die übriggebliebenen Poliziottos zu.

Rinaldo wird mit verbundenen Augen zum Richtplatz geführt. Eine vieltausendköpfige Menge umsteht das Richtgerüst. Verkehrspolizisten regeln den Verkehr. Rinaldo wird die Schlinge um den Hals gelegt. Die Televisione italiana will von ihm ein letztes Wort. Freunde, sagt er, dieser

Klüngel von Großgrundbesitzern, Weinfabrikanten, Chemiedirektoren und Kultusministern wird nicht mehr lange das Recht haben, ehrbare Räuber aufzuhängen, denn ... Da aber haut ihm der neben ihm stehende Polizist eine aufs Maul, und man schreitet zur Exekution.

Halt, ruft da eine ferne Mädchenstimme. Rinaldo erschauert. Es ist Rosa. Sie kommt über den Platz gerannt. Sie klettert auf das Brettergerüst. Ein Raunen geht durch die Menge. Rosa ist schön wie nie. Sie glänzt und glüht. Euer Gnaden, sagt sie zum diensthabenden Richter, ich bin bereit, nach uraltem Gesetz diesen Rechtsbrecher hier zu ehelichen und ihn dadurch vor dem Tod zu bewahren. Alle Zuschauer applaudieren wie wild.

Dieses Gesetz gilt nicht mehr seit 1933, ruft der Richter mit einem roten Gesicht. Ich weiß, wer du bist. Du bist Rosa. Ich werde dich neben ihn hängen, du linke Räubersau. Der Richter legt Rosa eine Schlinge um den Hals. Die Zuschauer stöhnen auf. Rosa faßt die Hand Rinaldos. Beide werden gleichzeitig vom Schemel gestoßen. Sie strampeln mit den Beinen, dann hängen sie still, Hand in Hand. Die Leute starren hinauf. Sie sehen das fette Gesicht des Richters, der eine Tablette ißt und dann seine Gehilfen anherrscht.

Sie knirschen mit den Zähnen. Dann gehen sie, schweigend, in die umliegenden Restaurants, das Gesehene zu bereden.

Ein ganzes Leben

7 Uhr Frühmorgens kräht der Hahn. Der Wagen des Milchmanns rumpelt durch die Straße. Wir spüren, daß unsere Leintücherchen und Deckbettchen starr werden. Unsere Mutter hat die Wiege im frostweißen Garten vergessen.

9 Uhr Eine schräge Sonne fällt uns auf die Nase. Wespen surren. Es ist warm. Wir glotzen aus dem Stubenwagen und sehen den Vater, der sich mit der Mutter balgt. Sie stehen in den Tomaten und haben rote Gesichter. Warum, warum schreien sie so?

11 Uhr Um 11 Uhr früh essen wir einen Pausenapfel. Wir schlürfen eine uperisierte Milch mit einem Strohhalm. Ohh, wir hassen Milch, handwarme, kuhwarme, brustwarme. Dann stürmen wir in die Klasse zurück, wo wir eine Schnur an den Stuhl des Religionslehrers binden. Wir lächeln ihm zu. Paul reißt, als der Religionslehrer seinen frommen Hintern auf den Stuhl tun will, an der Schnur.

13 Uhr Nach dem Mittagessen sitzen wir in unsern gebügelten Hosen an der Schwarzkaffeetafel. Vor der Hecke gehen die Arbeiter mit ihren Kappen vorbei. Wir paffen Rauch in die Luft. Wir denken, wortlos, daß wir Präsidenten der General Motors oder berühmte Nuklearforscher werden können.

15 Uhr Jetzt ist aber schon Nachmittag. Die Sonne steht hoch am Himmel. Unser alter Vater hat ein gelbes, faltiges Gesicht. Er ist tot. Wir müssen ins Kontor hinunter und die Kunden beruhigen. Tränenlos starren wir in die Geschäftsbücher. Wir addieren die Zahlen. Der Lehrling steht neben uns und sagt, 10 Mark mehr oder ich gehe.

17 Uhr Während des Fünfuhrtees treten die Honoratioren der Stadt mit Vorschlägen an uns heran. Sie lächeln uns an, reiben sich die Hände und werfen sich Blicke zu, während wir in den Papieren blättern. Sie bieten uns Zigarren an. Wir haben endlich genug von ihnen und werfen sie aus dem Haus. Die Herren schreien, daß sie sich rächen werden. Wir wissen auch schon, wie. Sie werden uns das Ladenlokal kündigen, und dann sitzen wir da, im Zenith unsres Lebens, mit dem Arsch im kalten Schlamm.

19 Uhr So kommt es. Die Sonne neigt sich dem Horizont zu. Wir haben keinen Laden mehr, und ein Erspartes, wie uns unsre längst tote Mutter geraten hat, haben wir auch nicht. Wir lesen in den Geschäftsbüchern. Es wird kühl in unserem möblierten Zimmer. Wir weinen. Wir haben keine Hauskatze.

21 Uhr Die Sonne ist untergegangen. In unserer uralten Hausjacke sitzen wir im Gasthaus, in einer Ecke, am Ofen. Wir trinken ein Glas Rotwein. Die Bedienung kassiert jedes Glas einzeln. Wir denken an die Zeit, wo ein Hahn krähte und die Wiege schaukelte. Wo nur? War es kalt, oder was?

23 Uhr Jetzt ist es dunkel. Wir zünden ein Licht an, aber wir sehen nicht viel. Wir hören, daß die andern Leute lachen und kreischen. Sie sprechen, auch mit uns, aber wir kommen nicht drauf, wovon sie reden. Wir lächeln und nicken mit dem Kopf. Jaja, sagen wir. Wenn wir nur unsere Geschäftsbücher noch hätten, sagen wir zu unsern Nachbarn, da standen herrliche Dinge darin. So etwas gibt es heute nicht mehr. Wir haben sie verloren. Sie enthielten unser ganzes Leben.

Ein Spaziergang

Karl sieht von seinem Schaukelstuhl hoch und flüstert Otto zu: »Die Feuer brennen in unsern Kaminen. Es ist still so allein in den Zimmern. Wir summen Melodien. Wir schauen durch unsere Fenster. Es geht kein Wind. In der Ferne ziehen Wolken vorbei. Wie sollen wir das jetzt ausdrücken, denken wir alle.«

Otto wispert gelassen, während er sich auf die Couch setzt: »Wir stehen also alle auf und gehen eine Weile hin und her. Wir schauen ein wenig auf die Straßen. Es ist warm. Leise ticken die Weckeruhren. Diese von uns stellen das Radio an, jene machen sich ein Vitamin C. Es ist still bei uns allen.«

Karl murmelt zurückhaltend und faltet die Zeitung zusammen: »Der Forscher, dieses Arschloch, in seinem Kammgarnanzug, ist schon längst unterwegs. Er sieht nicht rückwärts und nicht seitwärts. Er hat jeden Handgriff tausendfach geübt. Er ist stolz. Er atmet nach seinem Atemplan, und jetzt nimmt er eine Tablette.«

Otto tuschelt entspannt und holt die Rotweinflasche: »Plötzlich nehmen wir alle unsre Reiseta-
schen, packen die Dinge hinein und ziehen die
Schuhe an. Wir werfen einen letzten Blick ins
Zimmer. Wir schließen die Tür. Der Herbststurm
dröhnt durch den Park, aber schon sind wir im
Bahnhof, schon sitzen wir im Zug.«

Karl sagt bescheiden und stellt die Heizung
höher: »Ich trage mein Käppi. Du trägst deinen
Mantel wie immer, Hans trägt seinen karierten
Anzug und sein Monokel, Sepp trägt seinen Bür-
stenschnitt und den Hammer. Sepp hat eine kräf-
tige Stimme. Hans hat schlacksige Beine. Du
lachst. Ich schaue zum Fenster hinaus.«

Otto erwidert verträumt und ordnet die Blumen
in der Vase: »Ich sage, wo sind denn diese sagen-
haften Alpen? Ich lache. Ich kann doch nichts
dafür, sagst du bleich zu mir, der Vater von meinem Vater hat noch eine freilebende Kuh gesehen.
Wir löschen das Abteillicht. Es ist schade, daß wir
keine Kraniche sind.«

Karl spricht heiter und macht die Vorhänge zu:
»Nachts kommen wir dann doch noch in den
ersten Gasthof, der diese Bezeichnung verdient.
Der Wirt sagt uns, was er noch in der Küche hat

zu dieser nachtschlafenden Stunde. Wir essen. Jetzt erzählen wir, was wir alles noch für Pläne haben. Alle staunen.«

Otto bestätigt innig und verhängt die blendende Tischlampe: »Dann gehen wir alle zusammen ins Massenlager. Wir blasen die Kerze aus. Ach. Der Spaziergang morgen wird uns gut tun, sagst du. Ich höre dich rascheln. Aus der nächsten Pritsche kommen dumpfe Schläge, und aus der übernächsten kullert das Monokel.«

Karl versetzt herzlich und bietet Otto seine Flasche an: »Bald werden wir wieder richtig singen, flüstere ich. Vor dem Fenster rauschen die Arven. Als die ersten Sonnenstrahlen durch die Fensterläden dringen, drehen wir uns nochmals um in unsern zerknautschten Linnen, aber nicht mehr lange. Auf, rufst du, auf.«

Otto meint zart und zieht seine gefütterte Wolljacke aus: »Beim Frühstück studieren wir unsern Plan. Da, sagt Sepp, da muß es durch gehen, da wo die weißen Flecken auf der Karte sind. Dort oben müssen die Quellen des Flusses sein. Wir prägen uns den Weg ein. Der Wirt schüttelt den Kopf. Wir bezahlen.«

Karl stimmt empfindsam zu und stochert im Kohlenofen: »Wir gehen. Die schroffen Felswände ragen neben uns in die Höhe, und der Sand knirscht unter unsern Schuhen. Vor Hans zischt eine Schlange davon. Wer weiß, sage ich, ob da vorn die Quellen des Flusses sind oder die Bergschluchten. Du lachst.«

Otto gibt bewegt zu bedenken und nimmt einen Schluck Glühwein: »Der heiße Atem des Mittagswindes bricht auf uns nieder. Wir werden einen Sonnenbrand haben, wenn wir so weitermachen, sagt Hans, und wenn wir den Gletscher erreichen, droht uns die Schneeblindheit. Du setzt das Käppi auf. Ich lache. Sepp brummt.«

Karl teilt Otto beseelt mit, während er die Platte auflegt: »An den Quellen brauchen wir viel Phantasie, um uns vorstellen zu können, was aus diesen paar Tropfen weiter unten wird. Wir setzen uns in den glühenden Sand mit unsern Hintern. Komm, sagen wir, wir wollen unsern Bericht durchlesen. Es kommt auf jedes Wort an.«

Otto berichtet freudig und kühlt seine Stirn mit dem Eis: »Dennoch, wir können zufrieden sein. Höchstens die Beschreibung der Schluchten hätte uns lebendiger geraten können. Wir legen uns ein bißchen hin. Morgen werden wir Hungers sterben. Ein leiser Wind weht, und ganz hoch oben fliegt ein Flugzeug.«

Karl legt glücklich dar und gibt Otto die Früchte hinüber: »Wir keuchen. Schweiß steht auf unsern Stirnen. Es ist einfach zu trocken hier an den Quellen des Flusses, das wenige, was da herauskommt, reicht nicht aus für unsern Durst. Wir trinken, ich ein Tropfen, Sepp ein Tropfen, Hans ein Tropfen, du ein Tropfen.«

Otto äußert sich bezaubert und streckt sich auf der Couch aus: »Indessen stoffelt der Forscher durchs Unterholz. Er hat ein verkratztes Gesicht, seine Füße verheddern sich in den Lianen, und die Bienen haben ihn angestochen. Fieberhaft blättert er im Durchhaltebuch. Dieser Fall ist nicht vorgesehen, was nun?«

Karl erklärt warm und wischt sich den Schweiß von der Stirn: »Wenn wir nicht auf dem Löwenwechsel lägen, hätten wir eine ruhige Nacht. Aber immer wieder streichen uns die Mähnenhaare übers Gesicht, so daß wir schließlich ziemlich erschlagen aufwachen. Bis an den Horizont schlängelt sich der Sandpfad. Wir schnaufen.«

Otto stellt entzückt fest und wirft die Hose in die Ecke: »Endlich sind wir auf dem Gipfel. Wir haben einen herrlichen Rundblick, es ist fast so schön, wie wir es erwartet haben. Abwärts, sagen wir zueinander, können wir dann die Bahn nehmen, wir sehen, daß diese Unterländer sich schon zu uns hochbauen. Das können sie gut.«

Karl erwähnt lustvoll und setzt sich zu Otto auf die Couch hinüber: »Ich sage zum Ingenieur, der jetzt eintrifft, sollen wir Ihnen berichten, was wir für Erlebnisse an den Quellen hatten? Aber der Ingenieur ist damit beschäftigt, ein gefährliches Steinbockloch zuzuschaufeln. Jetzt aber kann es losgehen, sagt er dann, klar?«

Otto beteuert erregt und reckt und streckt und dehnt sich: »Wir schauen ein letztes Mal um uns herum. Die Berggipfel sind herrlich, weiß, aufragend, abweisend, eisig, großartig. Wir können uns nicht sattsehen. Ein kalter Wind pfeift uns um die Ohren. Wir haben die Münder offen. Wir machen uns auf den Abstieg.«

Karl ruft begeistert und schaut Otto in die Augen: »Der Forscher zappelt in der Nordwand. Er beißt auf die Zähne. Ein falscher Tritt, und er lernt den freien Fall in der Praxis kennen. Er wirft den Ballast die Felswand hinunter. Was bin ich für ein Tropf, denkt er mit Eistränen in den Augenwinkeln.«

Otto schreit atemlos und ergreift Karls Hand: »Plötzlich hören wir ein Poltern über uns. Ich lache, während ich wild einherspringe. Hans schlenkert mit den Beinen, das Monokel rutscht ihm aus dem Auge. Sepp wird vom Schnee einge- pappt, wie eine Kugel saust er abwärts. Du rennst wie der Teufel.«

Karl brüllt leidenschaftlich und drückt seinen Kopf an Ottos Brust: »Grausam donnert die Lawine durchs Tal. Sie schiebt Tannen, Stadel und Felsblöcke mit sich. Den Leuten im Tal stockt, als sie das Geräusch hören, das Herz. Im Schein der Blendlaternen stapfen die Frauen auf dem Ort der Katastrophe herum. Es ist eisig kalt.«

Otto heult überschäumend und preßt Karl an sich: »Mit langen Stangen stochern alle im Lawi- nenkegel herum, und es rächt sich, daß wir alle kein gutes Verhältnis zu Hunden hatten. Die Frauen weinen. Als sie uns dann ausgraben und in eine Reihe gelegt haben, sind wir kalt, steif und vereist.«

Jetzt kreischt Karl erschüttert: »Der Forscher, der jetzt auch da ist, zieht den Hut. In der Ferne klingt die Glocke, die der Abendzug aus dem Tal ist, den der Forscher nehmen muß, um den Bericht abzuliefern, der durch das unvermutete Ereignis naß, verspritzt und zerknautscht ist.«

Freitag der dreizehnte

Ich wackle mit dem Kopf, meine Rückenwirbel knacken, meine Muskeln schmerzen, und zwischen meinen Beinen sticht mich eine Nadel, zwischen Arsch und Schwanz.

Mein Vater hatte immer mehr Schmerzen, bis er starb. Er sah aus wie eine Maus in der Falle. Alles war ausweglos. Ich sah ihn an und war jung und schwor, nie werde ich den leisesten Schmerz in meinem Körper fühlen. Ich habe meine Mutter totgewünscht. Ist das jetzt die Rache? Damit ich nicht alles zusammenschlage, schreibe ich ortografisch richtig.

Einmal sagte ein kleiner Junge zu mir, deine Mutter ist eben gestorben. Ich hetzte nach Hause. Meine Mutter stand in der Küche. Ich starrte sie an.

Vielleicht habe *ich* die Ketten festgebunden? Vielleicht gehen andere frei und ungebunden durch Herbstblumen und Kiefernwälder? Ich will, daß da Ketten sind. Ich raßle mit ihnen.

Manchmal hoffe ich, wenn ich alt bin, kommt eine Zeit, wo jede Rücksicht von mir abfällt und ich kompromißlos wie ein Donnerschlag bin.

Schluß mit dem Blick zurück. Ein satter Messerschnitt, der alle Drähte nach hinten durchhaut.

Ich habe nicht das Gefühl, daß der Mensch eine zähe Konstruktion ist, und daß ich Herr über mein Schicksal bin. Ich ertrage *Filme* über den Faschismus nicht.

Reden ist besser als Schreiben. Schweigen ist gar nichts. Wenn ich stumm vor mich hindenke, komme ich bis zu dem Punkt, an dem ich die Dämonen wecke. Kaum knurrt einer, wende ich mich ab.

Eine Schlinge um den Hals: als Kind dachte ich, ich komme in den Estrich und da hängt jemand. Ich selber habe nie so Spiele versucht. Ich bin nicht verrückt. Meine Mutter hielt, glaube ich, jemanden schon für verrückt, der seine Mütze verkehrt herum trug.

Als ich *Une saison en enfer* von Rimbaud las, dachte ich, ich weiß jederzeit ganz genau, wie es weitergeht. Später ging Rimbaud in die Wüste und schrieb kein einziges Wort mehr. Die Schicksale der andern sind immer eher schwarz als hell. Ich liebe Verdi, weil er alt wurde, in Frieden starb, und weil seine Musik erwachsen klingt. Er war der Lieblingskomponist meines Großvaters, der meine Mutter so schikaniert hat, daß sie bis ins Alter wie Espenlaub zitterte. Wenn es ihr nicht ganz gut ging, war ihr Lieblingsthema, wie sehr etwas etwas anderes verunstalten kann: ein Pickel eine Frau, eine Marmelade einen Teppich, ein Ton eine Sinfonie. Immer konnte etwas Schönes noch schöner sein.

Warum sind Menschen keine Zebras, die aus dem Muttertier herausfallen, sich schütteln und, nach zehn Minuten, vor dem ersten Löwen ihres Lebens davongaloppieren?

Und so geht das immer weiter. Ich will aber nicht, daß es so weitergeht. Ich will nicht, daß ich Susanne böse ansehe, nur weil meine Mutter früher einmal hinter mir dreinging und in meinen Rücken hineinredete.

Ich träumte: ich stand in der Tür meines Zimmers und sah ein Treppenhaus hinunter in einen Vorraum, in dem eine junge wunderhübsche Frau vor einem Spiegel stand und sich ihre nackte Brust ansah. Sie hielt ihre Hände darunter. Plötzlich blickte sie nach oben. Sie lächelte, aber ich schämte mich. Später wagte ich mich wieder vor. Jetzt war sie weg, d. h. ich sah sie in ihrem Spiegel, sie lag auf einem Bett und zog sich eine Strumpfhose an.

Ich kenne die Requisiten meines Traums: der Spiegel ist der Spiegel meiner Mutter, und das Bett das meines Vaters. Vielleicht rief die Frau nach mir, aber wenn, dann hörte ich es nicht, oder ich traute mich nicht.

Der Flug von der Euphorie in die Panik dauert eine Sekunde. Wer verliebt ist, ist gut dran.

Vielleicht akzeptierten die Neandertaler ihre Grenzen? Heute gibt es Skiläufer, die glauben, daß das alpine Wetter vom Verkehrsverein gemacht wird. Wenn es windet, gehen sie hin und beschweren sich.

Mein Vater spielte zwei Wochen lang auf dem Grammophon in voller Lautstärke den ganzen Tag über ununterbrochen die Kantate von Bach: Ich freue mich auf meinen Tod.

Ich habe ein Tonband von ihm, von einem Vortrag, das ich in den elf Jahren, seitdem er tot ist, noch nie angehört habe. Manchmal, wenn ich eine Schallplatte suche, sehe ich es.

Ich bin 38, habe keinen Krieg erlebt, bin gesund, verdiene mein Geld, und ich beklage mich.

Wenn die Wirbel knacken, hoffe ich, daß, aller Evidenz zum Trotz, das ganze Elend der Welt und meines damit mit einem einzigen Ruck ins rechte Lot gerückt wird. Immer wieder versuche ich es.

Das Schreckliche an *Une saison en enfer* ist, daß Rimbaud überhaupt kein Prosastück schreiben wollte, sondern seine Existenz durch einen wilden Schlag ganz anders machen wollte. Wie im Fieber schrieb er. Als er fertig war und nichts sich geändert hatte als daß da ein scheißiges kleines Stück Prosa vor ihm lag, war er völlig verzweifelt. Noch zwei drei Mal versuchte er es, dann ließ er die Dichterei sein. Er konnte sich nicht daran gewöhnen, daß sie nichts veränderte, daß er er blieb, derselbe in derselben Haut, unausweichbar.

Das ist das Ende

Giacomo, es ist Winter geworden. Louis Armstrong in den glitzernden Bergen. Ich mit Puccini in Lianen verwickelt. Einmal muß auch Mimi sterben, aber noch nicht.

Vater, Vater, was ist das für ein Heulen?

Hier ist die Luft rein, die Verliebten springen Hand in Hand in den Tod, blöd glotzt der verhinderte Schwiegervater hinter ihnen drein.

Für Helen. Aber niemand weiß, wo sie ist, seit jenem Abend, als sie mich weinend verließ. Jetzt habe ich nur noch diese Schellackplatte, in die sie mit ihren Stöckelschuhen getreten ist.

Mord.

Sie saß einmal an diesem Tisch, aber jetzt ist sie längst weg. Soll ich das Getöse der Freunde in ein stummes Trauern verwandeln?

Immer auf dem Rücken liegen.

Vater, oder so ähnlich.

Als das Bier 30 Rappen kostete.

Das ist das Ende.

In der Mitte des Lebens klappert der Tod über den Horizont herauf. Schafe gehen blökend über die Grenzen. Die Sonne geht auch in den Städten unter. Aber was hatten wir gestern für Wetter?

Federico, du säufst. Du säufst ja.

Langsam verreckt das Schiff im Sand.

Herrschen, über wen, und warum?

Die Geliebten altern uns unter der Hand weg, und wir ihnen. Der Pfarrer geht mit einem Hammer durch das Haus und zerschlägt alle Spiegel. Später dann sitzen wir mit Augenkrebs am Bahndamm und schreien.

Giuseppe Verdi, übers rote Meer spazierend.

Vom heißen Geisir überrascht, knetet die junge Frau ihren verbrühten Hintern. Vierzigtausend Langläufer gleiten über den erfrorenen See, da bricht dieser endlich auf.

Vor die Wahl zwischen Bluthund und Abgrund gestellt, springen wir, Mund an Mund.

Jetzt, Mutter, jetzt.

Das Schwimmbad färbt sich langsam rot. Niemand kennt den Schmerz des Bademeisters. Über den eisharten Sumpf fliehend merkt der Gejagte, daß die Sonne immer wärmer scheint. Der Schauspieler schlägt seinen Kopf gegen den eisernen Vorhang.

Das ist das Ende.

$$\overline{\quad 5 \quad}$$

Schweizer Dialoge

Dialog über den 1. August

FRAU: Du. Hütt isch dr erscht Auguscht.

MANN: Heillandssack. Jetzt ha-n-i die bengalische Zündhölzli vrgässe.

FRAU: Worum isch hütt dr erscht Auguscht?

MANN: Erschte Auguscht isch jedes Johr.

FRAU: Nei. I mein, wenn isch dr erscht erscht Auguscht gsi, und worum?

MANN: Jä weisch das nit?

FRAU: Hett do dr Täll uff dr Öpfel . . .

MANN: Aber nei. 1291. Gründung der Eidgenossenschaft.

FRAU: Worum?

MANN: Will, do sinn fremdi Kaiser gsi und die hänn uns Schwyzer untrdruggt. Mir Schwyzer halte das nit lang us, wemme is d Freiheit ewägg nimmt. Drumm hämmer is heimlig uff em Rütli droffe und gschwore, daß mr die fremde Vögt dootschlöön.

FRAU: Hett me das denn dörfe?

MANN: I weiß nit. I glaub nit. Wart, i vrzell dr lieber d Schlacht bi Morgarte.

FRAU: Worum?

MANN: Paß uff. Unsri Find sinn uff ihre Rösser gsässe. Si hänn Rüschtige aakaa. Si hänn sich die schön Landschaft zeigt. Si sinn jo no nie in dr Schwyz gsi.

FRAU: Und denn?

MANN: Unsre Hauptmaa hett is d Taktik erklärt. Er hett müese improvisiere, es isch jo au *si* erschti Schlacht gsi. Denn simmer losgange. Plötzlig hämmer unde, am See unde, die fremde Ritter gseh. Mr hänn aafoo Schtei dr Bärg aberolle, und d Ritter hänn uffegluegt und hänn unseri Schtei gseh und hänn dänggt: O Tod, küßt du heute schon meinen rosenfarbenen Mund.

FRAU: Schön.

MANN: Mr hänn die Ritter in See kippt.

FRAU: O verreggt.

MANN: D Schlacht vo Sämpach isch no viil schpannender.

FRAU: Isch das die mit de Fraue?

MANN: Nei. Dasch Näfels gsi. In Sämpach sinn uff dr einte Site Basler, Baselbieter, Aargauer, Zürcher, Fricktaler und Schaffhuser gsi. Dasch dr Find gsi.

FRAU: Worum?

MANN: *Mir* hänn damals alli Mälchthal oder Winkelried oder Stauffacher gheiße.

FRAU: Hütt heißt niemerz me so.

MANN: Natürlig nit. Das sinn alles Helde gsi. Die sinn alli gfalle.

FRAU: Hänn die keini Kinder ka?

MANN: Helde hänn nie Kinder. Jetz baß uff. Do sinn mir und do isch dr Find. Do sinn Öpfel-bäum. Do oobe isch e Hügel. Do isch no-n-e Hügel, und do schtoots Beihuus mit dr Schlachtkapälle.

FRAU: Aha.

MANN: S Beihuus hett me erscht noch dr Schlacht baut. Me hett nämmlig nie gnau gwüßt, wo die Schlachte jetzt schtattfinde. Eimol do, eimol dört, die sinn wie verruggd gsi damals. Und s isch natürlig blöd, wenn de e düür Beihuus in, saage mr, Interlake bausch, und denn gits in Interlake überhaupt nie e Schlacht.

FRAU: Klar.

MANN: D Find hänn wahnsinnig viil Schpeer gha, ein näbenem andere. Do sinn si gschtande, zwi-schenem Hügel und em See.

FRAU: Hänn si sich scho widr näbene See gschtellt?

MANN: Jä. Abr mir hänn dismol vo vorne aagriffe, nit vo oobe.

FRAU: Worum?

MANN: Taktik.

FRAU: Aha.

MANN: D Harschthörner hänn bloose, mr hänn aagriffe und sinn in d Schpeer iinegloffe und doot gsi.

FRAU: Ohh.

MANN: Denn isch die zweit Reihe koo, in d Schpeer iinegloffe und doot gsi.

FRAU: Nei.

MANN: So sinn Schwyzer Soldate. Si folge uffs Wort. I ha ghört, s git hütt no e baar, wo sich sit em letschte Grieg im Wald vrschtegge und Wurzle und Beeri ässe und dr Rhy bewache. Si wänn nit ha, daß dr Aktivdienscht umme isch.

FRAU: Wenn das dr General Guisan wüßt.

MANN: Denn isch dr Winkelried uffdrätte. Er hett grüeft: Sorget für mein Weib und meine Kinder.

FRAU: Grad hesch gseit, daß Helde keini Kinder hänn.

MANN: Hänn si au nit. Abr si saage so Setz wie dä do.

FRAU: Worum?

MANN: Und denn hett er so viil Schpeer gno wie-n-er nur hett könne und hett si sich in d Bruscht druggt. Und mir sinn über si doote Körper in die hohl Gass gange und hänn d Schlacht gwunne.

FRAU: Hm. Wurdsch du so öppis mache?

MANN: Ich? Wieso ich?

FRAU: Saage mr, d Russe schtöön an dr Gränze, und alli hänn Schpeer bi sich.

MANN: I weiß nit.

FRAU: Odr d Italiäner.

MANN: Aso bi de Italiäner sofort. Vor däne hätt i kei Angscht. I nähmti die Schpeer und druggdi mer si iine.

FRAU: Worum?

Dialog über die Ausländer

MANN: Du, hesch du gwüßt, daß die ganz Bevölkerig vo dr ganze Wält uff em Bodesee Platz hett?

FRAU: Nei.

MANN: Das hett im Peschtalozzikaländer gschtande, wo-n-i e Bueb gsi bi. I ha au emol e Elektromotor usere Konsärvebüxe druss baut, abr er isch nie gloffe.

FRAU: Abr alli die Neger und Chinese und Inder und Russe, die kömme doch nie alli gliichzittig zum Bodesee.

MANN: I saag jo nur, si hätte Platz, si hätte. Das isch e theoretischs Problem. Wemme si alli druffschtell*ti*. So groß isch dr Bodesee, odr anderscht umme, so wenig Lüt gits, trotz dr Überbevölkerig.

FRAU: Die wurde doch versuffe.

MANN: Seich. Jede hätt genau e Quadratmeter.

FRAU: E Hindu us Nepal ka sicher nit schwimme, und scho gar nit uff eme Quadratmeter.

MANN: Bi uns im Schwimmbad hesch viil weniger als er Quadratmeter und kasch au schwimme.

FRAU: I saag jo nüt vo uns. Dr Bodesee isch jo au e Schwyzer See.

MANN: (*plötzliche Erkenntnis:*) Schtimmt. Das isch e Problem. Mir wänn sicher nit so viil Fremdi uff unserem See. Uff unserer Site. D Schwoobe könne uff ihri Site schtelle wän si wänn.

FRAU: Bi däne will scho kei Bayer näbe kei Preuß schtoo.

MANN: I ka au nit schwimme.

FRAU: WAS?! Jede Schwyzer ka schwimme.

MANN: I ka abr nit schwimme.

FRAU: Was machsch denn im Dienscht wenn de im Find entgegeschwimme muesch, wenn er übere Rhy kunnt?

MANN: I bi Briefdübeler.

FRAU: Ah.

MANN: Me hätt das Experimänt mit em Bodesee ebe vor hundert Johr mache sotte, nit jetzt. Vor hundert Johr hätte sich d Schwyzer sofort näbe jede Usländer gschtellt. Jetzt ischs z schpoot. Jetzt mache die das nümm.

FRAU: Möchtsch du denn mit ere Negere verhürotet si?

MANN: Vor hundert Johr sinn si us dr ganze Wält
zue-n-is koo, wenn si Schwirigkeite ka hänn bi
sich deheim. Italiänischi Revolutionär hänn
bim Regierigspresidänt vom Tessin gwohnt.
Schtell dr das hütt emol vor, dr Herr Baader
im Geschtebett vom Herr Furgler.

FRAU: Wär?

MANN: Weisch, im zweite Wältkrieg hänn so viil
Jude in d Schwyz iine welle, sit däm dängge
mr, das soll is nit nomol bassiere.

FRAU: Meinsch, me ka wähle, näbe wämm me uff
em Bodesee schtoot?

MANN: He?

FRAU: Denn will ich näbe zwei Neger schtoo, und
vorne und hinde an eine.

MANN: Gsehsch jo jede Daag, wo das mit unserer
laxe Usländerpolitik anegfüert hett. Zerscht
hett sich dr Lenin in Züri vollgfrässe, denn isch
er nach Rußland und hett dr Kommunismus
iigfüert. Me hätt dr Lenin sotte verhafte,
wo-n-er si erschts Gschnätzlets mit Röschti
bschtellt hett.

FRAU: Odr vier Inder? Oder zwei Inder und zwei
Neger?

MANN: Rußland wär e blüendi Oase, vomene
sanfte Zar regiert, mit güetige Großgrundbsit-

zer, wenn mir Schwyzer damals d Auge e bitz
offe ka hätte.

FRAU: Wenn d Wältbevölkerig uff em Bodesee
Blatz hett, denn hett si au uffeme andere See
Blatz. Zum Bischpiil uff em Baikalsee.

MANN: Do hesch rächt. Dä isch sogar no größer.
Do hett jede anderthalb Quadratmeter.

FRAU: Jä, denn ischs glaub besser, mr schicke si
zum Baikalsee.

(*Pause.*)

FRAU: Du?

MANN: Jä?

FRAU: Denn müeßte mir jo au zum Baikalsee
fahre.

MANN: Mir? Nie. Wär weiß, was es dört z ässe
git.

FRAU: Trockneti Rägewürm.

MANN: Zuckereti Ameise.

FRAU: Ischs, wemme Schwyzer isch, nit überhaupt
verbotte, ins Ussland z fahre?

MANN: Abr nei. Nur, s gitt dr Polizei natürlig z
dängge, wenn e Schwyzer im Usland läbe will,
wills em bi uns nit gfallt.

FRAU: Abr s gitt doch viili rächti Schwyzer, wo im
Usland gläbt hänn.

MANN: So? Wär?

FRAU: Dr Corbusier.

MANN: Dasch e Franzos.

FRAU: Dr General Sutter.

MANN: Dasch e Amerikaner.

FRAU: D Ursula Andress.

MANN: Isch das nit e Schwedin?

FRAU: Dr Albert Schwyzer.

MANN: Jä. Do hesch rächt. An dä ha-n-i nit dänggt. Dr Schwyzer isch e ächte Schwyzer gsi. Dä hett jede Daag e Neeger grettet.

Dialog über die Tiere

FRAU: Do bisch jo widr. Wie ischs gsi, hetts viil Schnee kaa oobe?

MANN: Schnee? Jä. Schnee hetts au. Du. I sag dr, was i hütt dört oobe gseh ha, das hett no nie eine gseh, was ich gseh ha.

FRAU: Was denn?

MANN: (*erschreckt*) Gämse.

FRAU: Dasch doch toll.

MANN: (*noch erschreckter*) Und Murmeldier!

FRAU: Schön.

MANN: (*entsetzt*) Und Bärgdohle und wildi Schööf und Hirtehünd und Schteibögg und Adler und ...

FRAU: Und was?

MANN: Männer und Fraue. Sonigi ha-n-i no nie gseh. Si hänn Fäll aa und sinn bruunbrennt wie

Araber. Wenn si sich rüefe, mache si so: *(Er macht einen Jodler nach.)*

FRAU: E Trachteverein.

MANN: Nänei. Si gsehn ehndr us wie Indianer. Si hänn Adlerfädere in de Hoor. Si schtöön uf Felsvorschprüng und luege uff d Paßschtrooß abe, schtundelang, ohni sich z bewege. Vo unde gseht me si nie. Si hänn Äxt mit Schteiklinge in dr Hand und Trinkhörner und roschtigi Morgeschtärn, und e baar hänn Fäldschtächer und Walkie Talkies. Dr lieb Gott weiß, wo si die här hänn.

FRAU: Und wo hesch du die gseh?

MANN: Uff öppe 3400 Meter. I bi schtundelang hinder eme Felse ghoggt und ha-n-ene zuegluegt. Ich glaub, dört oobe duet sich öppis Schreggligs.

FRAU: Aber kumm jetzt.

MANN: Doch. Mir hogge ahnigslos do unde und loose Radio und ässe und suffe, und niemerz merggt, daß d Wuet in de Bärg immer größer wird.

FRAU: Du schpinnsch.

MANN: Do oobe sinn hundertdausigi vo Gämse und Murmeldier und Schööf und Schteibögg.

FRAU: Jä und? Die sinn immer scho dört gsi.

MANN: Aber jetzt schtöön si alli uff eim Huffe. S isch wie-n-e Konferänz. Und die Bärgindianer göön zwischene umme als ghörte si drzue.

FRAU: Nei?

MANN: Du. Die wänn is an Graage.

FRAU: Meinsch, die kömme ins Daal abe?

MANN: E baar sinn sicher scho dunde gsi. Si hänn Raddeggel vo Autos als Helm. Ich glaub, die schliiche sich z Nacht an d Schtrooß abe und erlege sich e baar Automobilischte. S sinn jo wirgglig e baar verschwunde s letscht Johr, me hett nur no s läär Auto gfunde, ohni Raddeggel.

FRAU: Nei?

MANN: Sicher hänn die im Winter die viile Lawine abdrampt. Wenns denn so-n-e TEE verschüttet, denn hogge si obe uff de Felse und luege-n-abe.

FRAU: Aber das sinn doch keini Schwyzer, sonigi.

MANN: Immer hett me-n-is gseit, d Urbärgler sinn usgschtorbe. I sag dr, die sinn nit usgschtorbe. Si sinn ganz viili, s wärde immer mehr, si wohne ganz oobe uff de Bärg in Iglus und Höhlene. Bis jetzt sinn si schüüch gsi wie Okapis, bis jetzt.

FRAU: Die wänn is unseri Hüüser und Autos wägnää.

MANN: Odr si füere ihri alte Brüüch widr ii.

FRAU: Was für Brüüch?

MANN: Daß jede mache darf was er will. Daß jede

saage darf was er will. Das jede läbe ka wie-
n-er will.

FRAU: Meinsch?

MANN: Si sinn scho untrwäggs. Si göön übr die
höggschde Gletscher, vorne d Urbärgler mit de
Raddeggel uff em Kopf, denn d Schteibögg mit
de Hörner, denn Gämse mit de Bärt, denn d
Murmeldier, alli blitzwach, denn d Schööf und
hinde d Schoofhünd. Si kömme übr d Moräne,
über d Alpe, dur d Arve- und Föhrewälder,
dur die oberschte Bärgdörfer, dur dr Gmeind-
wald. Vo unde här höre mr si immr besser, si
kömme nööcher und nööcher. Bäum verschplit-
tere under ihre Füeß. Denn kömme si uff d
Autoschtrooß. Dr Verkehr bricht zämme. Si sinn
jetzt hundertdausigi, und viili vo unsere
modärne Bärgbuure laufe mit ene. Zvorderscht
sinn immr no d Urbärgler, si sehn schön us, mit
ihre bruune Hüüt und ihre Fädere.

FRAU: Meinsch, die mache-n-is öppis.

MANN: I weiß es nit.

FRAU: Villicht sott me zur Polizei goo und das
mälde.

MANN: Villicht.

FRAU: Villicht hänn si Militärberooter us
Hanoi.

MANN: Villicht hänn si sich das alles sälber
usdänggt.

Frau: Villicht.

Mann: Ich ha jedefalls immer gseit, s isch riskant,
immer mehr vo däne Schteibögg uszsetze in de
Bärg. Si wänn jo sogar Bäre und Wölf neu
aasidle. Wenn i ne verzell, was die Vicher dört
oobe mache, denn löön si si villicht doch lieber
in de Keefig.

Dialog *über das Glück*

Frau: Jetzt sag emol, Hans: Bisch glügglig?

Mann: Dasch e blöödi Froog. Frag *ich* di jemols,
ob du glügglig bisch?

Frau: Nei.

Mann: Also.

Frau: Bi mir isch das wie bi de Beduine. Die rede
immer vom Wasser. Die Arme rede vom Gäld,
die Verrägnete vo trockene Underhose, und ich
red vom Glügg.

Mann: Glügg, das isch eifach e Wort. Das gits nit.
Lueg mi aa. Ich bi au nit glügglig, und s goot
mr prima.

Frau: Jä. S Problem isch, du dänggsch immer nur
an di, und nur ich dängg immer nur an mi.

Mann: Meinsch öppe, anderi sinn glüggliger als
mir?

Frau: D Italiäner lache-n-immer und singe.

MANN: Was meinsch, was die mache, wenn mr um dr näggschd Egge verschwunde sinn. Denn haue si sich dr Sagg voll. Die singe nur für uns.

FRAU: Meinsch?

MANN: Mr hänn e Wohnig, e Arbet, e Auto und z ässe. Folglig simmer glügglig.

FRAU: Weisch no, wo de mr Liebesbrief gschribe hesch?

MANN: Ich? Dir?

FRAU: »Mein süßes Liebes, Tag und Nacht denke ich an deinen Rosengarten, den ich mit meinem Tau benetzen möchte.«

MANN: Das ha-n-ich gschribe?

FRAU: Jä.

MANN: Damals simmer au nonig verhüürotet gsi. Villicht bi-n-i bsoffe gsi? Weisch, früener ha-n-i nämmlig dänggt, Fraue sinn so öppis wie Fee. Die wänn nie, nur ich will immer, und damit me si ummegriegt, mues me-n-e so Feewörter sage. Jetzt weiß i, daß d Fraue au wänn, si sinn wie Männer, genau gliich.

FRAU: Und sit däm behandlesch mi wie-n-e Maa?

MANN: Richtig. So wie-n-i jede freie Schwyzer behandle, härzlig und korräkt.

FRAU: Aha.

MANN: Jä. Und will s is nit besser ka goo als es is goot, mues au alles bliibe wie s isch. Dasch

Logik. Me sott au nüt verbessere welle, das wär au falsch. Denn wenn me ei Schtei imene Mosaik veränderet, kunnt immer s Ganzi ins Rutsche. Sogar wemme öppis Guets will, gits gliichzittig immer e Unsicherheitslugge, wo s Böös iinewitsche kaa, schnäller als dr Geischt us dr Fläsche.

FRAU: Meinsch wirgglig?

MANN: Saage mr, Abdriibige wäre eifach so erlaubt. Das wär in Wirkligkeit jo gar nit so tragisch. Aber wenn de däne Fraue dr glei Finger gisch, hesch s Johr druff ganz Moskau im Land.

FRAU: Aber me hett doch s Rächt, emol öppis anders z dängge als was me immer scho dänggt hett.

MANN: Ich wär drfür, me sott e Haag um d Schwyz umme baue, mit Idrittskasse in Basel, Schaffhuse, Chiasoo und Gänf. Ich wurd us dr Schwyz e großes Museum für die andere Länder vo dr Wält mache. Si könnte bi uns go luege, wie me glügglig läbt. Immer bevor s irgendwo e Grieg gäbt, wurdi d UNO de Find befähle, e gfüerti Tour dur d Schwyz z mache, s ganz Programm vom Rhyhafe bis zum Jungfraujoch.

FRAU: Nit schlächt.

MANN: Gäll. Mir wurde ab sofort us pädagogische

Gründ schaffe. Das liggt is. S isch typisch, daß dr Peschtalozzi e Schwyzer gsi isch. Odr kasch dr dr Peschtalozzi als Türk vorschtelle?

FRAU: Wurd dir das gfalle, wenn dr im Büro immer e Dutzend Japaner und Chinese zueluege?

MANN: Wieso mir? Ich giengt doch nümm ins Büro. Ich ha doch die ganz Idee ka. Ich wär dr Diräggdr. Ich wurd das Züüg organisiere und luege, daß alles korräkt lauft.

FRAU: Jä so.

MANN: Zum Bischpiil dürfte d Bundesrööt kei bitz anderscht schaffe als bis jetzt. Alli müen immer einer Meinig si.

FRAU: Das gits in andere Regierige au.

MANN: Do wär i nit so sicher. Wo gits das sunscht no, daß d Sozi und die Großinduschtrielle zämme suffe und sich Witz verzelle?

FRAU: In Dütschland.

MANN: Dütschland isch z groß für e Museum. Und die Dütsche sinn nit so glügglig wie mir.

FRAU: Wohär weisch das?

MANN: Hesch scho emol ghört, daß e Dütsche seit: Herrgott, bin ich glügglig, daß ich e Dütsche bi?

FRAU: Nei.

MANN: Also.

FRAU: Was hesch denn do aa? Isch dr Grieg usbroche?

MANN: I mach mi letschte WK.

FRAU: Ah?

MANN: Lieschtel. Do kenn i sowieso scho alli Beize, usserem Ängel und dr Kanonebar. In dr einte sinn d Offizier und in dr andere d Fraue.

FRAU: Besser Dienscht mache als zahle.

MANN: Wenn ein nach Südamerika goot, macht er au kein Dienscht, und meinsch, dä zahlt?

FRAU: Nit?

MANN: Die schigge-n-em doch kei Polizischt an Amazonas uffe, nur wäg dr Wehrschtüür.

FRAU: Worum bisch du denn nit am Amazonas?

MANN: Wäg de Schnoogge und de Kampfbiene.

FRAU: De was?

MANN: De Kampfbiene. I ha vo däne gläse. Si sinn e Meter lang und wahnsinnig aggressiv. Wenn si e Mensch uff e Meter Dischtanz sehn, mache si e Schturzflug und schtäche-n-en doot. Si hänn irrsinnig gueti Auge.

FRAU: Nei?

MANN: Si kömme us Afrika. Aber so-n-e Forscher hett emol nit rächt uffbaßt und zwei so Biene sinn em abb us em Keefig. Jetzt isch ganz Brasilie voll drvo. Si wandere jedes Johr zäh Kilometer nach Norde. In zäh Johr sinn si in Amerika.

FRAU: Do gsehsch, wie schnäll sich s Unglügg vermehre kaa. Eimol z viil e Keefig uffmache, und hesch kei ruegi Minute me.

MANN: (*leise*) Me seit, dr russisch Gheimdienscht hett d Finger drinn.

FRAU: (*ebenso leise*) I verschtand. Aber worum hänn si si nit diräggt in Amerika abgloo?

MANN: (*leise*) Tarnig.

(Pause.)

MANN: (*normale Stimme*) Wenn i dä Schißdienscht hindr mr ha, will i nie vrgässe, was das für e Schißgfühl isch, wemme im Novämber uff eme nasse Acker schtoot und s Gwehrschloß usenander nimmt.

FRAU: Du bisch wie alli Schwyzer. De fluechsch über dr Dienscht und goosch gärn ane.

MANN: Seich. Wo-n-i jung gsi bi, hetts eifach keini Dienschtverweigerer gä. S isch au nie öpper us dr Kirche ussdrädde. I ha ehndr e-n-andere Fähler gmacht.

FRAU: Nämmlig?

MANN: I hätt sotte in Generalschtab koo.

FRAU: Worum?

MANN: Do wurd jetzt alles anderscht usgseh. Zum Bischpiil gäbts Soldate und Soldatinne gmischt.

Und wenn de d Nase voll hätsch, könntsch heim goo.

FRAU: Aber uff di loost jo nie öpper.

MANN: Isch dr das au scho uffgfalle? I ha dr ganz Daag die beschte Idee, und niemerz loost uff mi. Zum Bischpiil dät ich e Gürtel vo Waldärdbeeri um d Schwyz umme pflanze und ...

DEUTSCHER: Tach. Ist dieser Platz hier noch frei?

MANN: Ja.

FRAU: Ja.

(*Pause.*)

DEUTSCHER: Schlechtes Wetter heute.

MANN: Hm.

FRAU: Hm.

(*Pause.*)

DEUTSCHER: Ich habe meinen Urlaub, aber bis jetzt habe ich Pech mit dem Wetter.

MANN: (*schweizerhochdeutsch*) Wenn Sie schönes Wetter wollen, müssen Sie an die Riviera oder nach Tunesien.

FRAU: (*schweizerhochdeutsch*) Bei uns schifft es entweder oder es hat Nebel.

DEUTSCHER: Ach so.

(*Pause.*)

DEUTSCHER: Was tragen Sie denn da für eine Uniform? Sind Sie Briefträger?

MANN: Ich? Briefträger? Ich bin Soldat. Das ist unsere Soldatenuniform.

DEUTSCHER: Ach so. Verzeihung. Ich wußte gar nicht, daß die Schwyzer auch eine Bundeswehr haben.

MANN: Unsere Armee hat immerhin zwei Weltkriege gewonnen, unsere.

DEUTSCHER: Jaja. Da haben Sie sicher recht.

(*Pause.*)

FRAU: Wo kommen Sie denn her?

DEUTSCHER: Aus Münster.

FRAU: Was?

DEUTSCHER: Aus Deutschland.

FRAU: Aus Deutschland. Soso.

(*Pause.*)

MANN: (*zur Frau*) Worum bliibe die nie wo si sinn? Wo me hikunnt, schtoot ein vo däne und füllt sich unser Benzin in si Mercedes. Mi Vatter isch acht Johr mit em Gwehr in dr Hand am Rhy gschtande und hett d Flüchtling zrugggschücht. Und jetzt hogge si in alle unsre Beize.

FRAU: Schtimmt. Mi Vatter isch in dr Gotthardfeschtig gsi. Acht Johr kei Sunne, hett er immer gseit, aber wenigschtens keini Fremde.

DEUTSCHER: Merkwürdig. Manchmal verstehe ich Ihre Sprache, und manchmal nicht.

MANN: (*schweizerhochdeutsch*) Ich habe nur gesagt, wenn es diesen Tourismus nicht gäbe, sähe es auch anders aus in der Welt.

DEUTSCHER: Jetzt verstehe ich Sie gut.

MANN: (*schweizerhochdeutsch*) Nämlich, früher sind wir alle geblieben, wo wir gewesen sind. Darum hat es auch kein Biafra und Vietnam und so Zeug gegeben. Einmal im Jahr sind wir in die Stadt, und das hat uns genügt.

DEUTSCHER: Ja. Ich verstehe. Wir mögen die Schweiz sehr. Die Leute sind alle so freundlich hier, so viel herzlicher als bei uns.

MANN: (*schweizerhochdeutsch*) Das stimmt. Bei Ihnen will jedes Arschloch in den Ferien auf eine Südseeinsel. In Ihren Städten fahren die Jungen mit dem Auto in die Schule. Wenn dann wieder einmal eine Not kommt, dann sitzen die schön da. Sie tun den ganzen Tag über nichts und schimpfen über die Regierung und sehen aus wie die Mähnenschafe.

DEUTSCHER: Oh. Bei uns schon nicht mehr. Die meisten Jungen tragen bei uns wieder kurze Haare und Schlipse.

MANN: Ahh? So? Also ich gehe unserem Bub dann auch einmal mit der Schere dahinter, wenn er schläft, nachts.

DEUTSCHER: Aber warum denn?

MANN: Das Problem ist, der Bub schließt z Nacht die Tür ab, und manchmal schläft er überhaupt nicht daheim.

DEUTSCHER: (*lacht.*)

FRAU: (*schweizerhochdeutsch*) Da gibt es nichts zu lachen. Sie zum Beispiel. Sie sind sicher um die vierzig, und wie Sie aussehen! Das gäbe es bei uns nicht.

MANN: Wir würden Ihnen mit dem Sackmesser den Schwanz abschneiden. (*Mann und Frau lachen. Dann lacht, zögernd, auch der Deutsche.*)

MANN: Ja. Was ich sagen wollte. Unsere Jungen wären auch andersch, wenn es nur unsereinen gäbe. Zum Beispiel diese Bombenwerfer. *Wir* haben damit nicht angefangen, wir bestimmt nicht.

DEUTSCHER: Ich auch nicht.

FRAU: Aber einer von euch hat, glaube ich, das Schloß Sargans gekauft und überall Kachelbäder eingebaut. Ein anderer will das Gotthardhospiz kaufen und die Mönchszellen in eine Sauna umbauen.

MANN: Die letzten Bernhardinerhunde gehen ein, weil sich niemand mehr von ihnen retten lassen will. Heute holen alle den TCS.

DEUTSCHER: Sicher. Aber euch Schweizern geht es doch auch gut, nicht nur uns. Ihr kauft doch auch Häuser und baut sie um.

(*Pause.*)

MANN: Das ist etwas ganz anderes.

DEUTSCHER: Warum?

MANN: Wir sind Schweizer. (*Pause.*) Wir kaufen ja auch nicht ganz Deutschland auf.

FRAU: Wir finden Deutschland nämlich scheußlich, wissen Sie.

DEUTSCHER: Ohh. Kennen Sie Deutschland?

FRAU: Nein. Aber ich bin sicher, daß ihr etwas so Schönes wie die Klus von Balsthal in Deutschland nicht habt, da bin ich ganz sicher.

Dialog über den Sport

FRAU: Was hesch? Hesch e Depression?

MANN: Äntwäder i suff mi voll oder i nimm drei Valium oder alles zämme.

FRAU: Worum?

MANN: Bi am Matsch gsi.

FRAU: An welem?

MANN: FCB gege Sümüklü Bötschedler Ischtambul. 6 zu Null.

FRAU: Dasch doch guet.

MANN: Für d Türgge.

FRAU: Jäso. I ha gar nit gwüßt, daß die in dr Türkei au schutte.

MANN: So öppis wär früener nie vorkoo.

FRAU: Was isch denn früener anderscht gsi?

MANN: Alles. Dr Bickel. Dr Ballaman. Dr Schtuber. Dr Fatton. Dr Kiki Antenen. Dr Seppe Hügi. Dr Neury und dr Boquet.

FRAU: Du meinsch, die wurde gwünne, wenn sie jetzt no schpile wurde.

MANN: *(entrüstet)* Nie.

FRAU: Jä aber denn . . .

MANN: Aber schutte hänn si könne! 54, s 4:1 gege Italie, Zucker. Dr Fatton hetts viert Gool mit eme Fallruggzieher gmacht, und dr Seppe hett bi sinere erschte Kischte e Muul wie-n-e Forälle gmacht. Früener isch alles ganz anderscht gsi.

FRAU: Worum?

MANN: S isch ene nit so guet gange. Die sinn no ummegsegglet.

FRAU: Dasch doch guet, daß es de Lüt besser got.

MANN: Odr lueg dr Ferdi Kübler aa. Dä isch diräggt us em Sozialeländ koo, dorum isch dä Velo gfahre wie-n-e Deufel. Dä hett gwüßt, wenn er nit gwinnt, mues er widr go schaffe für 1.20 in dr Schtund. De Schportler goots hütte z guet. Das sinn Wärbeaagschtellti.

FRAU: Jä was sott me mache, daß die widr besser schportle?

MANN: Aabedrugge mues me si. Me mues uff langi Sicht plane, daß es immer gnueg Familie git, wo s ene richtig eländ goot, verschtoosch, daß ihri Söhn gar kei anderi Wahl hänn als Velo z fahre wie die Verruggde und z schutte wie die Wahnsinnige.

FRAU: Das kasch doch vo niemerem verlange.

MANN: Was nit? Frog dr Ferdi Kübler, ob en sini Erfolg glügglig gmacht hänn, odr dr Hugo Koblet.

FRAU: Dä isch doot.

MANN: Uff jede Fall isch so ein wie dr Pfänni nit so glügglig wie dr Ferdi.

FRAU: Bisch du denn glügglig?

MANN: Jetzt foosch scho widr aa drmit. Immer wotsch vo mir rede. Das hesch früener nie gmacht. Do hämmer immer vo Sache gredet, wo-n-is nüt aagange sinn.

Dialog über das Kinderkriegen

FRAU: Was hesch? Sehsch scho widr us wie drei Daag vor em Wältuntergang.

MANN: Do. Lis emol.

FRAU: Was? »Bundesrat gratuliert General Franco zum Geburtstag«?

MANN: Nei. Nit das. Do. »In der ganzen Schweiz nisten keine Störche mehr.«

FRAU: Jänu. S git jo au keini Wölf und Dinosaurier me.

MANN: Und wär bringt is in Zuekunft d Kinder, wär?

FRAU: D Kinder? Abr dr Schtorch bringt doch keini Kinder.

MANN: Sehsch. Sogar du bisch uf die modärne Uffklärigsbüecher iinekeit. Weisch, worum me-n-is schtändig uffklärt mit däm Gschwätz vo Penis und Eierschtögg?

FRAU: Nei.

MANN: Das isch, um e Panik im Schwyzervolgg z verhindere. Die schregglig Wooret isch, daß mir vomene usschtärbende Vogel brocht wärde. Wenn er ganz usgschtorbe isch, wär soll is denn bringe??

FRAU: I ha immer gmeint . . .

MANN: Im Elsaß gits no ganzi vier Schtörch. Vier Schtörch fürs ganzi Elsaß! Schtell dr das emol vor.

FRAU: Meinsch, was die ummeseggle.

MANN: Im Elsaß sinn si jetzt scho so wit, daß si in Nordafrika Schtörch fange und si mit dr Air France nach Mülhuuse fliege und si denn uff d Elsässer ablöön.

FRAU: Abr mir in dr Schwyz hänn doch scho lang keini Schtörch me.

MANN: Ebbe. Und wieviil Schwyzer gits, vergliche mit Bangla Desch oder Indie oder Pakischtan? Das sinn alles Schtorcheländer. Mir griege nur ab und zue e Schprutz ab, wenn sich e Schtorch verfliegt. Aber die verfliege sich fascht nie, die hänn e Radar wie-n-e Flädermuus.

FRAU: Aber das isch doch Blödsinn. Du weisch doch au, wie das goot. E Maa und e Frau – ka-n-i offe rede?

MANN: Also loos emol. Mr sinn doch schließlig verhürotet.

FRAU: E Maa und e Frau leere sich kenne.

MANN: Jä.

FRAU: Si luege sich in d Auge.

MANN: Jä.

FRAU: Dr Maa zahlt d Konsumation vo beide und seit, Fröllein, darf i Si no zuemene Tassli Kaffi iilade.

MANN: Jä.

FRAU: D Frau seit: Jä.

MANN: Jä.

FRAU: Daheim, in dr Wohnig vom Maa, ziehn sich beidi wie dr Blitz ab und leege sich uffs Bett und uffenander. Und kei Schtorch isch wyt und breit.

MANN: Jä. Jetzt bass emol uff. So lauft das jo oft, nur, das isch die reini Ideologie. Me hett is iigredet, daß das so goot. Dorum mache mrs au so. (*Eine leise Musik setzt ein:*) Aber in Wirkligkeit isch das mit em Kindergriege viil viil komplizierter. E Kind griegsch, wenn e

Frau bi dr richtige Temperatur am Fänschter
sitzt und dusse goot e Katz dur dr Härdöpfel-
agger und d Frau dränggt an e Matte voller
Blueme, und e Schtroß witer schtirbt e alter
Maa amene Härzschlag. UND WENN DENN NO E
SCHTORCH IN DR NÖÖCHI ISCH, denn klappts.

Dialog über das Kaisertum

MANN: Du. Jetzt kunnt mr grad in Sinn, mir
hänn als Buebe emol e Uffsatz über was mr
emol wärde wänn schriibe müese, und ein hett
gschribe: Kaiser vo dr Schwyz.
FRAU: Jä und?
MANN: Das wär i au gärn worde, Kaiser vo dr
Schwyz.
FRAU: Worum?
MANN: Denn dät ich alles umgrämbble, die ganzi
Schwyz, vo A bis Zett.
FRAU: Was?! Das hör i vo dir au s erscht Mool.
MANN: Mit de Schtedt dät i aafoo. I schmeiß d
Auti uuse, alli.
FRAU: Nei?!
MANN: I grab d Autobahne um und pflanz Tabak
und Knoblauch.
FRAU: Nei?!!

MANN: Vo de-n-alte Verantwortlige ka-n-i natürlig keine bhalte.

FRAU: Natürlig nit.

MANN: D Bangge sinn offe für alli. S hett sicher
gnueg Gäld drin.

FRAU: Sicher.

MANN: Dr Globi wird iigschperrt.

FRAU: Nei?!

MANN: Alli Globis in dr ganze Schwyz wärde
iigschperrt.

FRAU: Wie kennsch die?

MANN: Wenn me si ins Wasser keit, hänn si e
ganz schpezielli Schwimmtechnik. Sie heebe die
beide Düüme us em Wasser uuse wie zwei Ha-
seohre.

FRAU: Ah.

MANN: In de Alpe griff ich dure. Alli Beton-
hochhüüser über 1000 Meter Höchi wärde
gschprängt.

FRAU: Aha.

MANN: Wenn i öpper mit eme usgrissene Huus-
wurz entdegg, saag em, daß Huuswürz au
Mensche sinn.

FRAU: Hans. Du gsehsch diräggt zäh Joor jünger
us hütt.

MANN: I füer die völligi Gerächtigkeit ii. Dr
Herr Schmidheini und dr Herr Sacher hänn
nur no vier Hose und fünf Hemmli. Dr Herr

Bührle mues Schoggischtängeli fabriziere. D Fraue griege dr gliich Lohn wie d Männer. Am Radio darf jede sände, was er will, er mues eifach e Löösli zieh und warte, bis er draa isch.

FRAU: Das isch jo d Revolution, wo du do plansch.

MANN: I ha immer s Gfühl ka, daß de mi underschetzisch, Elsi.

Zu den Texten

Vom Fenster meines Hauses aus. Teil 1 zuerst in: Merkur, März 1977; Teil 2 zuerst in: Süddeutsche Zeitung, 1976; Teil 3: unveröffentlicht.

Gespräch mit meinem Kind über das Treiben der Nazis im Wald. Zuerst in: Das Tintenfaß, 12. Jahrgang, 26. Folge. Zürich 1976 (= detebe 122).

Die schreckliche Verwirrung des Giuseppe Verdi. Unveröffentlicht.

Der unbekannte Duft der fremden Frauen. Zuerst in: Akzente 2/1975.

Die Bücher von früher oder Ein Beweis, daß der Schnupfen der Vater aller Dichtung ist, ein Essay. Zuerst in: Protokolle 77/1.

Berufe! Unveröffentlicht.

Bildnisse von Dichtern. Zuerst in: manuskripte 47/48/1975.

Erinnerungen an Schneewittchen. Zuerst in: Tintenfisch 8, Berlin 1975 (= Quarthefte 73).

Rinaldo Rinaldini. Zuerst in: Märchen, Sagen und Abenteuergeschichten auf alten Bilderbogen, neu erzählt von Autoren unserer Zeit. München 1974.

Ein ganzes Leben. Unveröffentlicht.

Ein Spaziergang. Zuerst in: ZET Heft 3/1973.

Freitag der dreizehnte. Unveröffentlicht.

Das ist das Ende. Unveröffentlicht.

Schweizer Dialoge. Zuerst in: manuskripte 50/1975.

Urs Widmer
im Diogenes Verlag

Alois
Erzählung

Die Amsel im Regen im Garten
Erzählung

Das Normale und die Sehnsucht
Essays und Geschichten
detebe 39/I

Die lange Nacht der Detektive
Komödie
detebe 39/II

Die Forschungsreise
Roman
detebe 39/III

Schweizer Geschichten
detebe 39/IV

Die gelben Männer
Roman

Vom Fenster meines Hauses aus
Prosa

Nepal
Ein Stück

Außerdem erschien:

Hanns Grössel
Über Urs Widmer
In: ›Das Tintenfaß Nr. 26‹, detebe 122

THE KILLER GUN

A Western Story

LAURAN PAINE

Five Star
Unity, Maine

Five Star Western
Published in conjunction with
Golden West Literary Agency.

November 1998

First Edition, Second Printing.

Five Star Standard Print Western Series.

The text of this edition is unabridged.

Set in 11 pt. Plantin by Minnie B. Raven.

Printed in the United States on permanent paper.

Library of Congress Cataloging in Publication Data

Paine, Lauran.
    The killer gun : a western story / by Lauran Paine. —
1st ed.
      p. cm.
  "Five star western" — T.p. verso.
   ISBN 0-7862-1371-X (hc : alk. paper)
   I. Title.
PS3566.A34K55   1998
813´.54—dc21   98-28227

THE KILLER GUN

Chapter One

THE GUNSMITH

It was said of the old man that his pronounced limp was the result of a British musket ball during the War of 1812. If that was true, then he had to be very old, something his appearance left no one doubting.

It was also said the limp was the result of a Confederate bullet during the Civil War, but simple arithmetic made that a remote possibility. If he had been old enough to serve during the War of 1812, by the time of the Civil War, something like fifty years later, he would have been too old, but that kind of reasoning had to overlook that the Confederacy had soldiers in its armies as young as fourteen and as old as seventy.

In fact, the old man did not acquire his injury from a bullet or a musket ball; he was bayoneted while on the ground in the War of 1812.

Evidence of advanced age was not confined to his limp because, although his eyesight was excellent, his joints were troublesome, particularly during prolonged periods of wet weather. He made no secret of the fact that he had his gun shop, and his lean-to living quarters out back, in New Mexico Territory at the village of Pueblo Juárez. It was a small place that had doggedly retained its Mexican name — and culture — in the face of *yanqui* opposition subsequent to the U.S.–Mexican war when Mexico signed the 1848 Treaty of Guadalupe Hidalgo, giving the United States the

7

huge tract of land which became the southwestern United States. It was a hot, dry country ideal for arthritic joints.

The wars had been over a long time, but the people for the most part remained as they had been for hundreds of years. The raising of the North American flag signified ownership of land, but bodies and souls, religion and culture would require more centuries to change. Those who had survived other conquests shrugged off this one.

The old man's name was George Washington Mars, the first two names derived from his father's admiration for the first North American president. His passion since childhood had been weapons — rifles and hand guns — and he had made some of the most beautiful rifles men had ever seen. He was particular to the point of irritating exactness. His guns were expensive, but not so that he could live well. In fact, he lived frugally and untidily. Martha New, the midwife, said his living quarters put her in mind of a boar's nest. Those who had contracted him to rebuild neglected and abused guns as well as those who were willing to pay more for custom-made weapons never faulted the old man's work, but they complained about the length of time he required to finish a project.

They might as well have peed in the creek with the expectation of raising the tide. George Mars accepted complaints with the variety of indifference ducks showed to water on their backs. He tinkered, not only in his spare time, but also when he was supposed to be doing something else. He had spent nearly a year trying to re-tool a patch and ball hand-loaded Navy six-shot sidearm to accept the later cartridge-type bullets. However, the Navy pistol proved insufficiently sturdy to withstand exploding cartridges and would work satisfactorily only with a reduced charge; but such a reduction in powder load detracted from

8

both the velocity and power of penetration. Therefore, he abandoned the Navy model altogether and turned to the heavier Army revolver, and this time it worked. But by the time he could make the alteration to his satisfaction, he had spent so much time that the first reworked six-gun he had for sale had to bring an exorbitant price. Twelve dollars per pistol. He sold a few but not enough to pay him for his months of work, experimenting, and devising.

One thing the old man had inherited from an assortment of forefathers was stubborn persistence. He had the re-tooled revolvers suspended from nails on the wall behind his combination workbench and counter when he was struck by a fresh idea, which was the result of a gunfight he had witnessed between two half-drunk Texans in the center of the village's dusty, wide roadway. They had both been killed.

George had been sitting in front of his shop in summer shade and had seen the fight from a distance of no more than perhaps two hundred feet. As near as the old man could discern both Texans had drawn simultaneously. It hadn't been the killings that held his attention. It had been that both men were competent with six-guns. They had been so evenly matched, so fast and accurate, that both gunshots had sounded almost simultaneously.

That same night he stuffed his pipe, sat on the rickety chair behind his combination counter and workbench, fired up a fragrant cloud of shag, and gazed steadily at one of his re-tooled guns on the wall. Gunfights, while not commonplace, were not noticeably rare, either. It helped if the fighters had stiffened their resolve at O'Malley's saloon in *gringo* town.

It was late when the lame old man bedded down in his "boar's nest" lean-to, hours later than he usually retired, and the following morning he was up before sunrise. After a breakfast of stir-about that had been in the same pot on the stove for several days and was beginning to smell sour, the old man limped out front, found a pencil, took some brown wrapping paper, set a lighted candle close, and went to work.

There was nothing wrong with his idea. The more he sketched the more enthused he became. Hand guns were for killing. Ordinarily they lacked the range for hunting and were not to be relied upon for aiming. They served only one purpose, and those who might have contended otherwise had only to visit a cemetery.

The old man was still sketching, erasing, and re-sketching hours after sunrise. He had forgotten to unlock the roadway door. A large, gloved fist made the entire front wall rattle, and the startled old man swung his good leg first, then his other leg, and went to open the door.

The man in the opening was not only thickly massive and muscular, but had hooded, very dark eyes, and a bloodless slit of a mouth. His name was Austin Gorman. He was the town marshal of Pueblo Juárez, a man capable of handling trouble with weapons or fists, an individual who had detractors, but the kind of man towns and villages on the south desert needed because the entire territory for hundreds of miles had renegades and outlaws from both sides of the border.

The old man limped aside for the lawman to enter. Gorman went around the counter and removed a rifle from its pegs. He did this without speaking, but, when he placed the weapon on the counter, he said: "How much?"

The old man eyed the rifle. He had put in a new firing pin and had replaced a rusty spring. "Fifty cents," he told the large man, who put a silver coin atop the counter and left.

10

The old man filled a pipe and lighted it. There was one roadway window through which he watched Marshal Gorman growl and gesture with the rifle for a pair of wood gatherers with their laden burros to go to the side of the road, not the center.

There was no traffic.

Because the village was not large and also because it was roughly divided between natives and *norteamericano* late-comers, mostly store owners, traders, freighters, businessmen, not herders of small animals, maize and squash growers, wood gatherers, and laborers, there was little sharing of ideas, interests, and languages. The newcomers were often forceful individuals who lacked the native fatalism and cohesiveness.

Marshal Gorman made daily hikes through Mex town. It was known he did this usually about two in the afternoon, so those in the *cantinas* with their whiskey and beer remained inside. Mothers with children too young to understand were kept indoors as were the dogs. Chickens and wandering burros were corralled.

But if there was a soft side to Austin Gorman, it was the solemn, large-eyed, small children he encountered. Otherwise, he would collar drunks, break up fights, and haul anyone he thought might be a troublemaker up out of Mex town to his *carcel* and lock them up. Those who protested he slapped; those who resisted he struck.

The village was an ageless, enduring, mostly peaceful place. If outlaws fleeing south to Mexico stopped for provisions, they were not bothered. If they appeased a long thirst and got noisy or troublesome, the marshal disarmed them and locked them up, fined them two *yanqui* dollars when they sobered up, and released them. Those who mistakenly assumed the dark-eyed man was either a Mexican

11

or some kind of 'breed and reacted unfavorably to his presence were likely to get beaten. Their kind rarely returned to the village.

In early spring cowmen from the north drove cattle to the south desert for the brief period of grazing and browsing. Mostly they were men who had done this for years and warned their riders against angering the local lawman. As spring turned to summer and the feed began to cure and shrivel, the cattlemen made gathers and headed back northward.

These were traditions, customs, and habits which had followed patterns for generations. If the village had been on a popularly used road, it might have been different, but while other southwestern communities grew, some even becoming genuine cities, the village named for a hero of Mexico changed only to the extent of having *yanquis* arrive. Only one freighter served the community; other freighters ignored it; the reward did not equal the expense. The freighter's name was Robert Barber.

It was a serene settlement of great age whose lifestyle did not change much, even after the *norteamericanos* came, and whoever had enforced the law before the present town marshal, after six years of the Austin Gorman variety of enforcement life adapted without problems. For all his implacability he was neither biased nor needlessly cruel.

Because Pedro Amayo's *cantina* was occasionally the source of discord, Marshal Gorman had twice warned its proprietor, a short, heavy, graying man who smiled often to display two gold teeth in the front of his mouth. But there was trouble a third time. It resulted in a Mexican *arriero*'s shooting and killing a local *vaquero* because the little bells the *arriero* wore down both sides of his trousers made noise the local cowboy objected to, and since both

12

men had been drinking the argument which ended in the *arriero's* killing the local man was as final as it was ridiculous. Marshal Gorman told Pedro Amayo to close his saloon and emphasized this order with a huge balled fist striking the counter.

There was no other place for the old men to gather and sip liquor, reminisce, tell splendid lies, and smoke. One of them went to the *carcel* to plead. Marshal Gorman leaned massively on his table and told the older man the *cantina* would never be opened again. He also said, since he had been unable to catch the *arriero* who had made a beeline for the border and would probably never return, he was considering a prohibition against pack trains up out of Mexico. It was that which, even more than the shooting, resulted in a furor not only in Mex town but also among the *gringo* merchants.

Pueblo Juárez had a town council. It consisted of five local merchants. A spokesman was appointed to protest to Marshal Gorman, who drew his monthly eighty dollars from the council. He agreed to relent to the extent that, while pack trains could come up out of Mexico, he would post a large sign at the lower end of the village with block letters in Spanish saying that all weapons must be delivered to the marshal and would only be returned when the *arrieros* departed.

The councilmen were not appeased, but there was the matter of the lawman's unquestioned capability. They would compromise.

It was a hot summer, nothing unusual in this southwestern country. Adobe houses with walls of mud three feet thick were never either hot or cold, just ugly. Supper was at nine or ten o'clock at night when going outside was bearable. Breakfast was correspondingly well after sunrise.

13

George Mars heard of the killing in Mex town and limped over to Amayo's saloon to interrogate those who had been present. The closure of the *cantina* had forced its patrons to congregate on benches outside under the shade of an overhang, and to provide their own wine.

One old man, older than the gunsmith if such a thing were possible, said he had never seen such a fast draw. He said the *arriero* had to have practiced most of his life, and he was a young man. Pedro Amayo verified this with his own comment. "I knew Jorge Español since he was a child. He was good with guns. Everyone knew that."

The old man with the small glass of red wine at the end of a bench interrupted. "So was his father. Deadly with guns. No one could get out his pistol faster than Jorge and his father."

Amayo acted as though there had been no interruption. "Do you know Hernan, Jorge's brother?"

Mars nodded. He knew the brother of the dead man as he knew dozens of people in Mex town, although not very well and only rarely by name.

Pedro Amayo rolled his eyes. "He will not live with this."

The old man interrupted again, this time with a bony-shouldered shrug. "What can he do? The packer is a hundred miles down into Mexico."

Pedro, annoyed this time, spoke sharply to the old man. "The man he drives mules for . . . I know him very well. He will send the *vaquero* back."

The old man departed, carrying his glass of wine. Although his second home was the *cantina* and he liked its owner, he did not have to listen to such ridiculous talk. Moreover, it was time to feed the chickens. If he did not do this on time, his widowed daughter who weighed over

14

two hundred pounds would scold him. She had a voice like an enraged jackass.

The gunsmith limped along to the old man's *jacal,* found him feeding chickens from a tin can, and asked him to describe the gunfight in detail.

The old man gazed annoyingly at George Mars. "It was such a silly argument."

"No. Tell me about the shooting."

The old man emptied the tin and led the way to a shady *ramada* at the back of the house where he sat and offered the gunsmith red wine from a jug. Mars declined and pressed the subject.

"Which one drew first?"

The old man half filled a glass, made a small salute, and half emptied it before speaking. "It was so fast."

"You were looking . . . you saw everything?"

"Yes. Jorge was very fast getting his pistol out. I don't think the packer was any faster. But . . . this is good wine."

"No thank you. The packer was no faster?"

"I said that." The old man refilled his glass but spoke before lifting it. "But I can tell you because I was close enough to see . . . the packer cocked his pistol before it came out of the holster. You see? Jorge was cocking his pistol when he aimed." The old man drained his glass as he saw something large loom toward the *ramada*'s back wall, and swiftly arose. "I told you all I know. Now I must go inside."

George Mars limped his way back to his dingy shop and fired up his pipe as he sat studying his sketches.

That night after locking up he retired but did not sleep for a long time, and before dawn he stoked the stove but neglected the souring pot on the burner to go into the shop and light two candles. For breakfast he had his pipe and

15

his sketches. Old men have reserves of diminished energy. George Mars used his energy taking apart an Army revolver he had re-tooled for cartridges. He was still working at the bench when his stomach rebelled. He spread an ancient, moth-eaten, tan blanket over the dismembered six-shooter and went back to eat.

Outside, the killing of Jorge Español would remain a source of discussion for days, one might suspect, because the village now had something to talk about besides rainfall which never came after the heat arrived.

Chapter Two

MANUEL ORTIZ

Once he was dead, Jorge Español left behind an old mother named Carmen and an older brother, Hernando. Jorge was the love of the old woman's life. Even the priest who came monthly could not assuage her grief.

Hernan was six years older than his brother had been. He was a quiet, hard-working man, darker than Jorge had been, and still unmarried in his thirties, a man who rarely smiled and who with three burros ranged far and wide for loads of fagot wood which he sold in the village. Jorge had worked cattle, an occupation which by tradition was seasonal. During the months when there was no need for *vaqueros*, Hernan and his three burros provided for his mother and the younger brother he loved with all his heart possibly because they were as different as night and day, not only in skin tones but also in other ways.

Hernan had worried over Jorge's childhood illnesses more than a father could have done — their father had disappeared down into Mexico shortly after Jorge was born. Hernan taught Jorge to read, how to rope, why a man always cares for his animals before he cares for himself. He had also tried to teach Jorge the rosary. Jorge could not remember the little prayers. He would laugh, slap Hernan lightly on the shoulder, and head for Amayo's *cantina*.

When their mother complained, Hernan reminded her that Jorge was just a boy. But Jorge had been almost thirty

17

when he had been killed, and Hernan had still been making excuses.

The residents of Mex town said Hernan was morose, that he wasn't married because there was something wrong with him. A few old people said nothing. Hernan was polite. He took care of his mother. He treated his burros well. If he preferred burros to people — well, burros never lie or steal, never cheat, drink, and beat their wives. The older people remembered Carmen's husband. He had been a large, burly, dark man who regularly abused his wife, got drunk, and got into fights. He was, it was said, a bully. When he left the family, the older people considered it a blessing. He had been an evil, fiery-tempered man. It was only by the grace of God that he left behind two good, decent boys.

It would also later be said that this *bastardo* had left something else behind, his terrible temper, but that would not happen for almost a year after the death of Jorge Español, and it happened so unexpectedly people, even those in *gringo* town, were stunned. None remembered Pedro Amayo had said that *arriero* would return.

But he did.

It was the time of year when the ground had hardened enough so that mules did not sink to their fetlocks. *Gringos* used wagons with wide tires. Pack trains out of Mexico could have used wagons, and perhaps someday they would, but for a hundred years they had used trains of pack mules.

Mexican packers were unique throughout the entire Southwest. Not only was it the tiny bells sewn to the outside of their trousers, but the inside of a rider's leg was sewn from almost the waist to below the knees with buckskin. Unlike the little bells this was done so that trousers lasted longer. Some of them wore crossed bandoleers, but the owners of pack trains frowned on this because crossed cartridge belts to *gringos* were symbols of renegades, raiders who came in large parties to kill, steal, and burn towns. In fact, riders up out of Mexico wearing bandoleers astraddle *sillas de montar* — *vaqueros* with a saddle horn as large as a dinner plate and carrying machetes and saddle guns — were not uncommonly shot out of hand.

In Pueblo Juárez where *gringo* merchants knew the leaders of pack trains, their arrival was welcome. There was even a large brush corral at the lower part of the village for their animals and places for *arrieros* to eat and bed down in Mex town. But these pack trains rarely had the same *arrieros* because it was a tiresome, long drive with little diversion and not very good wages.

Among these men the older ones went to Mex town as soon as they could. Most spoke no English, and those who did felt more at ease away from *gringo* town. But the younger ones could be troublesome which meant that, although the town marshal had never put up his sign forbidding *arrieros* from carrying sidearms in his town, when he knew the train was coming, he geared up for trouble and hoped that, when it came, it would be, as had been the case in the killing of Jorge Español, confined to Mex town.

This particular train, one of the earliest of the season, corralled its animals, paid for their feed, and left the *jefe* to do transactions while the *arrieros* went to Mex town.

This time the *jefe* who had been patronizing Amayo's *cantina* for years was surprised, then angered, to find the place boarded up. He went to find Pedro Amayo who, after the closing of his saloon, had gone into the goat business. Pedro explained to the chief *arriero* why his *cantina* had been closed, and the *jefe* went directly to the town marshal. They were close to being equal in size and temperament.

19

The *arriero* told Austin Gorman that, if he closed a saloon because of a fight, then two-thirds of the *cantinas* in the Southwest should be closed, and the marshal gave glare for glare and said no one who wasn't a U.S. citizen would ever tell him how to do his job.

The *jefe* left, stormed down to Mex town, and told Pedro Amayo no damned *gringo* could close his *cantina* because of a fight Pedro could not have avoided. Pedro, always a heavy-set man but nowhere nearly as large as the *arriero,* said the town marshal was the law in Pueblo Juárez and, if the *jefe* was smart, he would let the matter drop.

It was during this discussion outside Amayo's corral, full of goats, that an expressionless, dark, lithe man came up, tapped the Mexican on the arm, and quietly asked if he had a packer with him named Manuel Ortiz.

The large, sweaty Mexican brought forth a limp bandanna to wipe his face and neck while looking steadily at the equally tall but not nearly so massive man and asked what business it was of his who his packers were. Pedro Amayo began to sweat like a stud horse and to wish he had wings.

The expressionless, younger man answered quietly: "I make it my business, *señor,* because Manuel Ortiz killed my brother the last time he was here."

The big Mexican stopped mopping, looked from the quiet man to Pedro Amayo who made a sickly grin and shrugged. He faced the younger man again and hesitated before speaking. "Listen to me. I bring pack trains. I deliver merchandise. That is all. If you have a quarrel with one of my. . . ."

"I asked you a question," the expressionless, dark man said. "A simple question for a simple answer. *Did Manuel Ortiz come with you?*"

The big Mexican was in his fifties. He recognized the set and cold expression on the face of the man in front of him. He had been angry over in *gringo* town. He had been angry while talking to Pedro Amayo. Right now he wasn't angry. A man doesn't live into his fifties without understanding certain things such as the unblinking, unwavering, very dark eyes of the man who was facing him. The *jefe* was tough, experienced, and no coward, but at a distance of no more than eight or ten feet he understood perfectly that there would be no survivors if there was a fight, just two fools who were dead.

Hernan said it again. "Did you bring a man named Manuel Ortiz with you?"

There was a brief scuffle in the goat corral. A billy was trying to mount an indignantly disinterested doe. Pedro looked back but for only seconds as the Mexican answered Hernan Español.

"If you have a quarrel with someone, don't talk to me about it. Talk to. . . ."

The blow was so fast and hard Pedro had no time to gasp, but the big Mexican did; he doubled over, staggered, and held his soft parts with both hands. When he could straighten up, he wasn't looking at a gun. Hernan had a two-sided, razor-sharp, ten-inch knife in his left hand. He used his right hand to get a handful of the Mexican's hair and jerked the man upright. When he spoke, his words were soft and without inflection. "Is he here?"

The Mexican was hurt. He hadn't expected the blow nor had he seen it coming. He answered through clenched teeth. "He is here."

"Where?"

"I don't know."

"*Where?*"

21

"In the *gringo* saloon. He and two others."

Hernan yanked the Mexican's sidearm from its holster and threw it into the corral among the goats, put up his knife, and walked away.

Pedro led the Mexican to his *ramada,* got a jug of wine from his house, and poured a full glass for the big man and half a glass for himself. The big man half emptied the glass, mopped sweat, and said: "Who is he?"

"The brother of the one your packer shot to death in front of my *cantina* more than a year ago. His name is Hernando Español."

The large Mexican emptied the glass and mopped off more sweat. "Ortiz will kill him."

"If he does, *señor,* if he shoots him over in *gringo* town, the town marshal will kill him. I swear to you, there will be a war. Why did you allow some of your packers to wear bandoleers?"

"Because one can never tell. There are brigands everywhere."

"Do you know what bandoleers mean up here? It means raiders. If there is a fight. . . ." Pedro Amayo tipped his own full glass.

The larger man struggled up to his feet. "I will get my men away from here."

Pedro shook his head. "It is too late. But maybe you can tell them to hide in Mex town." Pedro eyed the big, sweating man ruefully. "What a fool you have to be. Why did you bring Ortiz?"

"Because he is my best *arriero*. He can handle the mules better than any man."

"Did you know he killed a man the last time he was here?"

The big man made a gesture. "Men get killed every-

22

where. No . . . he said there was a quarrel."

Pedro Amayo rose, picked up the jug and glasses, and was heading for the back door when he said: "God be with you, otherwise it will be *Señor Satán.*"

The large *jefe* went to the packers' camp where only two men were tending a small fire to cook goat meat. They looked up and went back to their cooking. Their leader asked whether they had seen Manuel Ortiz. They were both older men and had slight interest in celebrating their arrival. They had arrived a hundred times. They only knew that Ortiz and two other men, both first-timers and young, had gone up to *gringo* town because the *cantina* was boarded up.

One older man held up roasted goat ribs, and the chief packer sat down, winced, and began eating.

It was suppertime in both parts of Pueblo Juárez. For single men supper could come any time, but the saloonman liked to close his establishment after dusk because the coal oil for lamps came by wagon from Missouri and was very expensive. He had been a cavalryman on the frontier for eight years. He was scarred, irritable, and gruff. His name was O'Malley. Orion O'Malley. He had no use for Indians, particularly Apaches and Comanches, but otherwise he was indifferent to skin color. But O'Malley could read men, something he had learned to do well for the eight years his life had depended on that ability, and the three *arrieros* at his bar had his interest. He knew none of them, but he knew the degrees of insobriety as they advanced and his interest encouraged an effort to wean them from whiskey to red wine. It failed. The Mexicans, one of whom could speak a variety of border English, spilled the wine and demanded more whiskey.

O'Malley was reluctantly reaching toward his backbar for

a fresh bottle, when a man spoke quietly from just inside the spindle doors.

He was tall, as lithe as a puma, dark, and expressionless.

"Manuel Ortiz!"

The Mexicans turned, slowly and sloppily. O'Malley also faced around. He forgot the bottle.

There were other patrons, all *gringos*. Some were playing cards, others were leaning at the bar talking, and one man with skin like parchment and hair as white as quartz rock leaned off the bar and started for the door. Hernan Español moved aside for the man to depart.

The three *arrieros* facing Español were steadily staring. Español said: "Which of you is Ortiz?"

The packer in the center nodded. "I am. What is it? Who are you?"

"My name is Hernando Español."

Ortiz's gaze cleared, not at the name but at the black, unblinking eyes and the frozen face.

"Ortiz, do you remember a man named Jorge?"

"Who?"

"Jorge, you son-of-a-bitch! *Jorge Español, my brother!*"

Ortiz's gaze flickered. "Your brother?"

"You shot and killed him last year in front of Amayo's *cantina*. Now you remember?"

"Well, I never knew his name. And you come to settle?"

O'Malley took advantage of the Mexicans having their backs to his bar as they faced the tall, dark man. He carefully and quietly gripped the ash wagon spoke he kept there beside the sawed-off shotgun and came up slowly.

Manuel Ortiz made a humorless smile. If drinking had done anything to him, it was to heighten and sharpen his perception. He had never been more deadly in his life. He was in no hurry, and so he said: "You want to settle things

24

about this, roadrunner. Your brother was fast. Not fast enough."

Hernan's shoulder dropped a fraction. Manuel Ortiz shot as Hernan's pistol was rising to be cocked. The bullet knocked Hernan back through the spindle doors. His shot was a reflex. It went into the ceiling just inside the saloon.

Men scattered. One *arriero* lunged clear of the bar as did Ortiz. Their companion was slower. O'Malley's ash spoke struck him squarely over the head. The man dropped like a stone.

Ortiz kicked past the doors, pistol ready. Hernan's eyes didn't focus. He may have smelled hell's fire because he tried to twist to one side and raise his gun.

A bass voice spoke from the settling dusk. "You shoot that man on his back an' I'll blow your gawd-damn head off!"

The exclamation startled the two packers, but two hammers being hauled back on a shotgun convinced them not to move, not even to breathe.

Marshal Gorman struck the nearest packer over the kidney with his butt plate, and the packer sank to his knees in pain. Ortiz turned his head. Both barrels of the sawed-off riot gun were six inches from his face. He dropped the gun in his right fist, and Marshal Gorman shifted the scatter-gun to his left and struck Ortiz alongside the jaw with his right hand.

Old George Mars appeared out of shadows in front of his shop. He said: "Christ Almighty, Marshal, you killed the son-of-a-bitch."

The marshal looked around as O'Malley appeared, dragging another one. This one had a bloody face. O'Malley said — "They're yours, Marshal." — and went back inside his saloon.

25

George Mars was kneeling beside Hernan Español when he looked up and said: "Broke his arm, Marshal."

"Help him up. Take him home. He's old Carmen's boy."

The old man could not do it, so the lawman growled for two bystanders to help. He then dragooned two other men to drag the pair of semi-conscious packers to his jailhouse and personally dragged the one named Manuel Ortiz.

Lamps and candles came alive. O'Malley growled the first round was on the house, and the talking started. Men who had heard but had not seen argued with those who had both seen and heard, several of whom had been having a relaxed nightcap in the saloon when the sky had fallen.

When they delivered Hernando Español to his mother's *jacal,* she hid her face in an apron and wailed. They got Hernan to bed about the time Martha New, the midwife, arrived. She was by nature a domineering individual and under these, and similar circumstances, she was loud, profane, and overbearing.

When she was satisfied about the nature of the wound, she tied off the bleeding and went to take old Carmen in her muscular embrace and speak soothingly. She endlessly repeated that Hernan would recover. She told the wailing old woman she had seen worse gunshot wounds and the victims hadn't even stopped talking.

26

Chapter Three

THE MARS GUN

Marshal Gorman — whose father had dropped the O' from O'Gorman — had a jailhouse with only one large cell. After locking his groaning prisoners in, he first went to O'Malley's place for eyewitness details, which the old horse soldier gave him in growling tones, adding that the Mexicans had been drinking steadily for about an hour before the shooting.

He went next to the Español house where the rooms were crowded with anxious neighbors and met the midwife, Martha New, for whom he had the identical feeling he had for scorpions, and listened through her entire recitation with undisguised disapproval.

"The bullet missed his chest and broke his upper left arm," the midwife explained. "He bled out some, but mostly it's shock. In a few days he'll be up an' around, but no liftin' or strainin'."

A dark Mexican woman brushed past to go to the bedside. Martha New gave her a caustic look and spoke again. "She's their *curandera*. A god-damned witch, if I ever seen one."

Marshal Gorman went finally to the packer camp where only coals showed. Mostly, the Mexicans were bedded down, but the man he sought was sitting with two older men, as lean as snakes and whose faces resembled those of monkeys. They looked up once and did not do it again.

Nor did they offer to leave as Marshal Gorman hunkered beside the *jefe*, who looked around from contemplating the glowing coals and asked a question. "They are dead?"

Gorman considered the pair of old gnomes to whom he might not have been present when he replied. "No. Headaches an' hurt a little." He paused to consider the other large man. "You never told me your name."

"No? Well, it is Alfredo Constantino Guzman y Arellegro."

Gorman nodded. He hadn't expected anything else. He did not ask — he said: "*Señor* Guzman, get your ass and the asses of your packers out of my town by tomorrow afternoon. Mules and all."

The large, dark man rolled his eyes. "One day? I have mules needing new shoes. I have men in your *carcel* which I can't leave behind."

Marshal Gorman eyed the pair of mahogany gnomes who were silently gazing into the coals. They seemed to be non-English speakers with their expressionless faces except for their clearly interested manner. He continued to ignore them.

"Tomorrow afternoon," he said as he rose.

"One day? Marshal, you ask of me the impossible." The large man looked up. "He caused the fight."

Gorman's answer was curt. "Ortiz caused it last year. Tomorrow afternoon."

As the marshal walked away, the old men looked at their leader without speaking. Guzman cursed in two languages, shoved up to his feet, spat into the fire, and left.

The following morning Pedro Amayo appeared at the *juzgado*. Marshal Gorman received him frostily. "If you've come to get more time for the Mexicans, forget it. This afternoon, no later."

28

Amayo said: "There is something. Their *jefe* and I talked. He will send Ortiz away and never bring him again. It was only Ortiz. You can't blame the others for Ortiz."

Gorman leaned on his table. "Pedro, it ain't just sendin' him away. He shot and tried to kill a man last night."

Amayo spread his arms. "But he didn't kill him. He only hurt him. And Ortiz was minding his business at the saloon when Hernan walked in to fight him. You should lock up Hernan."

The larger man leaned back off his table, looking steadily at Pedro Amayo. "I said this afternoon, no later."

Amayo was silent for a moment before speaking. "Then they will take Hernan with them."

Gorman snapped forward on the chair. "Did Guzman say that? Because if he did, if he tries to take Hernan, I swear to you, I'll come after 'em with every man I can muster and hang every damned one of 'em. Tell that to old lard gut!"

Pedro Amayo departed. On his way to visit the home of Carmen Español, he encountered George Mars. As they walked together, slowly because old Mars could not walk faster, Pedro related to the gunsmith what the marshal had said, and the old man, instead of looking anxious or worried, smiled, and Pedro was angered.

"You find humor in this? If the packers don't go an' if the marshal gathers men . . . do you know what will follow, for the love of Our Lady?"

The gunsmith said no more until they reached the Español house and were admitted by a thin woman with the face of a sour cactus apple wearing a black *rebozo* and a black dress. She seemed about to bar the way to the gunsmith, but from behind her Carmen said to let him enter.

The small, windowless room, where Hernando was lying

29

on an unsteady old iron cot with a bedside table crowded with amulets, medicines, and clean rags, had candles because otherwise it would have been dark.

Hernando's arm had been expertly cared for, set, and bandaged. He looked pale but otherwise no different when he greeted his visitors. The gaunt dark woman stood in the doorway like an avenging angel until Carmen called, and she left.

The men knew her. She was the healer of Mex town, a *curandera*. Her name was María de la Cruz. She also went with the priest when he arrived to make his rounds. She was a maiden woman of sixty, married, as she said often, to Christ. Before the death of her father thirty-one years earlier, he had told her it was good to be the bride of Christ, but on cold winter nights women needed something more substantial or they suffered. María de la Cruz suffered. She had never argued with her father, but three days after his funeral the name she had been born with, María Elena Alvarado, became Mary of the Cross — María de la Cruz.

Hernan had a jug on the floor which he offered, and both his visitors drank to his quick recovery, as well as to rain and to plenty of firewood for the cold ahead, until he took back the jug with his right arm and asked about Manuel Ortiz.

Pedro told him all that he knew, including the marshal's order for the packers to be gone by this afternoon and rolled his eyes in despair, but old George Mars looked steadily at Hernan, saying nothing until Amayo ended his recitation, then the gunsmith startled both Pedro and the wounded man when he said: "Can you stand up, Hernan?"

"He shot me in the arm not the leg. I can stand up. Why?"

"Do you feel weak or sick?"

30

"No. I feel well enough."

"Can you hold a gun?"

Amayo stared, and Hernan faintly frowned. "What are you talking about?" he asked.

Old Mars said: "Be grateful it was the left arm . . . not the right one."

His listeners looked steadily at the gunsmith, and, when next he spoke, Pedro Amayo forgot to breathe for three seconds.

"I want you to come to my shop. Can you do that?"

"Yes. I told you he didn't shoot me in the leg."

"Will you do it now?"

Pedro Amayo was staring at the gunsmith. "Too much wine. What are you saying?"

George Mars appeared not to have heard. He said: "Come to my shop before noon. I want to give you something."

María de la Cruz appeared menacingly in the doorway again. Pedro and George Mars left. Hernan sat on the edge of his bed, favoring the arm in its sling. María said: "I heard. You cannot leave this house for days yet. That old man with the wooden leg is evil. I saw the mark on his forehead. Your mother shouldn't ever let him come here again. I'll make you something to eat."

Hernan sat gazing at the empty doorway. He had lost blood. He could not go fagot hunting. He would even have difficulty doing chores. To start with he had difficulty getting into a shirt. He heard his mother snoring in her bedroom, listened to María's racket in the kitchen, and left the house.

The sun was hot. The sky was clear. There was a gentle little ankle-high breeze blowing. Bluish smoke arose from *jacales*. An old man as fair as a *gringo* but with obsidian-

31

colored eyes and a mass of unkempt black hair hailed Hernan.

"Good for you! It's in the blood. Your father could drink ten men to sleep with a broken leg."

Hernan turned. "I am going eastward where there is wood. Tomorrow, when I find such a place, I will go out with the burros."

The old man wetly laughed. He didn't have a tooth in his head. He also made a living gathering fagots to sell. He had been doing it for more years than Hernan was old. There was no wood east of Pueblo Juárez for a hundred miles. It would be a woman, then. Hernan Ortiz deserved and needed a woman. May God send him a good one, the kind that did not think of themselves and knew how to laugh.

Hernan approached the gun shop from the alley. It was already dusty, and full summer had not even arrived. The gunsmith let him in, locked the door after him, and took him through his dingy shop to the front. There Hernan got a shock. Pedro Amayo was standing with his back to the roadway door. Pedro nodded and told the gunsmith he had locked the door.

Amayo remained by the door as the old man handed Hernan an empty shell belt with an empty holster and helped him buckle it into place on the right side. Hernan considered the gunsmith quizzically and would have spoken, but George Mars shook his head. "You listen. Just listen."

The gunsmith slipped an Army model six-gun which was customized to handle brass-encased cartridges into the holster. Hernan felt the weapon. It fitted his right hand as any six-gun should.

The gunsmith said: "Now draw it. Do it again. You have to know your weapon." He looked at Pedro, who slowly shook his head as he said: "Jorge was faster."

32

George Mars gestured. "Do it again. Good. Now hold the gun. You understand? . . . it must feel like an extension of your fingers."

Hernan was sweating, and Pedro got him a tin cup of water which he drank as the gunsmith waited impatiently. When Pedro returned to the door, holding the cup, the old man said: "You had the cup in your hand. Move the fingers like this. Open and closed. Now . . . draw the gun. Pedro?"

Amayo shook his head, and Hernan finally spoke irritably. "What are you doing?"

The gunsmith said: "You are going to kill Ortiz."

"I tried. He shot me before I could. . . ."

"Draw the gun! Again draw the gun! Pedro?"

This time Amayo shrugged thick shoulders, and the gunsmith broadly smiled. "Hernan, draw the gun. Relax and draw the gun."

Pedro spoke from over by the door. "Maybe."

George Mars dragged up a stool and sat on it. He considered the younger man and spoke. "Ortiz is fast and fairly accurate. Hernan, only men who practice daily for years can be both fast and accurate."

"I can shoot straight," Hernan said, and the old man's look of satisfaction winked out.

"Just listen, damn it! You are going to kill him. You can shoot straight, fine, but he is very fast."

The old man took back the holstered gun and handed Hernan one like it. "Holster it. Now . . . draw it like you would shoot Ortiz."

Hernan obeyed. He drew, and raised the gun. The old man and Pedro Amayo exchanged a look, and Pedro smiled.

Hernan handed back the weapon and slumped. He was

33

tired. Old George got him a glass of red wine.

Within ten minutes he was ready to try again, but this time he had a question. "What is this about? Ortiz has friends. Even if I . . . ?"

Pedro Amayo interrupted. "There will be a celebration in Mex town for the packers. Meat and plenty of wine, and also twice their number of us slapping them on the back and handing the jugs around. If they hear a gunshot, we, too, will be armed. They won't be able to do a thing, and if they try. . . ." Amayo shrugged.

Hernan sat down again, looking from Amayo to George Mars. "All this so I can try to kill Manuel Ortiz?"

The gunsmith spoke adamantly. "Not try to kill the son-of-a-bitch." He gestured. "Draw the gun. Put it on half cock."

Hernan obeyed, drew the hammer an inch to half cock, and the hammer fell hard. He did that three times before looking up. George grinned. "There is no safety, no half cock. When you draw and squeeze the trigger, the gun fires. Remember that, or you might shoot yourself in the leg. Now do it! Draw and fire. The gun will buy you maybe two seconds. Ortiz draws, cocks, and fires. The reason he didn't shoot you through the brisket was because, when he cocked his gun, he pulled it sideways a fraction and hit you in the arm. You cut out two things, cocking and aiming. Now try it."

It was after the sun was sliding toward the west before Amayo and the gunsmith were satisfied. When Hernan put the gun aside and unbuckled the shell belt to toss it on the counter, he asked a question. "Ortiz in the *juzgado?*"

The pair of older men traded another sly look before Pedro lied with all his heart and a clear conscience. "The marshal will let him go with the others."

Hernan snorted. "He will never do that. You know him as well as I do. He will never free Ortiz until the pack train is on its way back to Mexico."

Pedro nodded. "That's it. You see? Ortiz will be turned loose to catch up . . . you see? You will be at the lower end of town, waiting. If he is a-horseback, it will buy you another two or three seconds."

Hernan sat gazing at the two older men. He rose slowly, shook his head, and started for the door.

The gunsmith called him. "You are forgetting something," and gestured toward the Mars gun.

Hernan went back for the gun. Without his holster, he shoved it in the front of his trousers. As he was ready to depart this time, the gunsmith said: "The alley door and, when you get home, practice. Come back after the celebration. Hernan, the timing has to be right. *¿Comprende?*"

The older men wasted little time. Both left by the alley door, too. When they reached Mex town, the fire glowed in a pit. Goat meat was cooking atop thick iron screening, and the red wine was already being passed around. The packers mingled. Possibly they had initially been surprised. They were men who had departed from dozens of villages without more than indifferent waves of people. This was like Christmas or a Name Day. They flirted, sang — badly — wrinkled their faces as the scent of cooking meat spread, and laughed.

Among the residents of Pueblo Juárez women sweated at the pit. The men, mostly older and wearing sidearms, unusual at fiestas, made it a lively affair. The jugs passed. The *arrieros*, normally treated indifferently in border towns they visited, sometimes scornfully, performed the traditional *abrazo* of warm friends and flirted outrageously even with grandmothers. A particularly undersize, wiry packer, whose

35

crooked nose suggested that leaning behind a Mexican mule was not a good idea, hovered around Carmen Español, who was old and flustered. It had been twenty years, but she was thrilled, although she would have died before admitting it.

The meat was handed out. Much of the noise and activity slackened. The pit-tenders wiped off sweat and took large wooden platters among the seated men. Old Carmen and two other women kept the cups full, while the sun slowly but inexorably marched westerly and got a faintly pink overtone from the rising dust.

Marshal Gorman leaned slightly apart, eating a greasy bone. He was affable but reserved. His order would be enforced, fiesta or not. The chief packer came up, wiping grease from thick fingers on a soiled bandanna. He smiled and said in Spanish this was good, that his men would never forget, and, when next he come north, they would fight to be among the drovers.

Marshal Gorman squinted in the direction of the sun before speaking in English. As with most people who lived in the borderlands, he spoke a second language but for serious conversation preferred his own. He told the portly Mexican he should send some men to get the mules ready, and the *jefe* offered a paternal smile and gestured. "It is such a good time. Look you, Marshal, everyone laughs." He dropped his arms. "We will go in the morning. Early before anyone is awake."

He should have known better. Austin Gorman's face was an open book. He neither backed down nor compromised. He repeated himself: the chief packer should send men to get the mules ready.

Alfredo Guzman exchanged a long look with the marshal, sighed, and turned away. Old George Mars limped over, wiped a greasy chin with an ancient, soiled sleeve, and said: "They are leaving?"

"Yes. Before sundown."

The old man wagged his head. "Look at them. Even the grandmothers are lively."

Gorman glanced around. "George, have you been to many of these fandangos?"

Mars broadly smiled. "Hundreds of them. Have you?"

"Some. Tell me something . . . do the men always wear guns?"

The gunsmith did not reply until he had disposed of an impossibly difficult piece of gristle, one of those bits of goat meat that the longer a man chewed the bigger it got.

"Different places, Marshal, different customs." The old man tossed aside his bone as he added: "Where are those men going?"

"You should know. They are to be out of Pueblo Juárez before sundown. I told 'possum-belly to get his mules ready to leave."

George Mars watched Mexicans detach from the crowd, and sucked his teeth. After a moment he had another question. "What about the ones you got locked up at the jail-house?"

"Guzman paid two dollars for each of them for disturbin' the peace. They go with the others."

The gunsmith drifted closer to the crowd, found Pedro Amayo, and repeated what the marshal had said. Pedro rolled his eyes. "Ortiz must be the last one to leave."

Mars staggered when a packer with a flushed face jostled him. The packer knew nothing of wooden legs, but his reflexes were excellent. He caught George Mars by the arm and made voluble apologies in Spanish. Pedro spoke shortly, and the packer departed.

37

George said: "Drunk son-of-a-bitch."

Pedro laughed. To Amayo, as to most of his people, the *gringo* epithet *son-of-a-bitch* was so ridiculous it was funny because as everyone knew it was biologically impossible for a man's mother to be a dog.

Carmen Español came by, flustered by the enduring attention of the Mexican with the misshapen nose. Pedro would have interceded, but the grim-faced, blacked-clothed woman of the cross caught his attention with a fierce look. She trailed after the wiry packer and Carmen who was heading toward her house. Pedro stepped back, watched briefly, and softly said: "If he tries to go inside, María will half kill him."

George Mars watched for a different reason — unless Hernan was in the house, his mother would be upset. More so, if she entered and found him practicing with the pistol.

Marshal Gorman came by on his way to *gringo* town and nodded. George Mars said: "Timing, Pedro. Come with me."

There were several ways to reach *gringo* town from Mex town. There were narrow openings between buildings. The natives called them *paseos,* the *gringos* called them dogtrots. The one George limped into was between the saloon and the harness works. Dogs were not the only creatures who used it. Because of the proximity of the saloon where most patrons drank beer, it was convenient, but over the years the dogtrot had acquired it's own individuality. It had a powerful smell.

The roadway was almost without life or movement. The gunsmith emerged first, barely in time to see the marshal enter his jailhouse. He said: "Maybe we have an hour." Then he led the way southward in the direction of the large public corral at the lower end of Pueblo Juárez.

38

Arrieros were rolling empty *alforjas* and securing them to harnessed mules, which were smaller than *norteamericano* mules and very hardy. They were also more individualistic. If they were cinched too tight or were overloaded, they bit. A Mexican mule could swing its head very fast, flatten its ears, and bite. Not nip in annoyance but bite with genuine intention to cause injury, and if, as was customary, the *arriero* was tightening a *cincha* with his back to the mule's head, he was unable to sit a saddle or a chair for a very long time, nor did he make that mistake more than once.

George and Pedro watched the rigging out, and were ignored except for an occasional acknowledging grin.

Marshal Gorman also appeared. He was looking for Alfredo Guzman who wasn't there. He was at O'Malley's place, exuberantly expressing his gratitude for all that the people of Pueblo Juárez had done and swearing a mighty oath that he would neither forget nor be gone so long the next time.

He was still exhorting — and drinking — when the marshal walked in. Guzman would have embraced the marshal, but Gorman kept his distance as he said: "Another hour, *amigo*."

Guzman dropped his arms and jerked his head for O'Malley to set up whiskey for the lawman, which O'Malley did, and the leader of the packers asked when his men at the jailhouse would be released.

Gorman's answer was short. "When you're on your way."

"But I need them to help with the getting ready."

"When I see your butt going down the road, I'll turn 'em loose," Gorman said, downed his jolt, and left the saloon.

Guzman looked at O'Malley who shrugged.

39

Chapter Four

AN AFTERMATH

George Mars did not carry liquor well. Common belief was that old men never did, and it might have been true because, after Pedro Amayo and the gunsmith paused for one drink at O'Malley's water hole and eventually departed, the gunsmith's otherwise pronounced limp was scarcely noticeable and his eyes were unusually bright — and wet.

They went to the lower end of Pueblo Juárez to fidget. Across the road Guzman's packers were almost ready for the road.

Pedro Amayo rolled his eyes pleadingly skyward. There was no response. George Mars swore, and moments later someone emerged from the alley behind them and softly said: "Where is he?"

The gunsmith answered. "He'll get set loose directly. Those mule men are about ready. Yonder . . . the fat man" — George paused to squint — "he's been drinking."

He got no refutation. As a result of the fiesta everyone had been drinking.

Pedro made an observation. "I know that name from somewhere."

"Guzman?"

"Yes."

Old George snorted. "You remember the man who used to carpenter hereabout, and it was not Guzman . . . it was Gustafsen."

40

Hernan eased up where he could watch the *arrieros* open the gate to line out their pack animals. Both men and mules knew which way was south.

Pedro breathed one word: "There."

Marshal Gorman was in his doorway watching three Mexicans walking southward. He may not have seen the large *jefe,* or he may have seen him with no interest, but, when Guzman twisted to look back with one hand on his mount's rump, one of the released packers gestured and called loudly. Guzman called back.

"Your animals are in the corral. Hurry!"

George placed a hand lightly on Hernan's arm and said: "Wait."

It wasn't a long wait. Two of the packers came out of the corral in a wide sweep. The third was behind them.

George Mars took his hand off Hernan's arm as he said: *"Now!"*

Hernan moved into roadway dust as the lagging rider came ahead. He called to him in Spanish. Ortiz had to recognize the man he had shot if by no other way than because of the sling. He didn't slacken his gait. Old George said: "Hernan!" He had seen Ortiz's right shoulder dip.

Ortiz had his weapon clearing leather when the bullet struck him. For a moment frozen in time he looked squarely at Español before going off his horse to land face down.

Guzman yelled, swung, and spurred his horse back the way he had come.

Hernan hadn't moved, neither had Austin Gorman who seemed rooted in the jailhouse doorway. When he did finally move, he yanked loose the tie-down thong over his holstered Colt as he approached. He and the chief packer reached the dead man about the same time. Guzman did not dismount or speak. Marshal Gorman knelt, rolled Ortiz onto his back, and slowly arose to look in Hernan's direction as he said: "He didn't get his gun out."

George Mars said: "He was goin' for it, Marshal. You was behind an' didn't see him do it. We was in front, an' sure as God made sour apples he was goin' for it."

There were people from both parts of town along the roadway, quiet and motionless.

Guzman started to speak, and the marshal snarled him into silence. "God damn you! Get his carcass out of here an' don't none of you ever come back!" The marshal motioned for Pedro and George to help him hoist the limp body up behind Guzman's saddle. Gorman stepped back, dusting his hands and glaring at the mounted man. "If I ever see you again, *amigo,* I'll slit your pouch an' pull your leg through it. *Get!*"

Guzman salvaged something of his pride. He rode southward to catch up with his train, but he did it at a slow walk.

Hernan went where Pedro and the gunsmith were standing. He addressed Mars: "More like six or eight seconds," he said. "I think I could have done it with my own gun."

George showed a persimmon smile. "That's your first mistake. Thinking you're better than you are. You had all the advantages. You keep thinking that way, and, old as I am, I'll outlive you."

George lifted away the Mars gun and went limping in the direction of his shop.

It was late evening when Marshal Gorman appeared at the gun shop. Usually a direct man, as he accepted the cup of black coffee from George Mars he said: "I heard talk you coached Hernan."

42

The old man did not deny it. "I helped him a little. That son-of-a-bitch had it comin'."

Gorman half emptied the cup and grimaced. "That's the worst god-damned coffee I ever tasted."

George kept a straight face when he said: "You're welcome. You didn't come here for coffee."

The large man ranged a look along the back wall with its pistols, rifles, and carbines suspended by nails. "Where's the gun Hernan Español used?"

George was brusque. "You want to buy it?"

"Maybe."

"One hunnert dollars."

The marshal brought his eyes down slowly. For a long time he said nothing, then he swore and stamped out of the shop.

The following day Pedro Amayo came by the shop, and, when George told him about the lawman's visit, Pedro nodded. "He was in the jailhouse doorway. He could see Hernan. He saw him draw and fire."

"Care for a cup of coffee, Pedro?"

"Red wine, *viejo*."

They were both enjoying a cup of red wine at the counter, when they both got the surprise of their lives. María de la Cruz appeared in the doorway in her habitual black attire, a gaunt, forbidding expression on her face, her black eyes fixed malevolently. She spoke cavernously. "I know!"

George recovered first. "You know what?"

"You two planned to get that *arriero* killed."

George was recovering fast. "You don't know any such thing."

She opened her fist, and something metallic struck the

43

floor. George looked down then said: "Where did you get that?"

She avoided an answer by asking a question of her own. "Who else makes bullets like that?"

George's temper was rising. *Where did you get that?*

"I help Carmen, who lost one son and almost lost another one because you made him a gunman."

"For the last damned time . . . where did you get that bullet?"

"I told you. I help Carmen when I can. She went to the *barbacoa* yesterday. I cleaned her house as a favor, as I often do. I was making up Hernando's bed. It fell out of the blankets. His *pistola* was hanging on the wall in its holster. You wanted to make a killer out of her only child. God will punish you both!"

She left as she had appeared. Without a sound Pedro looked at George who emptied his cup, cast a sulphurous glance in the direction of the doorway, and said: "Damned witch."

The inhabitants of Pueblo Juárez had something to talk about, and they talked. Eyewitnesses appeared whose versions of the killing varied except in one detail: since it was said the killer of Jorge Español was a deadly and dangerous *arriero,* very fast and unerring with a pistol, then what they had seen and would probably never see again was a miracle. Hernando Español only occasionally carried a sidearm, yet he had beaten Ortiz to the draw and the shooting. The only way to account for such a thing was to credit it to a miracle. On this point there was no question.

Marshal Gorman heard the talk at O'Malley's place and fixed the former horse soldier with a scornful gaze. "Miracle, my butt," he exclaimed. "It was the gun. Old Mars doctored it some way."

44

O'Malley had neither seen the killing nor was he especially interested in it. "How," he asked Austin Gorman, "could anyone make a gun to shoot like they say Hernan's gun did?"

"It wasn't Español's gun," the marshal replied. "It was a gun George fiddled with."

To O'Malley gunsmithing was a mystery. He made a wide swipe of the bar top and wagged his head. He had shot guns most of his life, particularly when he had served in the Army. Occasionally someone would file off a front sight on pistols or perhaps grease the inside of holsters, but from what he had heard Hernan Español had purely and simply been faster and more accurate than the *arriero*. But he knew better than to pursue the subject, so he got the marshal a jolt and left him.

It was inevitable that this *miracle* would be brought down from the realm of some unearthly intercession, and so, after a few days when this happened, old George began having visitors. Not prospective customers, but curious and wondering men to whom the old man, who did not welcome interruptions, brusquely advised that some men were born gunfighters and he was busy.

One man brooded after the other inhabitants of the village relegated the gunfight to something only worth recalling when the subject of gunfighters arose and that did not happen often. Marshal Gorman went several times to the gun shop. One time he did not ask to see the gun Español had killed the Mexican with, but demanded to see it. The old man arose from his workbench, removed a six-gun from its nail, and put it atop the counter.

As the large no-nonsense lawman picked it up and hefted it, he said: "How come you to have the gun?"

"Because I own it. You want to buy it?"

Marshal Gorman had been asked that question before and his shock and anger from that time had remained in the back of his mind. He swung the gun to dry fire it, and the old man stopped him.

"That ain't no cap pistol. You'd ought to know better'n to dry fire guns!"

Marshal Gorman put the six-gun gently atop the counter and leaned. "What did you do to it, George?"

"Do to it? I took it off its nail an' put it in front of you."

Gorman's neck swelled, and his face reddened. He left the shop.

For some reason known only to himself, Pedro Amayo avoided George Mars and his shop. Several times the old man saw the gaunt woman who wore black watching him. It didn't bother him. What did bother him was when the priest, who visited Pueblo Juárez as he made his loop of a large area inhabited by people who lived in tiny settlements or pueblos, came to the shop doorway one summer morning and hesitated before entering. He was one of those Irishmen whose pink skin never really adjusted to desert country and darkened. He was old, not as old as the gunsmith but close to it. His name was Shannon O'Rourke — Father Shannon.

He heard confessions, held Masses and evening prayer in what had once been a Mexican barrack. Its mud walls were badly eroded, its ridgepole sagged, but it served. There were Catholics among the *norteamericanos,* not many and even fewer attended services, but the arrival of Father Shannon made an impression, particularly in Mex town where men doffed their hats to him and women looked at the ground, some crossing themselves, others risking a shy smile.

A few with reason sought audiences. María de la Cruz

46

did. Among other local calamities she had warned him with a lowered voice and a piercing look that Pueblo Juárez was inhabited by *un espíritu maléfico*, possibly *Señor Satán* himself, and had told the story of the Ortiz killing.

The old gunsmith now peered from beneath unkempt eyebrows and called to the man hesitating in his doorway. "Come in."

The priest obeyed, smiling. He was of average height and from either training or habit had no difficulty raising a benign smile. He introduced himself, which was unnecessary, and gazed at the old man's array of weapons before saying: "Having no skill myself, I admire those who do have."

George smiled, too. "You might want to buy a little belly gun that you could conceal."

The priest's smile lost some of its warmth as Father Shannon said: "No, possibly some day, but I am protected."

The old man nodded, his faded, shrewd eyes on the other man. "Graveyards is full of fellers who didn't own weapons, Father."

The holy man reddened and widened his smile. He said — *"Touché."* — and continued speaking. "There was a young Mexican named Manuel Ortiz. . . ."

George nodded, but just barely. "Sure was, Father. He killed a lad named Español, an' Español's brother killed Ortiz." Old George raised a hand. "I know. . . . there's somethin' my mother told me better'n sixty years back . . . gittin' even is My business, said the Lord. Father, there's times when a man dassn't wait for the Lord to do it. He could get killed while he's waitin'. It happens all the time."

The priest considered George Mars without smiling. For a fact he looked like an imp, wizened, lined, unkempt with

47

piercing eyes and a glib tongue. Father Shannon eventually spoke again. "Did Hernan Español have help in that killing?"

George rummaged his pockets for his foul little pipe, couldn't find it, and said: "They say it was a miracle, Father, Hernan beatin' that gunfightin' *arriero*. I've lost my damned pipe again, Father, excuse me. It's hereabout somewhere."

When George found the pipe and returned to the counter, the priest was gone.

Two days later, when George returned from the village's small general store with tinned goods, he found the Mars gun was also gone.

What made it worse, the midwife had told him several times only fools went for groceries or anything else and did not lock their doors, and old George loathed the midwife above all the people in his circumscribed world.

Chapter Five

G. MARS

The loss of his Mars gun troubled the old man to such an extent that he scarcely noticed the wind storm that arrived along toward day's end and blew both fitfully and fiercely for two full days until dirt, sand, and dust were banked against doorways and people who ventured out returned with running noses and burning eyes. This was no novelty. Summer heat which became almost unbearable before winter arrived and winds which came out of nowhere for no reason were facts of life.

A person could find shade, or water in the creeks, to achieve coolness and escape from the desert heat, and during the cold winters, when darkness arrived at four in the afternoon, warming fires were built, but thus far no one had devised a method to escape wind. Inside adobe houses there was the fearful whistling; in wooden structures there was the creaking and groaning.

For traveling people there was no escape. Dust blinded animals and stung them unmercifully with jagged infinitesimal bits of sand and tiny stones. Robert Barber was a freighter who had left Pueblo Juárez with a gentle breeze at his back. He was traveling eastward to the border community of Scottville. It was such an habitual routine his mules knew every yard of the road, even places where arroyos broke the flatness, places where they hurried going down and across so that momentum would carry the big old wagon up the far side.

The benign breeze lingered until the freighter was about three miles west of Pueblo Juárez, then it began to increase. Barber cursed. He had been through this many times, and between Pueblo Juárez and Scottville there was no protection, no trees, no buildings, none of those rock fields with plinths higher than a mounted man, no shelter of any kind.

Not too many years earlier the natives had called this stretch of road *jornada del muerto* — day's journey of the dead man — because it was totally exposed and was through Apache country. There were still remnants of burned wagons and buggies, skeletons of horses, even shriveled black scraps of harness, but sand and wind had covered much of this débris, and the Apaches had gone down into Mexico where *Rurales* and routine Army patrols from this side of the border did not track them. A hundred Apache fighting men buried to their heads in sand had in the past ambushed ten times their number in this area.

The wind had blown then, too, and the Apaches had used it to advantage. Robert Barber went past the place where hostiles had decimated a train of emigrant wagons with a soldier escort, and, by the time he reached this place, his animals were traveling with heads down and eyes closed. The freighter covered his face to the eyes, otherwise the mules would have left the road and wandered miles out of the way.

The sun was hidden, and the sky was fish-belly gray as bits of ancient wood flew by. Once a slat struck Henry, then his near-side rear mule, and, except for flinching, the mule neither opened his eyes nor shied; he plodded along with no interest in anything in this world.

Scottville did not so much arrive where the road passed as it appeared ghost-like without clear definition, a mirage of a place. Barber held his mules to the wide roadway as

50

far south as a network of corrals at the lower end of town. Where he made a wide sashay, an apparition almost totally covered by a poncho appeared to open a corral gate.

Robert Barber climbed down to free the tongue, the single trees, and sweep harnesses off over rumps and drop them on the ground beside the old wagon. There was no point in forking feed. Wind would whip it away before his mules got a mouthful. They seemed more interested in the large, old, leaky stone trough.

Barber followed the man hidden beneath his poncho into the runway of a livery barn to the harness room where a stove popped and the room smelled powerfully of dried horse and mule sweat. The freighter vigorously scratched his beard where invisible bits of sharp-edge dust had lodged. He was fully bearded, almost to the eyes, and his hair was gray-streaked. He was a rawboned man of indeterminate age, thanks to the covering mat of face feathers.

The liveryman produced a jug, and Barber drank, blew out a flammable breath, and sidled close to the stove as he spoke loudly in order to be heard over the noise of the storm.

"Wasn't no more'n a breeze when I left Juárez."

The liveryman, like a monk, hadn't shed his poncho when he took back the jug, stoppered it, and shoved it out of the way before speaking. "They come sudden-like for a fact. You leave off freight over at Juárez?"

"Yes, some for the gen'l store, some for the saloon. I got to off-load here, then head for Buttonwillow."

The liveryman, whose name was Frank Barton, straddled a backless chair, cocked his head as a particular blast of wind scrabbled among the rafter ends, and wagged his head. "You should've been here last week. Sheriff Blount got shot."

"The hell you say!"

"Mort was too old. There was a day he'd have eaten that Texas drover for breakfast. Got himself killed. We buried him the next day."

Barber sat down on a small wooden keg, used an ancient bandanna to mop his eyes, and spoke while doing this.

"You catch the Texan?"

"Oh, yes. Like an idiot he hung around town. They come onto him from all directions, beat the whey out'n him, and locked him in the jailhouse. If the wind hadn't come, they'd'd've lynched him."

Barber dryly said: "I expect it's good for somebody."

The liveryman nodded as he asked a question. "You got much for us?"

"Some crates for the Emporium, some wooden boxes that look about right for havin' guns in 'em, an' some rolled hides an' what-not for the harness works." Barber was vigorously scratching his face as he nodded. "Two cases for the saloon." He finished scratching and arose. "Is the eatery open?"

"It was. You know Black Ben . . . he'll be snarlin' about the storm."

As Barber headed for the door, he grumbled aloud that he didn't blame the caféman or anyone else for grumbling about the weather, and the liveryman said: "It'll blow itself out in a day or so. It always does."

The freighter was bucking wind as he crossed to the plank walk and headed for a weak light showing through a foggy window. It was mid-afternoon, or a tad later, and already there was gray gloom and limited visibility. Barber had to fight the café door open and lean hard to close it. Behind an empty counter a black man watched and shook his head. "I think I'll build me one of them wind-wagons

52

an' leave this country," he said.

Barber sank down at the counter and, using his whole arm, made a dusting sweep. The caféman watched sourly without comment. He'd wiped the counter a dozen times today.

Barber's beard still itched. He ordered as he scratched. "Whatever you got that's hot, an' coffee."

As the caféman was filling a cup, he said: "You heard about Sheriff Blount?"

"Got himself killed, I heard."

"Yes, and they got the Texan in the *calabozo* who done it." As the caféman placed coffee in front of Barber, he added: "You been in Texas? No? Well, I have. There's a sayin' that the devil in hell was chained for a thousan' years an' remained there until God turned him loose." The caféman paused. "He went to Texas an' never left. I'll get your meal."

Barber's face would not stop itching. When the platter came, the caféman said: "I raised a beard years back. In Texas the wind blows, an' I'd itch for a week. Little bits of grit got in there. Liked to drove me to dippin' snuff."

Barber ate everything in sight, leaned back, rolled and lighted a smoke, and, when the caféman returned from clearing his counter, Barber asked about the Texan who had killed the sheriff.

The caféman leaned on his pie table opposite the freighter when he spoke. "I was in front of the apothecary. The sheriff was too old. Twenty years back it'd've been a dead Texan. This time the cowboy wasn't fast . . . he was half drunk . . . an' he still out-gunned the sheriff."

"What'll folks do?"

"Hang him, I expect. It don't take much for folks to make a lynchin'. You know what that Texan did? Offered

53

five thousand dollars in gold, if they'd let him go. *Five thousand gold dollars!*"

The freighter snorted, and the caféman held up a hand. "His name's John Parrot." At Barber's blank look, the caféman explained. "His pappy's Jefferson Parrot." Because the blank look remained, the caféman rolled his eyes. "Don't mean nothin' to you? Mister, that boy's daddy owns half of Texas. He's got more year-'round riders than we got folks in Scottville."

"He's rich?"

Again the caféman rolled his eyes. "Rich! You'd ought to quit lookin' at mule butts an'. . . ."

"He's more'n likely lyin'. I would . . . to keep from gettin' hung."

"He ain't lyin'. There was letters in his saddlebags from his pa."

The freighter began scratching again. "Five thousand. That's more'n a man would make in four, five years if he hauled steady."

Outside the wind was still howling, but now and then it would slacken a little. Barber returned to the livery barn, but the liveryman was nowhere around. Barber got grain for his mules and put it among them on the ground. Grain wouldn't blow away like hay would.

He bedded down in the mow which was directly below the roof. For a while he listened to the wind blundering overhead before he lay back with both arms beneath his head and said it aloud. "Five . . . thousand . . . dollars, for Chris' sake."

Something happened during the night. The wind departed. The damage for which it was responsible remained, but, when the sun came, while there was damage to spare, at least a man could see for miles. Barber hayed his animals, and, when the liveryman arrived, he paid him for the hay but did not mention the grain. The liveryman had been to the café where there was strong talk of a lynching.

The black man had been encouraging it. Several rangemen had eaten in silence and departed. The caféman had said: "They'll be back with others. Their kind pee through the same knothole. If he's goin' to get hung, it dassn't be put off too long."

When Barber went to breakfast, the normal customers had long since left, but there were a couple of old gummers noisily eating mush, and the caféman did as he'd done the day before. While Barber was eating, he leaned against the pie table as he spoke. "They're fixin' to have a lynchin'."

The freighter finished and shoved the platter away. "Is someone takin' ol' Blount's place?"

The caféman nodded. "The blacksmith's helper." He smiled. "He don't need a scatter-gun. It's unanimous, they're goin' to lynch that Texican. But if they wasn't," the caféman slowly wagged his head, "Marty's big enough to ride. No one'll get inside until they're ready to haul that Texas boy out."

The freighter returned to the roadway. Merchants and their aproned clerks were sweeping and swearing. Scottville seemed as normal as most towns would look that had just weathered a violent storm. There were no rangemen in sight, and from Scottville westerly sand yielded to soil, and wherever there was grass there were stockmen, owners, and riders.

Barber sauntered through town, considered a trim and haircut at the tonsorial parlor, and entered. The barber was using a turkey-feather duster to rid his place of dust. Across the road was the Scottville jailhouse. As the barber worked,

55

he and the freighter discussed the prime topic, the sheriff's killing and the Texas rangeman. There seemed to be a difference between the tonsorial expert and others. He said that as far as he knew, it had been a fair shoot-out. If anyone was to blame, it was Sheriff Blount who should have hung it up ten years ago.

The freighter asked about the sheriff and got a pithy reply. "Old buffler hunter. When I come here years back, he was right handy, but the years can make a difference, 'specially when Mort Blount was recoverin' from a bad case of lung fever. But, you know, there's folks you can't talk to. He was like that. He wouldn't give in to bein' old."

"You said it was a fair fight?"

"I'd call it that, except that the Texican was young an' the sheriff was old."

The freighter had a question. "You agree with the lynch talk?"

"Can't say as I do, but a man can get hurt mouthin' off against what folks want to do. You want the beard trimmed?"

"I expect so. I heard there's a feller in the jailhouse to keep watch."

The barber snorted. "Watch for what? No one's ever broke out of the jailhouse. That Texas boy sure won't."

"You know much about him?"

"I know the lies about his daddy bein' the richest man in Texas."

"Lies?"

"If your daddy was rich as Crœsus, would you ride for a livin'? I sure wouldn't."

When the freighter returned to the roadway, there were several groups of men talking earnestly among themselves. The largest bunch was in front of the saloon.

From the doorway the barber shook a cloth and said —
"Won't be long now." — and went back inside.

The freighter crossed over, went through a weedy place
until he reached the alley, then strolled up as far as the
jailhouse where he stopped to study the building. There
was an alley door. While he was doing this, a skinny wisp
of a nervous individual called to him from behind a fenced
yard. "You part of the posse? Don't worry, he can't get out
the back way."

The freighter gave a little start and walked northward to
an intersecting roadway that led around front. Those small,
congregating groups were getting larger; some were inter-
mingling with other groups. Morning was beginning to
shade into early afternoon. Scottville's main thoroughfare
had no women or children in sight, only men, a few tethered horses, and a fat black dog sitting solemnly in overhang shade.

Robert Barber got an unlighted cigar between his teeth
as he studied the roadway entrance to the jailhouse. It
would be risky. In fact, it would be downright unlikely, but
five thousand dollars! He crossed toward the jailhouse with
a feeling that eyes were fixed on his back, hesitated, then
knocked.

The door didn't open, but a man called. "That you,
Whit?"

The freighter muffled his voice with an upraised hand.
"Yeah, it's me. Open the door."

As the door swung inward, the freighter had a glimpse
of a very large, muscled-up stranger no more than
twenty-five years old and tow-headed. The tow head tilted
as the freighter held the six-gun close to his own middle so
it wouldn't be seen and said: "Back up, friend. Real slow
an' keep your hands where I can see 'em. Fine, now get

them keys off the wall an' open the cage."

The blacksmith's helper made no move to obey, so Barber tipped his pistol barrel a tad. "I don't have all day. Open the damned cage!"

From the strap-steel cell the prisoner said: "Disarm the son-of-a-bitch."

Barber ignored that, and, when the blacksmith's helper had a huge brass key in one hand, the freighter wigwagged with his six-gun. "Over by the cage. Closer. Now a tad to one side. Is your name Parrot?"

The youthful prisoner replied instantly. "John Parrot."

"What's your pa's name?"

"Jefferson Parrot."

"You got five thousand dollars, Mister Parrot?"

"Yes."

"Where is it?"

"In a Denver bank."

The big tow-headed man sneered but remained silent. Barber looked at him. "Use two fingers. Lift out the pistol an' drop it."

The tow-headed man obeyed as he spoke. "He's got no five thousand dollars in a Denver bank or nowhere else, an' his name ain't Parrot, it's John Stumpf."

"Stump?"

"S-t-u-m-p-f. John Stumpf."

The freighter's attention lingered on the tow-headed man. "You know that to be a fact?"

The blacksmith's helper jutted his jaw. "His picture's on the dodger yonder on the desk. Picture an' all about him."

Barber ignored the prisoner as he herded the blacksmith's helper to the desk, told him to go over by the door, then leaned to study the wanted poster.

Outside there was some kind of commotion. A man with

58

a growling voice rapped the door as he called: "Everythin' all right?"

Barber aimed the six-gun. "Answer him," he said, and the tow-headed man obeyed.

"Yeah. Everythin's all right."

"Get the son-of-a-bitch ready. Ike's gone for the rope."

Both the prisoner and his compromised guard regarded Barber, who stood behind the table, gun sagging, looking at the tow-headed man who made a cold smile and said — "Mister, we'll hang you, too." — and after a moment the tow-headed man added more. "Only a child would believe that story of five thousand in gold, an' that story about letters in his saddlebags. Folks just got to make up things."

Barber swiftly looked over his shoulder and that encouraged the blacksmith's helper to speak again. "Go ahead, mister, walk out into the alley. I'll yell, an' they'll blow you to hell."

The sheriff's killer spoke, his voice high and unsteady. "Mister, I'll take you to the bank in Denver. My pa's the richest. . . ."

"You lyin' bastard," the tow-headed man said without raising his voice. "You never even seen five thousand dollars. It says on the dodger you robbed stages. You should've gone after banks. Not the kind around here, the big ones up north. They'd have five thousand dollars."

Possibly the blacksmith's helper sensed Barber's quandary. It was just as possible he didn't, but he looked balefully at the freighter when he continued speaking. "You was goin' to break him out of here for that five thousand dollars? Mister, what you done was come in here without no chance of walkin' out with him . . . even by yourself now, when I yell."

Barber went to the only window and peered past the

59

bars. The groups of townsmen had become one large mob. A fat man with a gold chain across his middle was exhorting them with gestures. When he looked back, the tow-headed man had sidled closer to the gun rack. Barber raised the six-gun. He was sweating. All he wanted now was to get out of the Scottville jailhouse.

The tow-headed man froze. There was a look of challenge on his face. He said: "Scairt, ain't you?"

Barber involuntarily tightened his finger inside the trigger guard. The explosion was deafening inside. Outside it was less deafening, but it was unmistakably a gunshot. People were silent and motionless for a long time, during which Barber looked incredulously at the gun he was holding. The prisoner was screaming to be released. The freighter did not hear him. His ears were still ringing.

The blacksmith's helper had been punched against the wall beside the gun rack and slowly slid down the wall into a sitting position, eyes widely staring at Robert Barber. The bullet had struck him dead center. There was blood on his shirt front but not much.

Out front men were beating on the door and yelling. Barber looked at the frantic prisoner as he said: "I didn't cock it."

The Texan was screaming to be let out and probably didn't hear what the freighter said. Someone struck the heavily reinforced door with an implement of considerable weight. Above the yelling a man called for the others to stand clear.

Barber was already moving toward the alleyway door when whoever had told the others to stand clear fired his six-gun three times. Barber was at the alley door when shouting men burst in from the roadway. They shot the Texican in his cage screaming like a wounded eagle.

60

Barber got the door open. Most of the lynch mob was around front. Barber fled southward in the direction of the livery barn. When he got there, no one was around. He shoved the six-gun into his britches, hurriedly grabbed a bridle, shouldered a blanket and saddle, raced out back, and cornered a powerful, large, pig-eyed bay horse with a Roman nose and a stud neck. He bridled the horse, and the bit hung loose. He flung up the blanket and the saddle, caught the cinch, and was looping the latigo when two townsmen came out back from the runway.

One had a fisted six-gun; the other one had a shotgun. They stopped Barber with pointed weapons. One of them said: "You're the feller went into the jailhouse. I seen you from the harness works doorway. Shed that gun. *Drop it!*"

The townsman's companion raised his shotgun and hauled back both dogs. The liveryman came out back, breathing hard. He had run the full distance. He said: "Barber for Chris' sake. You was in the jailhouse?"

The man with the cocked six-gun said: "He was. He shot the lad. Couldn't have been no one else. You know him?"

The liveryman stared. "He's hauled freight for years. I've known him for. . . ."

"Put your god-damned hands atop your head, freighter. Now walk ahead of us."

The liveryman came abreast, looking baffled. "You shot the young feller in the jailhouse?"

"It was an accident. I swear to God it was an accident. The damned gun. . . ."

"Shut up," the shotgun-man said. "Keep walkin'."

When they were closer to the jailhouse, where a crowd was milling, the shotgun-man called ahead. "This here is the son-of-a-bitch. Ike, where's the rope?"

61

Barber struggled to avoid reaching hands. Someone struck him under the ear, and he sagged to the ground. For a few moments the lynchers looked down before the shotgun-man said: "Don't make a damn, conscious or unconscious. Ike put the rope on him."

Once Scottville'd had a hanging tree, a magnificent old oak beside the road north of town. After the last lynching, the Ladies' Altar Society had hired two men to cut it down in the middle of the night, so they took the freighter to a massive cross member above the gate of the tanning yard. Because it was a hot afternoon, there were flies by the thousands. There usually were at tanning yards. Men pulling on the rope had to free a hand to chase flies away.

The freighter may have been unconscious, but his body reacted. He jerked, kicked feebly, and twisted.

They didn't cut him down until dawn the following morning, which was about the same time the liveryman was choring and came across the gun the freighter had dropped in the corral.

He picked it up, wiped it off, and studied it. Beneath the steel back strap deeply engraved on the butt plate was a name:

G. Mars

Chapter Six

MAKING AN IMPRESSION

There was enough talk to keep people occupied through autumn and into winter. Most frontier towns had their legends and tales, and, also as time passed, the facts became embellished with myth. Unkempt Frank Barton, the Scottville liveryman, had the best souvenir, the Mars gun. Others had to settle for pieces of the hang rope.

Barton showed the pistol so many times he tired of rummaging in a drawer for the weapon. Eventually he offered the six-gun for sale, and, while he didn't lack for prospective buyers, because Barton had an exaggerated idea of its worth, he had the gun for a long time. Eventually he did sell it to a deputy U.S. marshal named Leroy Cain who heard the story twice, once from the man who had replaced Sheriff Blount, and the second time from Barton when the federal lawman went down to the livery barn and asked to see the gun.

Leroy Cain was a tall man, not particularly muscled and his head was noticeably small. He had stopped overnight in Scottville on his way south to investigate the killing of another deputy marshal at a place called Soda Springs. When he left town, the Mars gun went with him. While Scottville's liveryman was not sorry to see it go, he later encountered some annoyance because the six-gun had been the best memento of an event folks would not tire of discussing for a long time. Financially, Frank Barton did very well for himself. He received twelve dollars for the gun — and, by biding his time until he had a feed bill against the freighter's wagon, harness animals, and personal effects, he could lay claim to them according to the law and was justified in establishing ownership.

On Marshal Cain's ride to Soda Springs he examined the gun. It was a two-day ride, so he had plenty of time. Once he left the road, he went about a mile in a northerly direction to a jumbled field of big rocks, hobbled his animal, and stood facing a small rock balanced atop a large boulder. He dry fired the empty six-gun and discovered something odd about it. He then loaded it, tucked his coat behind it, and made a sweeping draw. He didn't cock the gun. It was on safety, and, although he barely touched the trigger, the gun fired. He didn't hit the rock. He sat on a nearby boulder to consider the gun. It had more than a hair trigger. He shucked out the loads, tried setting the hammer on safety, and the hammer fell again when he barely touched the trigger.

He did this three times before reloading the weapon and bracing the little rock atop the larger one. His draw was fast. He barely snugged up the trigger, and this time the small rock broke in all directions.

The marshal got on his horse, put his regular six-gun in a saddle pocket, and continued on the way to Soda Springs, arriving there about dusk of the second day. He had a hostler at the livery barn care for his animal and went looking for the jailhouse. It was one of those adobe structures with massively thick walls, and lettering on the door denoted what it was as well as being the office of Brant Clawson.

Marshal Clawson was a head shorter than Leroy Cain but easily wider and heavier. He was some kind of half-breed, Mexican or Indian. His hair and eyes were black.

64

He had a grip that would make a bear flinch, and because of his dark complexion his even teeth shone very white. He offered the federal lawman a seat and leaned forward on a scarred but solid wooden table on which some previous lawmen had carved their initials.

Brant Clawson had guessed why the tall man had come to Soda Springs. Because he was forthright by nature, he barely allowed Cain to get seated before he tossed a six-gun on the table top and followed the gun with a holster and shell belt splotched with a very dark stain. It was almost black. Over time blood became that color on leather.

Cain was also a direct man. "Do you know who killed him?" he asked.

The massively burly man with eyes blacker than obsidian replied in as blunt a tone as that in which the question had been asked. "Everyone knows. His body was found some distance from town to the north. That's the route Porfirio Miller uses on his horse an' cattle raids. Your marshal friend told me, an' most likely told others, he was goin' out yonder an' lay a trap for Miller." The dark eyes glowed with irony. "Porfirio sprang it first."

Marshal Cain took his time rolling and lighting a cigarette. He trickled smoke as he asked his next question. "You got a Mex town in Soda Springs?"

The dark man spread his hands. It was a foolish question. Every southwestern town had a Mexican section. "It's southward on both sides of the road."

Cain asked another question. "Have you done anythin' to find the local feller who warned Miller?"

This time the dark man leaned on the table, looking squarely at the federal marshal. "That's your job. Let me explain something to you, Marshal. Our Mex town is only a day or so's ride from the border. Folks got relations on

65

both sides, up here an' down there." The burly man paused. "Porfirio is a sort of hero up here an' down there. He's got a big band and plenty of gold pieces. I won't tell, but they'll figure it out . . . about you bein' another U.S. marshal." The dark man showed white teeth in a smile that was more bleak than humorous. "Get on your horse and vamoose. Make up a story, an' I'll back it up. You hunted all over and couldn't find nothin' about the other deputy marshal's killin'. Friend, they'll know you come to see me. They'll find out you're a federal lawman, an' they'll do it before breakfast tomorrow mornin'."

Cain's gaze neither blinked nor wavered as he said: "Whose side are you on, friend?"

Brant Clawson's smile faded. "I got a family. The cattle and horses Porfirio raids aren't owned by folks here in town. They're owned by cowmen who come down every year for the free graze, then they go back up north." Clawson spread his hands. "Porfirio don't bother us. In fact, he's good for the countryside."

"Is he? How?"

"He spends money here."

"In your town?"

"Yes."

"An' you set on your duff when he rides into your town?"

"I just told you . . . I've got a family, an' Porfirio is good for the community."

"It don't matter that he killed a U.S. marshal?"

The dark, burly man shrugged. "That's your job, not mine. I'm a town marshal, not even a sheriff. I'll tell you somethin' . . . if you're goin' to go after whoever killed your friend, you might want to use your head and call in the Army."

Marshal Cain killed his smoke and stood up, facing the seated man. "You mind if I ask you a personal question?"

"No."

"Did you take an oath to uphold the law?"

The black eyes got that ironic expression again. "The law, Marshal, that was wrote by *yanquis* six, seven hundred miles from here is for that country, not here. It don't work here. Our law's got to be different."

Cain nodded disinterestedly and went as far as the door before speaking again. "Nice talkin' to you," he said without a shred of sincerity.

He saw a sign that said **Rooms** and ignored it. Leroy Cain had been a lawman nine years, and during that time he'd ridden into a lot of places. After a couple of years he had learned the hard way that even in places where federal lawmen were welcome there were people who, for whatever reason, would kill them, if they could.

To trust was good. The difficulty was that men who trusted too much ended up under four feet of dirt. Leroy Cain trusted no one, except possibly his horse. In Soda Springs, where outlaws, fugitives, renegades, and raiders such as the raider named Porfirio Miller were known, men who lived dangerously and survived were heroes.

It was nothing new. *Barrio* people who existed poorly from day to day needed heroes. For the women there were the missions, the priests, the beautiful carvings of saints and Jesus, the incense, the murmured prayers; for the men there was the struggle to exist, to care for their families, to rob if necessary, and to admire those who appeared on fine horses, astride saddles with silver, had guns of quality, well-fed dark men who laughed and made good livings by stealing herds of horses and cattle and who also occasionally raided banks and wealthy storekeepers.

67

Leroy Cain knew all this. When he went to a local café whose owner was a lean, hawk-nosed *gringo* and ordered a meal, the caféman knew what he was but not who he was. Lawmen in pursuit of outlaws were not novelties. Even among Cain's own kind, in such places the risk was considerable. He struck up a conversation with the caféman, whose words were chosen carefully, and then let the conversation die. All the fleeing fugitives did not reach Mexico. Some settled in places like Soda Springs and opened cafés.

He camped north of town within walking distance of a leaky old stone trough where livestock drank and tested his surroundings by creating a bedroll of believable appearance and bedded down with one blanket farther out in the moonless night. He didn't hear them. He wouldn't have anyway, if he'd been in the bedroll, but, when the first streaks of dawn arrived, he stood above the bedroll, studying the three tears made by a sharp knife.

He returned to the café, nodded to the proprietor, and ordered a meal. Not a word passed between them. He went outside to roll and light a smoke, aware that dark eyes were watching. He went up to the saloon which was run by a scar-faced, thick-bodied man with hooded gray eyes and a wound for a mouth. It was too early for drinking, but Leroy Cain said — "Whiskey." — and the scar-faced man set up a glass and bottle. His gaze opaquely veiled his hostility. The marshal offered to buy the saloonman a drink and got a blunt refusal.

Cain said — "This ain't a friendly town, mister." — and got a retort that did not surprise him.

"Not for you it ain't."

Cain downed his jolt, pushed both glass and bottle away, and said: "I'd like to ask you a question, mister. Why do you waste your life in a place like this?"

The scar-faced man's stare was now openly hostile. "For one reason . . . because in Soda Springs folks mind their own business. For another. . . ."

"Does the idea of the law bother you?"

The saloonman got splotchy red in the face. He leaned across the bar. "I never seen a lawman I couldn't whip!"

Cain's gaze was stone steady. "I'm a newcomer here. Best way I know to get respect is for you 'n' me to step out front."

The scar-faced man's lipless mouth curved into a snarl. Before he could speak, two rangy, unshorn men came in and looked steadily and stonily at the federal lawman. One of them shifted a toothpick to the corner of his mouth before speaking. "Trouble, Sam?"

Cain stepped sideways as he faced around. "You want to buy in?"

The toothpick-chewer faintly smiled. "Might."

Cain pulled the tie down loose. "Fair odds, three to one . . . I'm waitin'."

It wasn't the toothpick-chewer who made the mistake. It was his companion. He didn't have to free the tie-down thong. He'd done that before when he and his friend had entered the saloon. The second his shoulder sagged, Cain shot him.

The toothpick-chewer looked from his collapsing friend to Leroy Cain who said: "What're you waitin' for?"

The saloonman was bringing a shotgun up over the counter when Cain struck him alongside the head. The man and his scatter-gun fell noisily behind the bar.

Cain turned. The toothpick-chewer was fixed in place. Cain nodded his head. "Spit or close the window!"

The toothpick-chewer held both arms wide, turned, and left the saloon. Cain emerged behind him. There were

69

people on both sides of the roadway fixed in place. The swarthy, bull-built town marshal was in front of his jailhouse.

Cain called to him: "Marshal . . . ?" At the same time he called, he kicked the toothpick-chewer as hard as he could. The man landed face down in the road. He floundered to twist around. Cain's un-cocked six-gun was aimed at his face.

The saloonman came out with his sawed-off shotgun in both hands. He had not fully recovered from being struck. Cain moved to one side and struck the man again. This time the man made no noise when he fell, but the scatter-gun did.

Cain stepped into the roadway, lifted away the toothpick-chewer's gun, and told him to get up, which he did. Cain kicked him again. This time the man curled up.

Cain called to the crowd and the marshal: "I don't want your friendship, you bunch of bastards. Anyone else want to go to the center of the road?"

No one did. A young mother broke the stillness when her little boy of five years ran out into the road. The mother screamed for him to come back. He went all the way over to where the burly town marshal was standing and tapped his leg. The marshal ignored him. The child then went back to the center of the road, walking toward Leroy Cain. His mother fainted. Two older women leaned over to care for her.

The child stopped, leaned back, and looked up. "Are you my daddy?" he asked.

The tall man leathered his sidearm and knelt. "Do you need a daddy?"

"Yes. Are you him?"

Cain smiled, held the child at arm's length, and said —

70

"I'm him." — and, lifting the child, walked down the center of the road and veered over to where the older women were tending the child's mother. She suddenly opened her eyes, saw the tall man holding her son, and screamed: "No! No, *señor*! He is only a baby!"

Cain knelt, put the child in his mother's arms, and said: "What's his name?"

"Raimondo."

Cain touched the child's cheek. "Take care of your mother, Raimondo."

He rose. Some of the onlookers had dispersed, but across the road the marshal called to the federal lawman: "Come over here. I have some good wine."

As Cain crossed the road, the toothpick-chewer he had kicked got unsteadily upright, saw Cain, and reached for his holster which was empty. Cain flung the gun toward the man and followed the dark, bull-built marshal into the jailhouse.

Brant Clawson went to a cupboard and returned with an earthen jug that he placed on his table. He said: "There is very little rain here, so the people who made this wine have to bring water on burros from a spring up north. The sun and sandy soil do the rest."

Cain took the jug, whipped it over one shoulder, drank, and put it back on the table. The burly man hoisted it the same way, drank, and put the jug aside as he sat down.

"Good wine, Marshal?"

Cain replied honestly. "About the best I ever tasted, an' I'm not a wine-drinkin' person."

The town marshal used a sleeve to wipe off sweat before he spoke again. "The little boy. . . ."

"Raimondo?"

"His mother is my daughter."

71

Cain was quiet for a moment before asking a question. "Where is his father?"

"Dead. Porfirio said it was a mistake. One of his men shot him. He was drunk."

"An' this is the man you protect?"

The dark man gazed out a small window in the roadway wall. "It was a mistake. It was late afternoon. My daughter's husband was crossing behind the horses. The Mexican saw him, thought he was trying to steal a horse, and shot him."

Cain slowly shook his head. "So you accept that. Does your daughter accept it?"

"She is young. Life can be unpleasant. He shouldn't have been walking in the late afternoon behind their horses." The marshal held out the jug.

Cain stood up. "Drink it yourself," he said, and left the jailhouse.

Chapter Seven

A MEETING

The next two nights Cain moved his bedroll, filled it each time with brush, and each morning, when he stood over it, there were no knife marks. When he returned to the café on the third morning, the hawk-nosed *gringo* said: "Good morning."

Cain said nothing, but he inclined his head and ordered a meal. Afterward, he went out front to lean on an overhang upright and watch a pack train enter town from the south. There were nine laden mules and six *arrieros*. As they passed the tall federal lawman, not one of them saluted or nodded.

The town marshal followed the packers, talked to several of them as the *alforjas* were being put on the ground, and the mules were cared for. When Marshal Clawson came back from the brush corral and saw Cain, he jerked his head.

It was early in the morning, chilly in the roadway, but inside the *carcel* it was warm as it would be on the hottest day or the coldest night.

Clawson said: "They bring trade goods from Mexico."

Cain nodded. He knew about the mule trade.

Clawson's brows dropped. "They know who you are."

Cain was marginally surprised. "Someone went down to meet them?"

"Yes."

"What's his name?"

Clawson spread his hands. "It don't matter. When they got here, they would have found out anyway. Listen. Ride away for a few days."

"Why?"

"Because two of them came to search northward for herds to stampede down into Mexico."

"Just two of 'em?"

"No. Don't ask so many questions. Just ride away until they are gone. I owe you this."

"You don't owe me nothin'."

"Well, my daughter, then. She. . . ."

"She don't owe nothin', either. You're warnin' me off because. . . ."

"Don't talk, just go. They will be an hour unloading, then eating. *Stay away for a few days!*"

Cain rose. "Tell me . . . you know who shot the U.S. marshal. Is he with this bunch?"

"No!" Clawson rose, went to the door, looked out in both directions, and then herded Cain out the back way into a dusty alley. He said: "Don't go north. Go in some other direction. They will go north looking for cattle and horses. *Now go!*"

Clawson closed the door and barred it from the inside. While Cain was standing in the alley, the marshal went to his cupboard for the earthen jug, drank deeply, and then went to his table to sit and sweat. What he had done could get him killed.

Cain's horse was hobbled but grazing in the area of the ancient watering trough, which was to the northeast. Cain kept to the alley, listened to sounds, and utilized every paloverde, every stone wall, every shadow, to get clear of the town. Beyond, there was manzanita, thornpin, flourishing clumps of chaparral. He threaded

74

his way, pausing occasionally to listen.

When he got to the trough, his animal was dozing. It didn't take long to rig out and get astride. The sun was climbing. As yet the heat was minimal, but within another hour or two it would be different.

He knew the road he had used to reach Soda Springs. He also knew the Mexican herd hunters would use it, so he only crossed it, went southward for a mile, then eastward. He stopped often to listen and to stand in his stirrups. The land was quiet and empty.

What he sought and eventually found after more than an hour was a deep arroyo where underbrush and several trees grew. The source of water wasn't a piddling creek so much as it was a rock-girt sump with water trickling in from the east and emptying out southward. There was no green scum which meant poison water. Such green water did not always kill varmints or horses, but it was fatal to cattle. They died even more quickly from drinking what was called "red water."

The first thing people looked for at such places was skeletons. Cain looked, found none, nor had he expected to, before drinking and allowing his horse to drink. There were dozens of tracks leading in and leading away, mostly made by small critters, raccoons, squirrels, the kind that lived underground, the pad marks of coyotes, foxes, even armadillos, and snake squiggles.

He was secure. The possibility of ranging *arrieros* finding him seemed remote, but there was the matter of sustenance. He had four flat tins of sardines, not enough for two days unless he found a method of augmentation which, while not impossible, was unlikely — some of the creatures who came here for water were not edible, except to Indians.

The first day went well. His horse did well on skimpy

75

graze and better forage. Cain himself spent time climbing the rims and lying in brush shade, watching.

He even took an all-over bath just before dusk and sat on rocks until dry. He was not ordinarily a meditative man, but with no recourse he did his share of thinking now. When it was time to bed down, he scuffed a place to avoid scorpions, creatures who sought warmth after sundown, shed his hat, boots, coiled the shell belt around the Mars gun in its holster, gun side up six inches from his face, and slept like a dead man until something walking across his face awakened him. It was a scorpion, tail poised as always, pausing occasionally to explore.

Cain lay motionless, watching. Any movement could result in getting stung with poison from the tail. He tried blowing. All that accomplished was to make the scorpion stop, stand high on all four legs, tail still poised.

Cain's eyes never wavered. The scorpion settled lower, ready to continue its exploring, when something moving with the speed of a shadow struck Cain's cheek and the scorpion. The scorpion was knocked violently away.

Cain squinted through dust, and for a moment his vision was blurry but not so blurry he couldn't see the unshaven, unkempt, dark, sweaty man looking down at him, grinning like a tame ape.

They were about of an age. Who could tell? — but for a fact the dark man had not been young for a long time. He said in border Spanish — "Lie still." — walked around to the coiled shell belt and tossed the Mars gun away. Then he squatted. His gaze was darker than the inside of a well. He spoke again in border Spanish, a combination of mostly bad Spanish, unintelligible Indian, and profanity in three languages, Mexican Spanish, Indian dialect, and English. Mostly what Cain understood was a scattering of the Mexican Spanish and all of the hair-raising profanity. No one had ever explained to Leroy Cain why people who learned English always learned the worst words first.

"Sit up. Both hands in front."

After Cain obeyed, the Mexican's humor surfaced again. It was the kind that laughed at death, the death of others or his own. He said: "Do you know the use of a blanket?"

Cain, whose shock had passed, frowned.

"*¿No habla ingles?*"

"No. You no espeak Spanish?"

Cain considered the dark man. "How did you know what I said? Why did you answer in English?"

This time the dark man threw back his head and laughed. "You *uno coyote gringo. Sí,* I espeak English. What is your name and why are you hiding in this place?"

"My name is . . . Smith."

The dark man laughed again. "*Uno furtivo. Mal hombre. Renegado.*" The dark man tapped Cain's chest lightly with his pistol. "Me, too."

That appeared to be the dark man's second question. At least, he did not repeat it, but sat like an unkempt, lined, and black-eyed interrogator, considering Cain. He holstered his weapon. "You don' move," he said, and went to drop flat and drink for a long time. When he rolled over, he had the gun in his hand again. Cain hadn't moved.

He rose, walked back, squatted again, and once more leathered the six-gun. "You have somethin' to eat?"

Cain gestured toward the saddlebags draped from a tree. This time as the dark man walked away with his back to Cain, he talked. "We are mature men. Mature men get that way because they learn things. I tracked you. Do you know how?"

"Fresh tracks?"

The *bandido* returned with the two remaining tins of sardines. As he squatted, considering them, he replied: "No, *gringo*. We don't shoe horses. When they limp, we steal better ones. How do you open this god-damned thing?"

Cain took the tin, inserted the key, and rolled it. The dark man watched. He ate the little fishes and drank the oil. He gestured. "We share. Now you."

Cain repeated the process, and, as he was later wiping his chin, which the Mexican hadn't done, Cain said: "You got a name?"

The dark man laughed again. "Many names. Which one you want?"

"How about Juan?" In Cain's experience, every third or fourth Mexican was named Juan.

The raider shrugged. "I be Juan. You be Smith." He considered Cain with shrewd eyes. "You Smith . . . my ass."

Cain retorted. "You Juan . . . *my* ass."

They both laughed.

Cain said: "Juan My Ass, are you goin' to use that gun, or is it to hold up your pants?"

The dark man grinned. "In time, Smith . . . *Mi Cola.*"

Cain had another question. "Where is your horse?"

"Why? You won't find him. I like your horse. It has shoes."

"It bites."

The black eyes returned. "Among friends we don't lie."

"Juan My Ass, among friends one always lies. Friends expect you to."

Again Juan My Ass laughed, rose, and drew out his six-gun but did not cock it. "You stay here until I come back. Lie to me, Smith My Ass."

"I will stay here until you return."

78

The dark man grinned and walked away, leathering his six-gun.

For a long time Cain moved only his eyes. He watched both rims of the arroyo, less for the dark man than for the sun's reflection off a gun barrel. When he was satisfied the dark man was not up there, awaiting an excuse to commit murder, he shoved the bedroll away, tugged on his boots, retrieved the Mars gun, returned, and pulled the bedroll back into place.

When the Mexican returned, he had a jug. He said nothing as he hunkered, put the jug beside Cain, and finally spoke. "Dead fish taste bad."

Cain drank, handed over the jug for Juan *Mi Cola* to drink, and, when Juan put the jug down, he looked steadily at Cain. "You dumb *gringo*. You shouldn't have put the boots on. A blind man could see what you did. And you have the gun under the blankets." The Mexican slowly drew his six-gun and cocked it. "Take it out slowly, Smith My Ass."

Cain obeyed. Juan *Mi Cola* took the gun, briefly examined it, and flung it over his shoulder. "I should kill you."

Cain considered the cocked pistol no more than six or seven feet from him and shrugged.

The dark man laughed, lowered the hammer, holstered the gun, and asked a question. "*Gringo bandido,* what did you do?"

Friends lied to friends — acquaintances, too. "I robbed a bank."

The dark man was contemptuous. "That's all?"

"It's enough. You . . . ?"

"It don't matter. I was a peon. I starved. No one wanted me. I stole until I was older, then I joined raiders, even *pronunciados*. The army beat us, but I had two sacks

79

of Church gold. Now . . . I have hurts. I am tired of running, first one way, then another way. How old are you,
Smith My Ass?"

"Fifty one."

"Hah. When I was only fifty-one. . . ." Juan cocked his
head. "You look older."

Cain said — "Friends only lie to friends." — and they
both roared with laughter. When that moment passed, Cain
asked a question. "You don't raid alone?"

"No. With Porfirio. We come up as packers, as people
who do business. We scout. Sometimes we find dumb
bastardos, gringos renegados riding shod horses. We spy for
Porfirio. When we get back, he makes up the numbers to
ride with him."

"Do you know Porfirio?"

Juan made a gesture. "Like a brother. His father was a
gringo. He hates *gringos*." He made a shrug of indifference.
"The last time we came here a drunken idiot named José
Arredondo shot the town marshal's daughter's husband.
Porfirio was mad. Him and the marshal are like this." Juan
held up his first two fingers, side by side. "When we got
back, he took José aside and shot him."

"José shoot a lawman, too?"

"No. That was Henrique." Juan looked up. "How did
you know? Have you been to Soda Springs?"

"You followed the tracks."

"Not from there . . . from a mile or two north of there.
Smith My Ass, friends lie to each other, yes?"

"Yes."

The six-gun was drawn out again. "Sometimes, no, eh?"

"All right. Tell me Henrique's last name, and I will tell
you my last name."

There was no hesitation. "Henrique López. He found

80

the *gringo* lawman hiding in some rocks, came up behind, and shot him in the back."

The black eyes became, as they had originally been, unwavering and merciless. "Your last name?"

"Cain. Leroy Cain. Don't get nervous. I have something inside my shirt." He removed the small circlet with black letters around it that Juan took, turned it over, and handed it back. "You are a sheriff?"

"Did Henrique López show you the badge from the man he shot in the back?"

"No. He gave it to Porfirio. He wasn't a sheriff?"

Cain was putting the badge back inside his shirt when he answered. "He was a United States deputy marshal."

"That is bigger than a town marshal or a *gringo* sheriff?"

"That is the biggest, Juan. That is a lawman from Washington."

"*Guazington?*"

"Yes. *Sí.*"

"You are such a one from *Guazington?*"

"*Sí.* I mean, yes."

"And that means the Army is coming?"

"Do friends lie to friends? I don't know."

"Mother of God. That bastard let us walk into this!"

"What bastard?"

The black eyes came up unblinkingly steady. "The town marshal, Porfirio's friend, Brant Clawson. That . . . !"

"No!"

"He knew about you, then?"

Of all the reasons to lie, what better than to save a life? Not always, no, but Cain had no time for a determination. "He didn't know about me. I saw him once. We talked at the saloon. He didn't know who I was."

Juan My Ass considered Cain over a long moment of si-

81

lence during which he slumped, fondled the medallion of the Holy Virgin at his throat, and put more feeling into a *gringo* expletive than Cain had ever heard from a man before. *"Son-of-a-bitch!"*

He shifted his stare to the pond, to the tree where a *gringo* saddle hung, and then came back to Cain as he drew his six-gun without cocking it and stared. Cain recognized that this was the moment when life ended in a miserable country out of sight in a peaceful arroyo with his horse dozing and birds sounding.

Juan let the barrel tip. "Smith My Ass, how much longer? Two years, five years? I am older than you. Five years at the most. Let me tell you, I have two caches in Mexico. My idea has been for some time to dig them up, buy a nice house with land, find a woman who can cook, who is fat enough to protect me in winter. I get tired sometime. How about you?"

"Have you seen the marshal's daughter?"

"Clawson's daughter? No. Is she fat?"

"No. Juan . . . I, too, get tired of riding, of. . . ."

"Fish in tins?"

"Of fish in tins."

"She is pretty, then?"

"Very pretty, Juan. Young. She has a little boy named Raimondo. He asked me if I was his daddy."

Juan put up the gun, studying Cain. "Someday I want to come and talk to you. Now I go back. I saw no horses or cattle. The others will have found them. We go back, and later Porfirio comes." Juan My Ass stood up and unconsciously brushed off. "Smith My Ass, I never disliked all *gringos,* some, but not all. What will you do?"

The tall man also stood up. His Mars gun could still be seen where it had landed. Neither of them looked at it.

"Talk to the marshal. I am much older, but the boy needs a father."

"You will tell him about me, about our talk?"

"Not as long as I live."

"Smith My Ass, my name is Esteban Castillo. *Adiós, compañero*. Someday. . . ."

As the Mexican went among the underbrush, Cain called to him. "Someday, *compañero*."

Maybe he heard, and maybe he didn't. He continued to walk until Cain lost sight of him.

He retrieved the Mars gun, spent time cleaning it with his handkerchief, leathered it, rigged out, and rode southward until the arroyo gradually tipped up and met flat ground, then rode west, but slowly. The *arrieros* would still be in Soda Springs.

There was an ancient, dilapidated, adobe mission southward whose lopsided ocotillo cross attracted attention. Cain made for it. Sundown was close. He would reconnoiter tomorrow, looking first at the road southward where mule tracks would be topmost. If they were, he would return to Soda Springs; if they weren't, he would find another place.

Like most nights, this one was warm until after three in the morning, then predawn chill arrived, but Cain's problem was neither the moldy smell of the old mission nor the weather. It was rats, some almost as large as cats who clearly had no idea how dangerous the creature in the bedroll was because they ran across him from side to side, changed course, and did the same from head to heels. He swore, but that only frightened timid rats. He got up and brought his riding equipment close. He knew from long experience that rats would kill to find salt-sweat impregnated leather, even leather without salt. During Cain's lifetime, he had had headstalls chewed in two, saddle skirts eaten al-

83

most to the tree, and hadn't laughed when greenhorns had awakened swearing to high heaven when harness had been half eaten, clothing, too, if it was where a rat could climb, and seemingly there was no place a rat couldn't climb. If he had fired the Mars gun, they would have squeaked in terror and fled, only to return.

There were two things a man who lived in a saddle could find no reason for the good Lord to have created. One was wind. The other was rats.

Chapter Eight

ROSALIA

On the third day, hungry enough to eat a rattler if someone would hold its head, Cain came up the southward road, riding over the sign of mules going southward. The burly dark town marshal had been watching and came to meet the federal lawman, wearing a smile reflecting relief. "They are gone. Rode away yesterday afternoon."

Cain let Brant Clawson walk with him to the livery barn where he off-saddled and nodded for the Indian hostler to lead the animal to water, hay, and a dry stall. They went to the jailhouse where Clawson brought forth the jug and set it between them, sat down, and smiled broadly.

"They knew you had been here. There is always someone. Mostly they were told you had ridden away."

"Porfirio?"

Clawson leaned back, spreading his arms wide. "He believed me. Why shouldn't he?"

Cain nodded. Of course, Porfirio believed him. Friends only lied to friends. "Will someone tell him I'm back?"

Clawson leaned forward again before replying. "Only God knows, an' He don't tell. But it will take time to overtake them, and meanwhile I have news for you. The man who killed the other federal marshal is Carlos Domingo García."

Cain nodded without expression. *Cagadao del toro.* Old Juan My Ass would have laughed. Cain gazed steadily at

85

the constable. "How old is your daughter?" he asked.

Clawson's smile fell inward. "Well . . . twenty six. Does it matter?"

"Raimondo matters," Cain said.

He got up to leave. At the door he turned to ask one more question. "When will Porfirio return?"

"Who can say?"

"You can, Brant. *When?*"

Again the burly town marshal spread his arms wide, but this time he avoided Cain's gaze. But when the federal lawman started to turn, Clawson answered shortly. "Six days." Then he added: "You must be gone."

Cain walked out into midday heat and went to the café where the hawk-nosed caféman with the knife-scarred cheek nodded. "You missed 'em," he said.

Cain nodded, ordered a meal, and asked the caféman the name of the marshal's daughter. The man paused before offering a reply. "Rosalia Benevides. Friend, don't do it."

"Why?"

"Her father will kill you."

Cain paid for his meal and asked another question. "Where does she live?"

The caféman almost imperceptibly shook his head when he answered. "In Mex town, the second *jacal* on the west side, not far from the *acequia*." The caféman raised hooded eyes. "Her pa lives next door."

Cain nodded and left. The heat was bearing down. Only among the *gringo* stores were there overhangs to provide shade. Where they ended, Mex town sweltered, and heat danced an undulating fandango.

Cain stopped at the last store with an overhang, bought some of the local candy, small squares of squash soaked in

86

sugar water. It was also sold in Mex town but on tables outside where flies congregated by the hundreds.

The woman who opened the door, when Cain knocked, was not the woman as he had last seen her. Then she had been wild-eyed with dread, her hair loose. This time her hair was somehow pulled back and braided up from behind. And her expression, when she saw Cain, reflected something like confusion, or fear.

He removed his hat. Raimondo came out of the interior gloom and squeezed past his mother. Cain leaned and handed him the bag. Raimondo held it, looking up. Cain said: "It's candy."

Raimondo's mother moved slightly aside for Cain to enter.

The *residencia* was typical except that it had three rooms instead of one. It was probably always gloomy without candles, but it was cool and immaculate except for some children's clothing on a string in a corner. It was the custom. Anything with color or designs was dried inside. Outside the hot sun faded them.

She swept the clothing from its string and shoved it into a cupboard. When she faced around, he told a lie. "I came to see Raimondo."

He knelt, and the child offered him a piece of candy with wet and sticky fingers. Cain took it, chewed, looked up, and rolled his eyes. Rosalia Benevides laughed.

She started to thank him for what he had done during the fight, and he stopped her with an upraised hand.

"You don't thank me *por nada, señora*. I didn't even see you." He looked down. A pair of very dark eyes were looking up. Cain winked. Raimondo did the same but with both eyes.

The woman asked if he would care for wine. Cain was

87

tempted but declined. He felt awkward, oversize, and intimidating. But not to the child. Except for being larger, he could stand beside Raimondo who had candy. Life, it seemed to Cain, was a matter of priorities, and in the very young they were oriented to the stomach.

He had never known a family. Not that he could remember. He went to the door. For some inexplicable reason the house seemed stifling. The woman followed, thanked him. He waved, and the child waved back with bulging cheeks.

Cain turned, and Brant Clawson barred his way. Cain would have moved past, but the burly marshal blocked that way, too.

Cain said: "I brought Raimondo some candy."

The marshal's black eyes showed points of fire. "He is my grandson!"

"I know."

"Stay away from him!"

"And your daughter?"

"Her, too, *gringo*. Stay away from them!"

Rosalia was leaning on the door, frozen. She knew that expression on her father's face. She would have spoken, but Cain gave the marshal a shove hard enough to make him struggle for balance.

Clawson said — "You son-of-a-bitch!" — as his right shoulder dropped.

The explosion could be heard all over Soda Springs. Dust rose in roiled violence from between the marshal's spread legs. Rosalia cried out, but her father seemed to have turned to stone. His sidearm was only half out of its holster.

Cain waited. For seconds they regarded each other before Cain took two steps and shoved the marshal aside. He softly said: "Want to try again, you son-of-a-bitch?"

Clawson raised his hand from his holster. As Cain walked past, the marshal turned only his head. Rosalia recovered first. She took her father into the house. There was no sign of Raimondo.

Cain went to the barn to look in on his horse. The liveryman neither approached nor spoke, but his eyes remained on Cain until he left the barn, crossed the road, and by-passed the eatery in favor of the saloon where the barman asked him if he'd heard a gunshot. Cain nodded, pointed, and, when the bottle was set in front of him, he asked the barman a question. "What kind of a man is your town marshal?"

"Brant? Well . . . why?"

"Because he just run me off from takin' candy to his grandson."

The barman rolled his eyes. "That's his only grandchild. The mother is his only daughter. His wife died six, eight years ago. Mister, he's a decent feller. You just crossed the line. Don't no men go down there."

Cain said — "Yeah." — paid, and walked out where the heat was enough to fry eggs on a rock.

Six days, and he would now be as welcome in Soda Springs as a broad-assed rattlesnake.

As he passed the café, its proprietor came out. "I seen it," he said. "You should've aimed higher."

"Why? You don't like him?"

"I like him. He'll kill you, mister. Lawman or no lawman, he'll kill you!"

Cain made a humorless, small smile. "Not until he grows up, and maybe not then."

The ride to the old abandoned mission was under a scorching sun. He led his horse inside, too. Old Juan My

Ass would have doubled over in laughter. "Is she pretty? Is she fat?"

She is pretty, and, no, she isn't fat, but her father is. Fat in the head, jealous of his own daughter and her little boy.

Now Porfirio would hear the U.S. Marshal had returned.

He rolled a smoke, watched his horse sleep standing hip-shot, and for lack of anything better to say he told the horse they were both tired of this business of manhunting. The horse opened one eye, and Cain nodded. "I know."

He fell asleep where some other transient had shoved two pews together. The overhead ceiling had been leaking water for generations, so one interior wall was a mess of soft-hued figures that could have been hallowed saints in prayer. Their faces were darker than the adobe and contorted.

He had no idea how long he had been asleep before the rats found him. He caught one by the tail and hurled it in the direction of the distorted art work across the room. It squeaked only when it hit and fell. It ran.

For a while the rats stayed away. He got up to bring his leather gear closer and was bending over to lift the saddle when he heard a whisper of sound as though someone wearing moccasins, or hide sandals, was behind him. He rose slowly, twisting from the waist. If there hadn't been more light in the doorway than there was inside, he would have killed her.

She said: "I came to talk."

It was like an apparition. She was faintly backgrounded by starlight. She stood with a hand on one wall, looking at him.

He put the saddle down and motioned her forward. His first question was: "How did you know I was here?"

"By your tracks?"

"In the dark?"

90

"No. I brought a candle."

He pointed for her to sit and swore that in the morning he would find someone with shoe-pullers.

She said: "He would have shot you."

He sat down beside her. "I don't blame him, because it was my fault. I was told to stay away from both of you."

"Everyone knows who you are, and why you are here."

"An' they want to kill me."

"No! But they are afraid of you. They heard how you could have killed my father and shot dirt on him, instead."

He faced her. "They'll know I'm out here, too."

"No! I told the man where you put up your horse you left Soda Springs because you know my father would kill you. I told him you went east, back the way you came."

"But you tracked me here."

"They won't. I dragged a blanket to cover my tracks as well as yours."

"Who's lookin' after Raimondo?"

"My father. He lives only for Raimondo."

"And you?"

Rosalia shrugged slightly. For a long moment she regarded the hands lying in her lap like dying birds. "I came to talk to you."

Cain relaxed where he sat. Dead ahead was an old altar. It had been vandalized. He leaned back and closed his eyes, waiting.

"Why are you here?"

"You know why. By now everyone knows. I'm here to settle for the lawman who got shot in the back trying to spy on Porfirio. Do you know Porfirio?"

"Yes."

He opened both eyes and turned his head. For a moment he looked at her profile, before her head was lowered. He said: "You . . . ?"

"Yes, and my father is willing. He needs Porfirio. Our town needs him."

"He's comin' back in six days. I figure they found someone's livestock. Is that it?"

"Yes. The ranch of two old people fifteen miles northwest. Horses mostly. Three days, not six."

Cain stiffened. "Three days? That's only until the day after tomorrow." He asked if she knew the nearest Army post, and she gave her head a shake before she spoke.

"I know there is one because soldier patrols pass through once or twice a year, but I don't know where it is."

"Your father would know."

She looked up at Cain. "How could I bring up such a subject. We have never talked of the soldiers."

Cain had been tired. Now he was not.

She touched his arm. "Why I came was to tell you to go away. A long way this time. Maybe never come back."

He faced her. "If I never came back . . . would you remember?"

She rose so abruptly it startled him. She was at the far door before he stopped her.

"Rosalia . . . ?"

"I would remember. So would Raimondo."

She was gone before he could reach the door. She had snatched up a heavy blanket as she disappeared in the shadowy gloom.

Cain didn't sleep, hardly heeding the scampering rats. Three days! The back shooter who had killed Rosalia's husband was dead. Porfirio had seen to that. The other one, Henrique López . . . *son-of-a-bitch*.

He left the mission before sunrise, riding northward, still shadowed by the night, almost a phantom horseman. He had been told a dozen times by older lawmen, grizzled and disillusioned, never, no matter the circumstances, get emotionally involved. Do a job, say little or nothing, avoid unnecessary risks, and come back in one piece.

By sunrise he was miles north of Soda Springs. With the arrival of daylight he picked up three sets of barefoot horse tracks and followed them to a topout overlooking a green place with old trees, old mud buildings, and about two dozen horses, mostly in their prime, some older, some younger.

The tracks led around from an overlooking height until Cain saw where they had turned southward. He rode down into the yard. An old woman with skin the color of tanned rawhide came out to watch Cain dismount and leave his horse tethered to an ancient stud ring in one of the big trees. She turned and seemed not to speak, and, when Cain was closer to the *ramada*, an old man came out carrying a Winchester saddle gun in both hands. Neither of them spoke English, and Cain's knowledge of Spanish was shaky at best. He introduced himself, showed them the badge neither could read, and explained clumsily as best he could why he was in their yard.

The old man erupted into an explosion of words. The old woman did not take her eyes off Cain nor did she speak until she stepped past her husband and pushed the door wide as she gestured.

As Cain passed the old man, he turned him by the shoulder so the old man preceded him inside. He took the Winchester and leaned it in a corner. He told them to sit down, please, straddled a bench, and over half an hour of using terrible border Spanish and gestures told them what he thought was going to happen to their horses within a day or two.

93

Again the old man spoke excitedly. The old woman spoke very slowly. Cain understood Spanish better than he spoke it. They had seen tracks of riders on the hills above their yard. Fresh tracks.

The old woman leaned forward as she said: "¿Bandoleros, señor?"

"Sí, señora. En dos días. For your hor . . . your caballos."

The old woman spoke aside sharply to her husband. She had to speak loudly. His eyes were fixed on Cain when he asked in Spanish where Cain's posse riders were.

Cain spread his arms wide. "No possemen. I am alone."

The old man's eyes widened. He repeated it to himself. "Alone?"

The old woman stood up. She would feed Cain.

He thanked her and returned the old man's stare. "Solo, señor."

The old man flung up his arms and made a wailing sound. The old woman among her pots and pans called to him sharply. "Muy matador, Papa. Look you, what do you see? . . . this one is a killer?"

The old man still wailed. "There were three of them. There will be more."

"Be quiet. Are you hungry?"

"Sainted Mother," he replied. "Who can be hungry?"

She brought Cain a large bowl of carne con chili and a tumbler of red wine, then sat opposite, watching him eat. When she spoke, slowly for his benefit, he understood. She and her man raised fine horses. That was how they lived. He could no longer break them, but in his youth he had been a caballista. There was no finer horseman than a caballista. There were people who spread their legs and pulled a horse between them. There were vaqueros, she said, who rode horses and knew nothing except to stay on top. Cabal-

94

leros were different. They were *gentes de razón*. They were also very rare. Her father had been a *caballero*. He had fled Mexico for being on the wrong side during an uprising.

Cain thanked her for the meal and rose. He needed a place for his horse. She told the old man to show where the horse could be cared for. After they left, the old woman went to a wall niche, lighted the votary, and with closed eyes prayed fervently to the small wooden Virgin in her recess.

They cared for the horse, and then the old man, who didn't walk very well, took Cain on a tour. Everything was old, and, although effort had been made to make repairs, clearly deterioration was proceeding faster than two old people could keep up.

There was an empty *jacal* where the old woman's mother had lived, and died. There was also a tiny adobe chapel with an oversize crucifix, exquisitely carved out of one solid piece of wood by someone no one would remember.

They wanted Cain to stay in the house. There was enough room. He wanted to sleep in the abandoned *jacal* where the old woman had died.

The opposition was slight, but he noticed it. Old people were religious for a fact. Where did religion and superstition meet? Indians would not sleep in a house where someone had died, and they were simple savages. Juan My Ass would have laughed.

They fed him again before he went to the empty *jacal*, and again in the morning. The old woman went to milk a goat, and Cain insisted on helping. They had no box for the goat to stand on, so they knelt. Cain knelt, too, but couldn't bend low enough. The old woman hid a smile behind her hand.

Inside, the old man had laid out an assortment of weap-

95

ons. Some had been old already when the old man was a boy. Two were fairly new, less than fifteen years old. One was a Colt revolver for which the old man had only the loads in the chambers. The other was the saddle gun. The old man had two boxes of bullets for it, which were slightly green in places despite the oil.

There was also a sword, sharp enough to shave with, but Cain shook his head, and the old man leaned it aside. His woman asked if the weapons would help, and Cain smiled at her, which left her free to interpret the smile as she wished.

She had no illusions. She was more calm than her husband, who was never still and staggered often to the only window, facing north, to peer out until his wife told him the riders of other people's horses would not arrive until tomorrow. The old man went into the back of the house and slept.

Dusk eventually arrived. The old woman and Cain sat across from each other. She was clearly an individual who had been born with a ramrod up her back. She asked in Spanish if she should go for help, and Cain answered matter-of-factly that, unless she had close neighbors, there would be small possibility of getting help.

They had no neighbors. The closest was nine miles westward. She made a small smile and told Cain she was eighty-six and Manuel, her husband, was almost ninety. Then she said something that straightened Cain in his chair. She said her son-in-law was the marshal in Soda Springs and asked if Cain knew him. Cain nodded, so she told him the rest of it. Brant Clawson had wed the old woman's daughter something like twenty-six years earlier. She and her husband had opposed it. They did not believe Clawson was good enough for their daughter.

Cain interrupted. "Rosalia is your granddaughter?"

The old woman's shriveled face became almost radiant. She told him her granddaughter was beautiful, sweet, caring, and unselfish. She also told him what had happened to her granddaughter's husband, and her expression showed bitter resignation.

He asked if the granddaughter visited, and the old woman made a wistful, small smile. "Not so much as we'd wish. She has her child, and her father doesn't like us. But, someday. . . ."

Cain held up his hand. He heard horses. The old woman explained. "They come every evening for water in the corral. There is no other water."

Cain excused himself, left the house with darkness increasing, was careful not to be heard or seen, and reached the corral gate before the *remuda* knew he was there.

At one time the log gate had been strong and sturdy. Now, Cain had to lift it at the far end and carry it to close it. There was a large harness snap held in place by leather as old and dry as the old man, Manuel. He fastened it and leaned in poor light from half a moon. There were about thirty animals clustering at an old stone trough. Some were fine bred, some were old, and there was a scattering of colts, mostly yearlings and better. It was anyone's guess how many were broke to saddle.

Cain returned to the house. The old woman had set up a large glass of red wine and had lighted four candles — her wish to be hospitable. Each candle cost four cents in Soda Springs. She and her man rarely used candles. They went to bed before dark.

Cain told the old woman to go to bed. She stiffened and shook her head. He patted her shoulder and went outside to smoke.

97

He had to guess about numbers, but there would be too many, and, being experienced raiders, they would approach by stealth. But they would have to open that forty-pound gate, which couldn't be done without noise.

A dog would have helped, but evidently the old people did not have one. Everyone young or old, who lived isolated, should have a dog. At least one.

The stars were dazzlingly sharp with their brightness. The moon — well — it was better than no moon.

He killed the smoke, settled comfortably in an old chair which had been repaired with a green hide with the hair on, but it had dried as hard as all rawhide did.

Rosalia was their granddaughter. It was easy to imagine why her father disapproved of her visiting the old couple. They would make cookies and squash candy for Raimondo.

Cain cocked his head, but the night was without sound. Brant Clawson was a hard individual to understand. He loved the child and his daughter. He had lied to Cain about when the raiders would return, and Cain smiled in the quickening darkness. Were they friends? They must be, because only friends lied to friends.

He went inside. The old woman was asleep in her chair. He took the Winchester, a box of bullets, tiptoed back to the *ramada,* and lengthened his stride in the direction of the corral when he heard a coyote sound.

He had heard that howl all his life. This was the first time he heard it end with a noticeable trill.

Chapter Nine

AN OLD WOMAN AND A RED SKY

Seasoned raiders didn't come charging in, shooting and howling. Drunken renegades might, but their life span was short. Not everyone used a coyote sound to signal, and coyotes had no Spanish echo when their trill tapered away.

Cain knelt alongside the rough-walled *jacal* where the old woman had died, with the old man's Winchester grounded between his legs, and the tie down hanging loose from its holster. There would be a surprise, of sorts. They knew the people were too old and had no dog. He had to guess how many would sneak to the gate to open it, rout out the horses, then get astride, and whoop and yell to head them south.

If it had been possible, he would have tried to find men to ride north with him. He was not in a territory he knew or among people he knew. There was one he could have wished to be with him, but by now he was somewhere far south, digging up caches. In the Southwest borderland treachery came cheap, a *centavo* a ton.

Darkness was not especially his friend, but it would be his ally. The night was warm. What light came earthward was adequate when a man's eyes adjusted. Cain could see the gate clearly. He alternately watched it, and the corralled horses. When they came, they would appear as *fantasmas*, soundless wraiths with only one objective. The horses would detect them, less by movement than by smell.

Cain's legs hurt from kneeling so long, but he couldn't move. The horses would peer in his direction. An old mare nickered for her yearling. It ignored her. It was standing at the trough, head up, little ears pointing, water dripping. Cain raised the old Winchester. It had steel buckhorn sights, the kind men kept filed to catch light. Cain could see the sights well enough, but swore to himself. He should have pared the sights with his clasp knife.

Several other horses stood with raised heads. One snuffy horse blew its nose. Another one softly snorted. Cain saw the wraith. He was not a large man and moved like a cougar. He had a sidearm but no carbine. Where weak light showed best, Cain saw the big, sheathed fleshing knife on the left side of his shell belt. Another one appeared. This one's hat was down his back, held by a thong, and this one was carrying a saddle gun.

Cain tracked the first raider through the sights to the gate, was snugging up his finger inside the guard, when the raider tried to open the gate. The second raider came up. He was a little taller and heavier. This one jostled the gate, then softly cursed and lifted it, which was when Cain fired.

The Mexican fell in the scant opening he'd made. His companion whirled in a crouch. He fired from the hip and missed even hitting the *jacal*. Cain levered and fired again. This time the wraith was down flat. The bullet passed above him. The raider had seen muzzle blast. When he returned Cain's fire this time, a fist-size chunk of adobe struck Cain on the left cheek, and he instinctively flinched.

The Mexican fired again, twice, very fast. Cain saw him clearly because he had raised up like a lizard. He shot the man.

For a long moment there was silence before a third raider appeared, this time sneaking alongside the old adobe horse barn which had dead grass atop its roof. Cain didn't see this one because he moved in fits and starts, but the snorting horses did and strained in the man's direction.

Cain flattened, began crawling backward. The invisible raider fired where Cain had been, not where he was. Cain fired at the muzzle blast — and missed, but came close enough to panic the raider who twisted swiftly and ran, staying close to the adobe wall.

A man called loudly in Spanish. "Cease you! Come back!"

Cain fired in the direction of the voice, and someone howled a hair-raising curse and yelled for Cain to be flanked, to be shot from behind the *jacal*.

Cain had no choice. He sprang up, raced to the front wall, and kicked open the door. There was only the door, no windows. He flattened inside the front wall and fumbled to determine how many bullets remained in the old man's saddle gun.

One bullet.

The man who had called before called again. "Get the gate open!"

Cain got belly down, crawled to the opening, dropped his hat, and eased his face out. No one was at the gate. He waited, but no one seemed willing to approach the gate.

The angry yelling began again, but this time promising whoever the defender was, he would be boiled in oil.

Cain was soaked with sweat. He ran a sleeve over his face. When he lowered the arm, a raider had soundlessly crept along the front wall. Cain had seconds to look up. He and the raider stared briefly. Cain hoisted the old man's saddle gun about the same time the raider brought his right hand around.

The gunshots sounded almost simultaneously. Cain

didn't miss, and the Mexican sprang backwards and yelled. Cain dropped the old man's gun, drew his sidearm, leaned recklessly where the now blinded raider was groping toward the *jacal's* corner, making small sounds. Cain shot him again.

A high-pitched voice cried out as a raider fled, and Cain moved to get upright. One leg would not act for itself. There was no sense of pain, but the trouser leg was sticky with something warm.

Cain propped himself against the wall, removed the belt from his trousers, cinched it around the leg, and twisted it with his left hand. His right hand held the Mars gun, but no one appeared, no one called, only terrified horses in the corral shook the ground with reverberations.

Later, as Cain was straining to get upright by leaning against the wall, the horses became calmer. Some still snorted and moved stiff-legged, heads and tails high, but after a time that also stopped.

The last gunshot came from the house, and it sounded like a cannon.

Cain sucked air. When the pain came, it was like red-hot pokers were in his flesh. He got as far as the door. Distantly, he heard riders going southward, and two bewildered and riderless animals came to the outside of the corral to smell noses with the animals inside. Both wore Mexican saddles with huge horns and boxy steel stirrups.

He let himself down the wall and waited. They were probably gone, but graveyards were full of people who put faith in "probably."

Inside, it was warm even with the door open. Outside, it was chilly, and beyond the big swale, where the buildings were, a thin streak of peach-pink crossed the sky.

Cain fainted.

* * * * *

When he awakened, Cain was in the house with the old woman spooning *tizwin* into him. It burned in the mouth and all the way down. He was on the floor. His trouser leg had been cut its full length. He had a bandage as thick as his arm most of the way down his right leg, and the old woman was tying it off with tears streaming down her face. When their eyes met, she tried to smile and repeated what she had told the old man the night before, but this time with something close to either pride or gratitude.

"*¡Mucho matador!*"

Cain closed his eyes. He was sore everywhere. The old woman finished the bandaging and spooned more *tizwin*, until Cain raised an arm to push her hand away.

She sat back on her heels and spoke slowly and softly. "My husband is dead."

Cain opened his eyes. His brain was fuzzy, but he did not think any shots had been fired in the direction of the house. A stray bullet?

The old woman jutted her jaw in the direction of an ancient buffalo rifle. "When he fired, it knocked him almost to the fireplace. His heart stopped."

Cain closed his eyes again. The Indian whiskey was working.

The old woman disappeared in the back of the house where she knelt beside an old bed, held the cold hand of her man, and cried.

The sun was high before Cain opened his eyes again. Now the pain was from the right hip almost to his ankle. His head ached, too.

The old woman brought him a bowl of something hot and highly flavored, got him propped up, and spoon fed him. She was no longer crying. Her face was set in the expression most familiar in the border country — resignation. How could God allow such things? But He did, and people still prayed to Him. Maybe He only worked small miracles. Maybe pain and loss were necessary, even if they made no sense. What was left? God's will, which was resignation.

By late afternoon Cain could move, painfully, but there were required things a person could not put off long, particularly after eating, and the old woman had something for Cain to eat every time he opened his eyes. The headache departed, but the leg hurt worse. She would have helped him, but there are things which are best done alone.

Movement, painful or not, helped clear his mind. He sat on the rawhide-upholstered chair under the *ramada,* gazing in the direction of the dead woman's *jacal* and the adobe barn. The old woman brought a glass of red wine and joined him. She was expressionless and silent as she stared far out.

Cain eventually said: "Something's got to be done. It's too hot to leave them lying for long."

Without agreeing or looking at Cain, the old woman said: "How many?"

Cain wasn't sure. "Four. Maybe five."

She faced him slowly. He emptied the glass of red wine. She was looking northward again when she said: "There is an old mare with a white mane and tail. I rode her for twenty years. I'll ride her to Soda Springs."

Cain said nothing. It had to be done, he supposed, but she was very old, it was hot, and the ride was a good six or better miles. If there was a buggy? . . . he asked, and she shook her head. "You couldn't get in it, if we had one. No. I will go and be back before dark. No! No! No! I have saddled horses all my life. You sit here. I'll bring the jug."

When she brought the jug and placed it beside his chair, she said: "You will give me your word . . . ?"

He smiled and nodded. "I'll be settin' here when you get back. Listen. Don't use the road. Keep out of sight. You understand?"

She nodded and went down to the barn.

Cain slept until shadows were gathering, and this time, when he awakened, the leg was acutely painful, but otherwise he ached from exertion. He was hungry and had to pee. It was not too difficult to stand, favoring the bandaged leg which he could not bend, and pee off the edge of the porch. Getting up and sitting down were both painful and awkward. He considered trying to reach the kitchen while he was still standing, but three steps convinced him to return to the chair. He had some wine and watched the sun redden as it settled lower.

The old woman had removed his shell belt and holstered sidearm. They would be inside somewhere.

He was awake when the corralled horses began fidgeting and lining up on the east side of their corral. He thought at first they were hungry. There was nothing to eat in the corral, but it had to be more than that. They shoved one another, nickered, and stood like crows on a tree limb looking intently eastward.

Cain could not see beyond where the eastern land swell obscured his vision. Someone was coming. He wanted his sidearm. He couldn't get it nor did he intend to make the effort until he saw who was coming.

The old woman most likely. She had been gone long enough.

The first movement atop the land swell wasn't a rider. It was a light dray wagon. Behind it were several horsemen.

Cain strained to recognize any of them. Only two were even possibly recognizable. One was a hatless woman whose raven black hair was pulled tightly back on both sides. The other was a thick, dark man riding beside her, followed by three people Cain could not make out well because they rode bunched up. Not until the three widened slightly did Cain recognize the old woman riding a faded old palomino with a flaxen mane and tail.

He hoisted himself upright, used the back of the chair to lean on, and watched.

They entered the yard without haste. They had evidently set their pace to that of the wagon animal, but every one of them was looking in the direction of the house.

The old woman got stiffly down. A man took her mare. The burly, dark man looped his reins at a rack and tipped down his hat while he stared at the standing man on the *ramada*. Someone spoke to him. He turned his back to help care for the animals, and Cain formed a word with his lips. *Bastard!*

The two women started toward the house. Cain's gaze was fixed on the one whose hair was tight on both sides. He could not see behind her, but he knew there would be an upward braid.

The old woman was deliberately slow reaching the porch which allowed Rosalia to get there first. Cain smiled. She stood in silence for a moment, then said: "You need a shave." She was solemn as an owl. She left him standing there and entered the house with the old woman. There was her grandfather to be seen to first. Why was it that there was always more time for the dead than for the living?

No one else approached the house. They were busy with dead raiders, animals to be released from the corral, other animals to be watered and fed, and because the town marshal kept them busy. They were fascinated by scars of the fight which also kept them away. One man eventually came toward the house. He was carrying something loosely in one hand.

When he stepped onto the porch, he held out whatever he had been carrying, and Cain took it. Neither of them offered a hand nor smiled.

It was a nickel-plated revolver with ivory grips bearing the initials H. L.

Cain looked up. "Which one?"

"The one trying to get around the front of the barn. Henrique López."

Cain handed back the gun as the marshal said: "I wanted to kill him myself."

Cain's lips curled. "Why didn't you?" The dark, burly man's gaze flickered, and Cain said: "Because he rode for Porfirio, and you 'n' Porfirio was friends? I know . . . Soda Springs needed Porfirio."

The marshal changed the subject. "You did well for these old people."

Cain replied dryly. "The old man's inside. He's dead."

Clawson entered the house. It was like walking into a den of wildcats. The old woman struck and cursed him. He backed out of the door, protecting his face. The old woman slammed the door so hard the house quivered.

Cain smiled.

The marshal said: "She's goin' to come to town. She has a sister there, older'n her." He paused to reset his hat. "She give the ranch to Rosalia." Clawson looked across the yard. "It is a place for starving."

Cain waited until Clawson was leaving the porch to speak. "I'm coming to town, too. If you get in my way, I'll aim higher next time. *¿Comprende?*"

107

★ ★ ★ ★ ★

The ground was like iron, so each grave hole was soaked overnight with water. Cain was unable to help, but he went with the diggers and watched the marshal sweat and dig. The old man was the last one they buried. He was put down with prayers, with Rosalia holding the old woman and looking over her head at Cain. Her father and the others left. Rosalia told Cain she had arranged for the wagon to stay. When Cain was able to travel, she would return and drive him to town.

The old woman would not hear of such a thing. She said for Rosalia to drive the wagon to town, load it with her things and Raimondo, and come back. She insisted the ride would open Cain's wound. She made gestures. "He would bleed to death!"

Rosalia put an amused look at Cain, kissed the old woman, and went to drive back with the wagon. As soon as she was out of sight, the old woman sat with Cain on the *ramada* with a dying day making the sky red. She said: "I can't stay here. Not now. I gave the ranch to her." She smoothed her skirt very thoroughly. "But what can a single woman do?"

Cain squinted into the reddening sky. "Can't do much."

"Did you know she wants to marry you?"

The squint widened.

"Well? She said that to me. She is very pretty. She is a fine cook. She will never be fat."

Cain rolled his eyes. Juan My Ass would have got up and walked away.

"Well, *Señor Matador?*"

"She never said anythin' to me."

"Do you need a rock in the head? Mother of God. Men

108

are so strong, like an oak. And twice as thick! I'll get us some wine."

Cain leaned back, considering the reddening heavens. He looked upwards and softly smiled. "Juan My Ass . . . He is up there, and for a fact we don't understand His ways, but He understands ours."

They were married in the autumn. Cain sold the Mars gun to a tired outlaw for nine dollars.

Chapter Ten

THE HAWKS' PLACE

Tyler Heinz was a large man, big-boned, and rangy. He was neither agile nor graceful. He established a reputation near the hamlet of Virginia Dale in southern Colorado when he met two rough, unkempt, hard-eyed men named Croft and Turpin, part of the outlaw band known locally as Jake Slade's crew. In a face down he killed them both at the same time.

Tyler, who had once been an outlaw, was a traveling livestock buyer at the time. The last bunch of animals he bought came from the ranch of a limping, tall man named Leroy Cain, who had a pretty wife and two children. He also bought a six-gun from Cain that had most of the blu-ing worn off. Tyler paid nine dollars for it.

After selling off the Cain horses in a sleepy place called Colorado Springs and heading north, he arrived in Virginia Dale on a cold and windy springtime evening, looking for a place where he and his horse could get fed and bed down.

Virginia Dale was a stage stop and little else. The coun-try was rough, rocky, and timbered. Cattlemen got by when their cattle could graze over thousands of acres. No one else could make a living in such country, although some had tried: homesteaders, pot hunters, even sheepmen. The sheepmen did not last long. The squatters lasted slightly longer, usually through one winter with drift snow five feet high and never enough firewood. Pot hunters lingered, but the markets for meat were dozens of miles apart and, again, meat was scarce when wildlife left the high country every fall.

As there always were somewhere, a handful of people lived on. The stages ran north and south from Denver to Cheyenne and elsewhere, summer or winter. There were way stations at intervals, which is how Virginia Dale came to exist. Slade's crew weren't the only highwaymen. Between Fort Collins and Laramie, the country was ideal for stopping coaches. Not only was it timbered, but there were rocks taller than a mounted man and miles where sunshine didn't reach the ground. Robbing stages was mostly seasonal, although highwaymen operated during the bitter winter months, too, only not as consistently as during summer when a coach and four could not only move fast, but armed outriders went ahead, if highwaymen were unusually active.

The blustery late day when Tyler Heinz reached Virginia Dale the proprietor of the combination way station and general store, Potter Jackson, a dour man whose face was darkly shadowed even after he shaved, had just been paid in coins for whiskey and two glasses. His bar was an afterthought extension of his grocery counter.

Potter left his two customers to show Tyler where to put his horse, where the hay was, and gestured indifferently in the direction of a log cabin with a sagging roof where someone had piled several armloads of firewood on the small porch. Potter said there was an iron cot in there and an iron stove. Tyler returned to the store with him, settled at the bar, and nodded for the drink he needed to warm his insides.

One of the sullen-looking pair, also at the bar, studied Tyler for a long time, then asked a question.

111

"You travelin' through, mister?"

Tyler downed his jolt and pushed the glass forward for a refill as he replied: "All the way to Cheyenne. I figure to lie over in Laramie." Tyler downed the second jolt and began to loosen. He addressed no one in particular when he said: "I never been in this country when it ain't either windy or cold."

The second unshorn, unwashed man spoke. "You a travelin' man, friend?"

"Livestock buyer," Tyler answered, and looked at Potter Jackson. "You feed folks?"

Potter nodded. "Give me fifteen minutes."

Tyler moved toward the large iron stove, placed his back to it, did not keep watch over the pair of burly men in muted conversation, and let his muscles relax and his bones stop aching.

Both of the shaggy men at the bar now faced him. One had reddish hair, lots of it. The other one had his right hand resting atop the saw-handle grip of a six-gun holstered in old leather, scratched and scarred. This one's name was Andrew Croft. He studied Tyler Heinz from an expressionless face, noticed the large man remove his woolen coat, and said: "Can't do much livestock buyin' this time of year, can you?"

Tyler agreed. He was warm. The whiskey had helped, and he smiled. "A tad early but I like to be handy when the time comes."

The man with carroty hair smiled. "I got a cousin who buys 'n' sells over in Missouri." The smile widened. "He told me one time he's been robbed so often he thought he might find another way to make a livin'."

Tyler also smiled. "I've known it to happen. Not to me, but to others." As Tyler was speaking, he turned slightly to

112

one side as though seeking heat on that part of his body. When he turned back, the tie down thong was hanging loose. He said: "Buy you gents a drink?"

The man standing slightly to one side of the red-headed man said — "That's right decent of you." — and dropped his right shoulder. His pistol was half clear of leather when the bullet hit him squarely in the brisket. The man with carroty hair leaned slightly. Tyler's second bullet hit him higher, in the throat.

Potter Jackson in his skimpy cooking area dropped a fry pan, and the grease spilled against his lower left leg. He let out a howl and groped for the water bucket.

The red-headed man bled like a castrated bull. When Potter Jackson came in behind the bar, Tyler Heinz was standing like a wooden Indian, his back to the stove. Jackson stared at him before going around the counter and looking down. This time, when he looked at Tyler, his gaze was disbelivingly wide.

Tyler said: "Livestock buyers don't always wear a money belt stuffed with greenbacks. I'll stand you a drink."

Potter Jackson neither spoke nor moved for a long time. Not until a howling blast of wind hit his building, making it groan at every joint. After the blast passed, he said: "You know an old man named Ezra Hawks?"

"No. Why?"

Jackson went back behind his bar, set up a bottle, two jolt glasses, and filled them both before answering. "He's an old soldier . . . gets a pension. The third of every month he rides in for his check." Potter gestured, and Tyler moved to the bar. They emptied the glasses.

"Go on," Tyler said.

"He has bred-up cattle. That's what he does to make money. He's lost about half of 'em the last year or so."

Potter Jackson held the bottle poised. Tyler put a ham-size hand palm down over the glass. Potter Jackson refilled his own glass and hung fire before speaking again. "He told me last fall he was goin' to hire a feller to ride for him." Potter paused again. "Said he'd pay dear to the right man."

Tyler leaned on the bar. "You know these fellers on the floor?"

"Yes. They sometimes ride with Jake Slade."

"Who is Jake Slade?"

"Cattle thief, horse thief, highwayman."

"You know him?"

"He comes here now 'n' then. There's a reward on him, if you're interested."

Tyler shook his head. "What're you goin' to do with these two? Ground's too hard for digging."

"Put 'em in the freezer house until I figure what else to do with 'em."

"Friends of yours, are they?"

Jackson curled his lip. "No good sons-of-bitches. But Jake won't like this. If I was you, I wouldn't be here come sunup. He might not come, but if he did an' you was still here. . . ."

"I figure to be gone about sunup. It smells like something's burnin'."

Potter Jackson yelped and ran back to his cooking area.

Tyler went back to the stove, lifted out the six-gun that graying man down yonder had sold to him for nine dollars, considered it and what it had accomplished lying not fifteen feet away face down, and eased the Mars gun back into its holster.

That tall, graying man down yonder with the pretty wife and two children had taken the livestock buyer behind his barn and startled the hell out of him. After firing, he had

114

handed Tyler the nine-dollar gun and said: "You don't have to pull it all the way back to a full cock. The pin's been blunted, an' the firin' spring's stronger. If you carry it at half cock, be careful you don't snag the trigger, or you'll likely blow your foot off."

Tyler had practiced with the gun, loaded and unloaded, between a place called Soda Springs and Virginia Dale.

Potter Jackson took a long time bringing the platter of food and the mug of coffee. He had larded his left leg from halfway below the knee to the ankle.

After eating, during a lull in the wind, Tyler helped Potter Jackson drag the bodies to a small log building and leave them there. As he was turning toward the cabin with firewood on the porch, he called to Potter Jackson. "Does this feller named Hawks have cattle to sell?"

Jackson called back just before another blast of icy wind hit. "I'll make a map to his place." As things turned out, the map wasn't needed.

Tyler went inside. It was like an icebox. He fired up the stove, sat on the edge of the old iron cot until the room was warm, then shed off to get between two moth-eaten old Hudson Bay blankets bearing the trade bars used by the company when dealing with Indians.

In the morning it was colder than a witch's bosom, and Tyler shivered for half an hour until the stove did what iron stoves were supposed to do.

The sun was fully up. In front of the way station men were harnessing a change of animals to the stage, and one passenger, so muffled in a buffalo-robe coat only his nose showed, drained a mug of Irish whiskey the way station manager had provided.

Tyler entered through the rear door. The only noise was outside until he heard someone noisily drinking coffee and

115

saw the wiry, older man all dressed in gray, even to his hat and his necktie, hunkering at the bar. They exchanged a nod. The stove was crackling, but clearly it hadn't been fired up long, because the store was chilly.

The older man pointed. Tyler filled a mug from the pot and went to sit near the older man who ignored him and was holding the hot mug in both hands. There were no fingers in his gloves.

Without looking at Tyler, the old man said: "Cold for spring."

Tyler replied: "It's always cold in spring in high country."

The old man drained the cup but still curled his hands around it. He grumbled. "What's takin' Potter so long? It's only the mail coach."

Tyler explained that, too. "Leather's like wood when it's close to freezin'."

The old man finally looked at the younger man. "Are you a leather man?"

"No, sir, I'm a cattle buyer."

The old man straightened slightly. The room was getting warm. "Are you? In this country it's too early. Cattlemen won't have anythin' to sell for another four, five months. By any chance . . . what's your name?"

"Tyler Heinz. What's yours?"

"Walter Hawks." The all-gray man paused. "Mister Hawks."

They didn't shake, but both nodded.

Potter Jackson came in, threw a stiff nod, and got as close to the stove as he dared. Outside, someone whistled up the fresh hitch, and the passenger buried to the nose in his hide coat was carried southward.

Without making a move away from the stove, Potter

116

asked if Tyler wanted breakfast. He did, but Potter did not move for another ten minutes, then he did it reluctantly.

Mr. Hawks pulled a thin smile. "I don't know why he stays. He hates the cold."

"For the way station an' the store?"

"I expect so," Mr. Hawks replied, and went to refill both their coffee mugs. When he was back on his seat with both hands curled around his cup, he said: "What'd he spill on the floor?"

Tyler neither looked down nor answered as Potter reappeared with a platter of fried meat and a pair of spuds that were very small.

Mr. Hawks said: "He's a cattle buyer. Potter, what'd you spill on the floor?"

Potter shot a glance at the man having breakfast and back before he said: "There was an accident in here last night."

Mr. Hawks wasn't really interested. "You been through the mail yet?"

"No. I'll get it directly. You want breakfast, too, Mister Hawks?"

"Don't believe so. I ate before sunup. I'd like to get up the Laramie today."

Potter Jackson reddened, went to the stained canvas sack, rummaged through until he found the envelope, and handed it to Mr. Hawks with his usual comment. "Make it last."

The old man pocketed the envelope, which contained his pension check from four years in the Union Army. He considered the large man eating for a moment, then asked a question. "If you're interested, I got some cattle to sell."

Tyler swallowed, then spoke. "How many?"

"Well, maybe all of 'em, about eighty head. Bred-up

117

quality." Mr. Hawks looked at Potter Jackson, who seemed surprised. The old man babied his cattle like some folks babied children. Hawks said: "It's nothin' I want to do, Potter, but the sons-of-bitches raided me again day afore yestiddy, an' this time they got both my Durham bulls."

Tyler spoke. "Get the law to track 'em."

Both the older men showed expressions of scorn and disgust — scorn at the cattle buyer's ignorance, and disgust for another reason that Mr. Hawks explained.

"The law's in Laramie, a long ride from here. I been there before. They tell me they'd like to come help, but they ain't enough money in their budget to keep at full strength, let alone send someone down, lookin' for rustlers who likely went south into Colorado where they got no jurisdiction."

Potter inclined his head. After an interval of silence he said: "The law from Denver don't know we're up here, an' the law in Laramie don't care." He was about to add more when Mr. Hawks darkly scowled.

Tyler made a fair guess and spoke next: "So you got a nest of outlaws."

Neither of the other men spoke.

Tyler finished breakfast, and Mr. Hawks had a long ride ahead. The old man called to Tyler: "Make you a good price. They're goin' to steal 'em all anyway."

Tyler told the old man to wait. He paid Potter Jackson, rigged out his horse, and came around the side of the way station as Potter and Mr. Hawks broke off a hurried conversation.

Mr. Hawks had a top buggy that showed much use. The horse between the shafts was beginning to shed and looked like a bear with the mange.

They didn't say much. Tyler rode beside the rig on the

far side. They had progressed northward about two miles, when Mr. Hawks hauled up and pointed in the direction of twin ruts going southwest. "I'll get back before supper-time," he called, and flapped the lines for the shedding horse to move out.

It was picturesque country, rocky with timber, small clearings called parks, and creeks with fresh growth showing on willows and in the grass. The ruts ended in a spacious clearing where three log buildings stood. They were old, color leached out with straight ridgelines, and the pole cor-ral made of draw-knifed lodgepoles had no sag anywhere. Clearly the old soldier cared for things.

Tyler put up his horse, explored, decided no one had used the anvil or forge for years. He was midway to the shaded porch when he heard cattle bawling. It wasn't the lowing of mammy cows seeking calves. It was the sounds of distress.

He placed the direction, got his horse, and rode into a stand of ancient, overripe pines, emerging on the edge of a huge meadow.

Two riders were gathering cattle. Both were well mounted, but neither man had been near soap or a hair cutter in months. The cattle were bred-up animals. Not a one of them had a set of horns more than four feet long from tip to tip. Nor were they razor-backed nor long legged. Mostly, they had the brown color of Durham.

Tyler came out of the timber, riding at a walk. Neither of the rangemen saw him. They were busy holding their gather before they began the drive, but eventually one man saw him and yelled to his companion.

They both faced Tyler, and their bunched-up gather be-gan to spread. The bellowing almost ceased.

Tyler raised his right hand, palm forward. Neither of the

unshorn, unshaven, and unwashed men responded.

Where he drew rein, the distance was about thirty feet. One of the rangemen said: "Who'n hell are you? What you doin' here?"

Tyler's horse fidgeted to the right. When Tyler brought him back around, the tie down thong was hanging loose. He said: "I come to look at Mister Hawks' cattle. He figures to sell down."

One of the furry-faced men with coarse features studied Tyler. "A cattle buyer?"

"Yes."

"You got a money belt?"

Tyler let his left rein-hand rest atop the saddlehorn when he nodded. "You can't buy 'em on trust, mister."

The second man slowly straightened in the saddle. Before he could speak, his companion said: "Take the belt off, mister, an' let it drop."

As he said this, the rangeman reached for his holster. He did not move fast. He was clearly relying on intimidation, and for a fact he was a surly, vicious-looking individual.

It would have made no difference if he had been faster. Tyler's slug hit him high. He lowered his head, hung briefly, and, when the horse shied, the man went off and landed like a sack of wet grain.

The second man's horse was in a hackamore. It was a colt. The gunshot turned him inside out. He didn't unseat his rider as much as he fled out from under him. The man landed in a sitting position. Tyler leaned, waiting. The sitting man was dazed. His eyes seemed not to focus. Tyler swung down, hoisted the man with one hand, flung away his sidearm, and pushed him toward the dead man's horse.

He said: "Mount. Ride ahead of me an' don't even sneeze."

Chapter Eleven

OLD MEN

By the time Mr. Hawks returned, Tyler knew quite a bit about his cow-stealing prisoner. For one thing, his name was Lemuel Wilhite. He was nineteen years old. His pa had died under a train. His ma had just upped and disappeared. He didn't really ride with the Slade crew. They didn't want him, but the dead man in the big meadow had brought him along to help steal the Hawks cattle.

After Tyler fired up the parlor stove and heat spread, he wrinkled his nose. "You smell worse'n dead," he told the cow thief. "Where'd you get them britches an' that shirt?"

"I taken 'em off a clothesline up near Laramie."

Tyler adjusted the lamp as he said: "Good thing the feller who owned 'em didn't catch you. He was big enough to ride." Tyler turned. "What was the name of that nasty bastard I shot?"

"Alex Moorer. He told me he'd killed seven men in fair fights."

Tyler cocked his head. The old man was coming. He looked at his prisoner and spoke dryly. "Eight was his unlucky number. Now you set there. Don't move and put both hands atop your head."

It took time for Mr. Hawks to care for his buggy animal and the rig, and, when he stamped up onto the porch and entered the door, he squinted his eyes nearly closed, but only for a moment. As he opened them wider, Tyler said:

"That's one of your cow thieves. His name is Lemuel Wilhite. There was another one. His name was Alex Moorer. He's dead out in that big meadow to the west."

The old man went to the stove, put his back to it, and looked at the cow thief as he addressed Tyler Heinz. "How many'd they get this time?"

"None, but they had about forty head in a gather."

Mr. Hawks slowly put his attention on Tyler. "I'll be god-damned," he said, recovered from shock, and spoke again. "What'd you say your name was?"

"Tyler. Tyler Heinz."

"Mister Heinz, you had anything to eat?"

"No."

"I'll get us somethin'. Don't he seem young to be rustlin' cattle?"

"From what I know, Mister Hawks, age don't have much to do with it. You want to hang him before we eat or after?"

The old man disappeared into a dingy kitchen without answering. The cow thief looked steadily at big Tyler Heinz. "Mister, if I give you my word I'll never. . . ."

"A cow thief's word isn't worth a coal in hell. I've had 'em sneak out of the trees and cut out a critter or two while I was drivin' past."

"I never stole cattle before."

"Don't lie to me. Of all the worthless sons-of-bitches on this earth I hate liars first."

The old man stood in the kitchen doorway. "It's ready," he said, and added: "I don't cook good."

It was gospel truth. He didn't.

Mr. Hawks was a whiskey drinker. He gave the cow thief whiskey and water in a separate glass, but for himself and Tyler Heinz he only filled glasses a quarter full of whiskey, which was a lifesaver because the old man's dinner beef was like chewing sun-cured leather, and the potatoes, which ordinarily were difficult to make inedible, bounced like rubber and never completely broke down before being swallowed.

The cow thief ate hurriedly, like someone who'd missed more than his share of meals. He washed everything down with the watered whiskey, and, when that was gone, he did the same with water. Mr. Hawks seemed not to notice, but he did, and, when they'd finished, he went to a crate nailed to a wall with two handmade shelves, groped, and muttered to himself until eventually he brought forth a tan bag. He put it in front of the cow thief and smiled. "Jelly beans," he said. After filling two coffee cups, he sat down.

The coal-oil lamp had an untrimmed wick and a sooty mantle that eliminated any ordinary brightness. By this light Lemuel Wilhite looked closer to fifteen than to nineteen.

He ate the jelly beans, smiled at the old man, and was careful not to look at Tyler until he finished eating. Then he hitched up his courage and asked a question.

"Mister Heinz . . . you're faster'n lightnin'. Do you hire out?"

Tyler considered the pinched face with large blue eyes when he shook his head. "I'm a travelin' livestock buyer."

"Well . . . ?"

"Help Mister Hawks clean up," Tyler said, and arose to return to the hearth in the parlor.

The cattle he had seen in that large meadow were slick as moles, no bones showing, and, while some were butt-headed, mostly the horns were half the usual length. They would bring sound money in Laramie and maybe four bits more a head over in Cheyenne.

Mr. Hawks and the cow thief continued to talk in the

123

kitchen. When they entered the parlor, Tyler looked steadily at the old man, and Mr. Hawks looked into the fire. Lemuel Wilhite sat on the edge of a cobbler's bench, hands pressed together between his knees.

Tyler sighed.

The old man talked of cattle. He knew livestock, but, when Tyler pressed him about price, the old man avoided a direct answer. Instead he said: "I raised 'em from calves, mostly. When a man gets old bein' alone. . . ."

"The rustlers come," said Tyler, and the old man nodded. "They're quiet animals, Mister Hawks. They'd drive good."

The old man nodded again, filled a foul, small pipe with shag from a bowl, and fired up. Tyler throttled a cough. The cow thief fished forth a nearly empty sack of Durham and painstakingly rolled a cigarette with a hump in the middle and lighted up.

Mr. Hawks finally spoke. "I'll pay you for your time, Mister Heinz. I don't think I want to sell down."

Tyler moved slightly so the old man could put a split round into the fire. It had enough fat wood so that Tyler had to move again.

Mr. Hawks finally faced the larger and younger man. "In the kitchen," he said, "me 'n' the lad talked."

Tyler looked at the cow thief whose eyes were watering from cigarette smoke. "Mister Hawks, he was goin' to steal your cattle."

The old man puffed a small cloud before speaking, and his voice was stronger. "I'll pay you for the inconvenience."

Tyler considered the cow thief and shook his head. He said the old man owed him nothing, and that he'd be coming back south in a month or two. If there were any cattle left, he'd like to buy them then.

Mr. Hawks jerked his head, and the cow thief went down a dingy hallway to a windowless, dark room with a bed, a chair, and a commode pot. Mr. Hawks's pipe went out. He put it aside to speak without looking at Tyler Heinz. "Did you have a family, Mister Heinz?"

"Well, no."

"Neither'd I. Not after the war. I was gone four years. They was gone when I come back. Scattered to the wind. Mister Heinz . . . ?"

"First chance he gets, he'll brain you, steal everything he can carry, and drive off the cattle. Mister Hawks, cow thieves don't change."

The old man's shoulders slumped. After a silent period he said: "He's sixteen."

Tyler was not surprised. When he'd been the cow thief's age, he'd lied about how old he was, too.

"Mister Heinz, I've seen 'em wanderin' in rags, nearly starved to death, folks gone, cabins burnt." The old man raised his head. "The lad needs folks, Mister Heinz."

Tyler sighed, asked where he could bed down, and left the parlor to find the tiny log house with the small pot-bellied stove. He told the stove the old man was a damned fool, shed down, and rolled into some blankets that smelled of mildew.

Before leaving after breakfast, with sunrise brightening an otherwise drowsy world, he took the cow thief aside, poked him in the chest with a rigid finger, and talked to him like a Dutch uncle.

"Boy, if it'd been left to me, I'd have left you hangin' from a tree. I'll be back this way someday. You remember that. No matter where you go, I'll find you."

Tyler rode back to the way station where Potter Jackson was surprised to see him and would have got a conversa-

125

tion going, but the livestock buyer neither listened nor spoke, not even when horsemen clattered into the yard with the sun climbing and a new day's warmth spreading.

Tyler had returned to buy canned peaches among other things to tide him over until he reached Laramie.

He was considering the canned goods on a grocery shelf when Potter Jackson seemed turned to stone. The three men were dangerous-looking, and for a fact they were dangerous. Two were average in most ways including soiled clothing and too-long hair. These two had cuds in their cheeks. The third man was slightly taller and was also unkempt and unshaven. He had dark gray eyes and a set of thin and bloodless lips for a mouth. He stood briefly, thumbs hooked in his gun belt, before moving closer as he addressed Potter Jackson.

"Is this him?" When Potter Jackson did not answer, the man faced Tyler Heinz. "If you ain't," he said, "you'll do."

Tyler put his back to the counter. "For what?" he asked.

One of the individuals back by the roadway door said: "It'll be him."

While the man facing Tyler seemed not to have heard, he nodded his head, looked askance, and asked Potter Jackson if the stranger was the man the southbound's driver had said was at the way station.

Potter Jackson was between a rock and a hard place. He almost imperceptibly inclined his head.

The beard-stubbled man kept both thumbs hooked in his shell belt. Tyler Heinz was a large, muscular man. The man facing him was a head shorter and thick-bodied. He said: "Friend of ours got hurt in a meadow some miles north 'n' west of here. Someone ridin' a horse with three nails on each side of his shoes rode here from the Hawks place. We looked at your animal. Three nails instead of

126

four on each side of its shoes. Mister, we pay our debts."

While the unwashed man had been talking, Tyler had let his right hand dangle. When he raised it, the tie-down thong was hanging loose. One of the men at the door said: "Jake."

Before he could speak further, Potter Jackson interrupted. "Take it outside, gents. I got a glass mirror that cost me seven dollars."

The man who had tried to warn the man facing Tyler made a low, sweeping gesture, and he was fast, but the difference was the matter of seconds required to haul back at full cock before firing, and not having to. The explosion sounded doubly loud inside the building. The man by the door struck the wall so hard he was propelled forward and collapsed, face down.

The man called Jake looked down, then up. His companion by the door didn't seem to be breathing.

Tyler didn't raise his voice. "Shuck 'em, both of you. Good. Now come to the counter." They obeyed that order, too, and Tyler hit them both hard with the six-gun barrel. Blood mingled with their hair. They fell very close to the place where floor planking was stained almost black.

Tyler considered Potter Jackson, jerked his head, and herded the way-station man out where four horses were at a tie rack. He backed his own horse clear, swung up, and mounted. His last words to Potter Jackson were: "Thanks for nodding, you gutless son-of-a-bitch."

Potter watched the livestock buyer lope northward. It was too late in the day for him to reach Laramie before dark. Potter went back inside. The survivors were moaning, sitting up now on the floor. The one called Jake said: "What was his name?"

And this time Potter lied. "He never said what it was."

Potter Jackson went over to where the dead man was lying and systematically emptied his pockets and appropriated his gun, while his friends watched indifferently, nursing their injuries.

The sun was directly overhead. The blustery last gasp of winter had spent itself. The day was warm. The sky was clear. Dust showed for a mile, and Tyler Heinz faded from sight among forest giants until the coach passed. It was heading northeast in the direction of Virginia Dale. Tyler was riding southwest, in the opposite direction.

He reached a place called Cache Le Poudre an hour or so ahead of sunset. It had a large general store, some scattered sheds, and a large, old barn with a butchering post up near the peak and a block and tackle in place. It wasn't even a settlement.

The store itself had been whitewashed. In a country where colors were basic, it stood out for miles. A limping old man, badly bent, helped Tyler care for his horse and outfit. The old man did not say ten words, not even when Tyler asked where a man could bed down. All the old man did was point.

The store was large, well-stocked, and not only looked prosperous but smelled it. The proprietor was gone for the day. His wife was a dumpling of a small woman. She had bright eyes, a shoe-button nose, and perfect white teeth when she smiled.

When Tyler asked about bedding down, she said: "Pick a cabin. Ten cents a night." She held out her hand.

Tyler passed over the coin. "Hay, dry stall, an' grain for my horse?"

"Fifteen cents more."

Tyler paid and considered the stocked shelves.

128

In anticipation the small, round woman said: "Five cents a can. Help yourself."

By the time he got to one of the crib-like, small, log sheds he had spent almost a dollar.

While he was eating, the old man came to knock timidly and say: "Mister, I didn't grain your horse. The oats is wormy."

The old man stared at the open tin Tyler was eating from. Tyler jerked his head for the old man to enter. He gestured toward the tins. "Help yourself."

The old man did. He produced a large, double-edged knife to cut off the lid and afterwards ate with it. He sat in the only chair. Tyler perched on the edge of the wall bunk.

The old man spoke around a mouthful. "My name's John."

Tyler had to swallow before answering. "Tyler Heinz. Don't they pay you, John?"

"No. Scraps for breakfast an' supper. They don't have to pay me, an' they know it."

Tyler lowered the tin from which he was eating. "Why? Because you're old? Everyone deserves to be paid for what they do."

John ate in silence. Some sticky substance got into his beard. He mumbled, fished forth what had once been a red bandanna, and went to work trying to remove it. Tyler got a bucket of water from the well to wash with and drink. He put it on the table, and the old man soaked his faded bandanna and continued to work vigorously on the sticky substance. When he was satisfied, he pocketed the bandanna and discreetly belched behind a scarred and discolored, upraised hand. Afterwards he said: "Excuse me, mister."

Tyler was drying his fingers and smiled. "Take a can with you," he said.

The old man eyed the remaining unopened cans, selected one, and looked at Tyler. "This one would be all right, mister?"

Tyler nodded with his smile fading. He held out his hand with a silver cartwheel on it, and the lame old man's brow wrinkled. "A Yankee dollar."

"Take it."

"Well, mister. . . ."

"Just take it."

John did and made a sweep with a ragged cuff across his upper face. "You'll want it back," he mumbled, and Tyler slapped the old man's shoulder.

John stood as straight as he could, which wasn't very erect. With all his weight on one leg he repeated: "You'll want it back."

"No. Why would I?"

"My name's John Wilkes Booth. They know it at the store."

130

Chapter Twelve

TOWARD NIGHTFALL

The morning was still with air as clear as glass. Tyler had no illusions — early spring or not, it was going to be hot. His horse had an advantage. He never knew what the weather would do until it did it.

They didn't stay to the road. Tyler had no reason to believe the gray-eyed man with a slit where his mouth was supposed to be would shag him. Men like Jake Slade were murdering bullies. They did not take chances, nor was the loss of companions important to them.

Tyler liked the country south the best, but, wherever a man's trade took him, he went. That was what life required unless a man got rebellious. Then he sacrificed his income and more.

The day did, in fact, get hot, but by the time this happened Tyler was in a fair way of skirting one city and several towns. Once, when he was near the road, he encountered a buggy listing to one side because a wheel had come off, something buggy makers sought to avoid by using a reverse thread on hubs and wheels. He would have ridden past, but a tall woman gestured with a parasol. Tyler rode over, leaned from the saddle, considering the buggy. The woman neither mentioned her name nor the accident.

She said: "The burr came off."

Tyler dismounted.

The woman lacked no more than four inches of being as

tall as he was, and she was dark with fine, thin features. She said: "A dollar if you'll fix it."

Tyler considered the woman. It was one of those meetings when instinctive dislike was paramount. He handed the woman the reins to his horse, went behind the light rig, and lifted. The woman didn't move until Tyler said: "Pick up the burr, lady, an' screw it on."

"What about your horse?"

"Put the god-damned burr on!"

The tall woman dropped the reins and went to kneel in dust. Tyler's horse nuzzled the buggy mare. The rig wasn't heavy to lift, but it got heavy if it had to be held up very long.

The woman dropped the nut and nervously groped for it. On her second try she got it in place.

Tyler said — "Turn it the other way." — which she did. When the bolt was in place, Tyler eased the buggy down, went where the woman was cleaning her hands on a tiny lace handkerchief, and shouldered her out of the way.

The bolt was firm. Tyler said: "Get the wrench."

"What?"

"There'll be a burr wrench under the seat."

The woman went forward, grunted as she lifted the seat, and returned with the wrench. Tyler leaned, exerted muscle to tighten the bolt, and straightened up to hand the tall woman the wrench. She recoiled. The wrench was sweat-slippery and dirty.

Tyler dropped the wrench at the woman's feet and went up to his horse. Behind him the woman said: "Here's your dollar."

Tyler turned. "Keep it. Your husband hadn't ought to let you out of the yard."

That stung her. "My husband is a territorial judge."

132

Tyler digested this scrap of information with quiet skepticism. "I didn't think he knew enough to make sure burrs are tight."

The tall woman's nostrils flared. "What is your name?" she asked him sharply.

Tyler answered her from the saddle. "Grattan Dalton. What's yours?"

There was no answer. The woman's mouth hung slack. Her dark stare was glassy. The only thing she could think to say was: "A Dalton?"

Tyler evened up his reins. "Get in your buggy," he said without looking at the woman. Grat Dalton was almost as notorious as his relative, Jesse James.

Dust rose because the tall woman put her harness animal into an abrupt lope. Tyler looked after the buggy and softly said: "You're welcome."

By late afternoon he and his horse were tiring. They were also hungry, but there wasn't a rooftop in any direction. There was tree shade beside a piddling, little, warm water creek, so they spent better than an hour there. Tyler dozed. What awakened him was riders over on the road. They were blue-uniformed soldiers, a squad of them complete with sabers and guns. They loped northward.

Tyler watched until they were lost in dust, got his horse, snugged up, and left the creek and the shade, riding eastward.

Somewhere ahead there was a town with singing wires. That pinch-nosed, condescending woman had sure as hell sent a telegram from somewhere close to Denver to some place southward where there was a soldier post. Grat Dalton was worth sound money dead or alive.

For supper Tyler had a smoke. His horse did better. It

133

cropped grain heads from stirrup-high grass as they went along, something riders did not often allow their mounts to do, but that hadn't been the horse's fault. Tyler's irritation had made him shock hell out of the tall woman.

Dusk arrived with a faint aroma of supper-fire smoke. There still wasn't a rooftop in sight. He let the horse pick a direction, and after an hour they found the source of the smoke scent. It didn't come from a kitchen stove. It came from the supper fire at the tailgate of a canvas-topped range wagon.

Tyler helloed before riding in. Four men sat cross-legged on the ground, eating. The cook sat among them. He was a burly individual with a beard. He rose, peering into the settling night. When he could make out the big man on the ground beside his horse, he sang out: "You timed it right, mister. We got plenty."

After Tyler off-saddled and hobbled the horse, he approached the fire. The rangemen considered him in silence but continued eating from tin plates. The cook filled another plate and handed it to Tyler. He also did what the others had not done. He spoke.

"You lost?"

Tyler sat down to eat and thumbed back his hat. Firelight had a way of showing the evil in men, even when they weren't really bad.

A graying man with a prominent Adam's apple leaned to look closer, leaned back, and said: "You from down south, friend?"

Tyler waited to swallow before answering. "Up north, near the Colorado-Wyoming line."

The man with the prominent Adam's apple persisted. "But you been down south?"

Tyler lowered his clasp knife which served as a fork and

134

looked steadily at the speaker. "I been down south."

"Pueblo Juárez?"

"No, Soda Springs. Why?"

The other man's answer was solemn. "That gun . . . an old feller in Pueblo Juárez made it. Well, he doctored it. I knew him well."

Tyler scooped the plate clean and put it aside. "I bought it for nine dollars from a rancher named Cain in Soda Springs."

The man with the Adam's apple nodded. "Soda Springs is a hoot an' a holler from Pueblo Juárez. I know that gun. Mind if I look at it?"

Tyler made no move to hand over the sidearm. All four rangemen were looking at him from expressionless faces. The man with the Adam's apple said: "It's got the old man's name on the butt plate . . . G. Mars."

A rider held up his hand for silence. They all heard it — riders coming, riding slowly, cautiously. The cook called out. "Come on in." And they emerged, nine of them in blue uniforms that showed indistinctly in the night. One of them held up his hand and came ahead alone. He was an older man, his face lined and showing evil by firelight. He was an officer.

The rangemen were too shocked to move. The soldier said nothing for as long as was required to look at each squatting man individually. He raised a gauntleted hand, pointing at the rider with the prominent Adam's apple. He said: "Stand up. Shed that pistol. Come over here. You're goin' back with us."

The rangeman dropped his six-gun but otherwise did not move. Before he could speak, the cook said: "Who the hell are you?"

"Captain Evans. I want that man."

135

The cook did not yield. "For what?"

The officer put a hard look on the cook. "For breakin' half the laws of the gov'ment. Who are you?"

"My name's Abel Stearns. We ride for Mister Hamilton of the Double H Livestock Company. You know who Mister Hamilton is?"

"No. You there . . . walk over here."

The cook spoke swiftly. "Canby, stay where you are. Captain . . . whatever your name is . . . you don't take nobody from here. Mister, turn that horse an' get your blue-bellied ass out of here, or, by Christ, we'll bury you."

The soldier considered the cook, the other riders who were now all getting to their feet, and said: "That man's Grat Dalton. If you make trouble, whiskers, I'll come back with the law from Denver and a slew of federal lawmen."

The cook didn't look at Tyler, but the other rangemen did. The cook was winning, probably because he wasn't bluffing. "You can come back with half your damned Yankee army. We'll be here or at the home place, an' Mister Hamilton ain't goin' to like this. Get your damned ass off Hamilton range. *Get!*"

The soldier was an old campaigner. No rangemen in the world would back him down. What had bothered him from the start of this business was that it wasn't the Army's business to chase outlaws. It was the business of civilian lawmen. It also annoyed him that the order hadn't come from a commanding officer. It had come from some damned civilian judge.

The cook went to reach inside the chuck wagon and face around, holding a Winchester saddle gun. He didn't say a word, but he cocked the carbine.

The captain raised his rein hand, but he wasn't being routed. He said — "You son-of-a-bitch." — and rode back where he growled an order.

The rangemen listened until the sound of horsemen faded completely, then the cook carelessly tossed the carbine back inside the wagon, and turned. "Grat Dalton, for Christ's sake? I thought you boys stayed over in the Missouri country."

The tall man named Canby spoke before Tyler could. "Someone stole that gun from the old man down in Pueblo Juárez. He said he figured it was a damned freighter. Mister Dalton . . . ?"

"I told you, I bought the gun near Soda Springs."

This matter of ownership of the Mars gun wasn't what kept the other rangemen silent. One of them eventually said: "Grat Dalton? I seen Jesse 'n' his brother once over in Kansas."

The cook scratched inside his beard and leaned on the tailgate of the wagon. He blew out a noisy breath and moved closer to the fire, holding out both hands and not looking at anyone as he said: "Mister, I'll make up a bundle for you, but you better ride all night because sure as hell's hot that son-of-a-bitchin' Yankee'll be back."

Tyler thanked them and went to rig out and ride into the night. A couple of miles along he fervently told the horse he would never again as long as he lived scare the pee out of an irritating female by using a name to do it. The horse was reasonably rested and willing. Its rider was not willing. It was dark with no moon. He had no landmarks, but he needed none. He had a traveling man's instincts.

By first light he saw farms, stippled fields, yards with houses in them, and fences. He had been avoiding places where people put up fences all his life and was tempted to swing northward. It didn't take more than a moment of re-

137

flection to know that riding north would be the worst possible direction. By now, there would be posses and soldier patrols like ants, scouring for miles, so he paralleled the fences, riding south. To get farther from that settled, civilized country, he also angled to the west.

Eventually he saw two mounted men in a circular corral, trying to head and heel a savvy old cow who knew exactly when a lariat was flung and either put her head on the ground or stopped stone still. The buildings were made of adobe. The corral was woven brush. The ropers were lithe and horse-handy. When he entered the yard, the ropers watched him tie up, left their mounts in the corral, and crossed the yard. One of them was lighter than the other one. He called out: "Welcome. It's time to eat."

The shorter, stockier man did not speak, but he smiled broadly.

There were outbuildings, and the main house had a roofed-over porch of rough lumber. Two women were standing over there, one older than the other. The younger one called that a meal was prepared.

The riders did not ask Tyler his name. They asked no questions at all. When they were inside where the aroma of spiced cooking made Tyler's stomach think his throat had been cut, the younger woman smiled and introduced herself. "Esmeralda Leary."

Tyler removed his hat. "Tyler Heinz."

The older woman herded them like geese toward the kitchen without speaking. She had dark, expressive eyes like the shorter and darker of the two men.

Tyler was starved. The old woman kept platters and pans full. Once she and the quiet, shorter man exchanged glances.

When the men returned to the corral, it was empty except for the horses. The fairer of the two men swore in

138

Spanish but spoke in English. "Again. Twice now she's jumped the fence."

Like all corrals built by real stockmen, the woven brush-work of the corral was close to six feet in height. The dark, silent man laughed. It was an odd sound. His brother didn't laugh. He cursed. Tyler wagged his head. From what he had seen of the old cow, she was mostly red-back or Durham. Her horns were negligible, and she was slab-sided. He hadn't seen her legs. She was one-third razorback out of *Tejas*. Longhorns would fight a buzz saw, and they could clear a six-foot fence.

They saddled up to find her, herd her back, and that was a circus, too. They found the old girl standing in tree shade. She had seen them first. Her head was high. Her body was stiff and poised. The other cattle didn't flee, but they discreetly sidled. Not the old cow.

The taller and fairer man said: "Frank, go far out an' around. Come up behind her." As the squatty dark man rode off, his brother said to Tyler: "He can't talk. Neither can our mother. Only my sister an' me can talk."

Tyler looked after the distant, dark man. He had never before encountered a person who could not talk. He asked no questions, sat his saddle, watching and waiting.

Frank was *coyote*. He kept the thick tree trunk between himself and the cow so that, while she warily watched the stationary riders, Frank got close enough. The old girl whirled, tail high. It was too late. Frank rode at a dead walk straight toward her. She flung her head, whirled, and ran. Tyler and his companion didn't move. She went past them with her tail in the air like a scorpion. They got on both sides of her and loped without pushing the cow so it wouldn't panic and run blind.

Getting the old girl into the corral was another matter.

139

She had been in there before. She veered hard left. The fair man went at her. His mount's shoulder hit the cow's shoulder. She stumbled badly, righted herself, and ran easterly. Tyler allowed her to get within fifteen or so feet, then put his mount straight at her. Collision was unavoidable. The old girl swung wildly and ran through the open gate.

The fairer man laughed, swung off, closed and chained the gate as Tyler rode up, and said: "If there was another one or two in with her . . . but we don't have no other cattle."

Tyler led his horse inside, off-saddled, stalled the horse, and searched for the three-tined fork and some hay.

The fair man came up and pushed out a hand. He was smiling. Tyler gripped it. "Tyler Heinz."

Tyler released the other man's hand and waited until the man said: "Reynaldo Leary."

They drank at the trough with the old cow at the far end of the corral, head up, watching. Frank appeared out of nowhere with an earthen jug. He was sweaty and smiling as he handed the jug to Tyler.

As Tyler handed back the jug, he said: "Good . . . thanks."

The fairer man shook his head. "In Spanish. He can tell when you talk but only in Spanish."

"Bueno, gracias."

Tyler never did find out why they were so fixed on the idea of corralling that old cow. They took him to the porch with its planed-wood overhang, not only a rarity the farther southwest he would go, but also expensive.

Esmeralda came out and flirted very noticeably with Tyler. Reynaldo growled, and she went back inside. Tyler relaxed. Frank pointed to Tyler's holstered six-gun and held out his hand.

Tyler handed over the gun as he told Frank in Spanish not to cock it. Frank nodded, rose, and went inside with the gun. Tyler looked inquiringly at the fair man, who said: "He will bring it back. It takes time. But Frank has a talent in his hands that God must have given him to make up for Frank not talking."

Tyler sighed, drank red wine, relaxed, and watched the day end. Shortly before the handsome girl came to announce supper was ready, Reynaldo asked a question. "Would you stay for wages and keep?"

Tyler smiled. "Three of us to watch one cow? I can't stay, but I'd like to. Maybe someday. . . ."

"*Seguro*. Someday."

After supper they returned to the verandah. Tyler was beginning to worry about the Mars gun. He was ready to say something to Reynaldo when Frank appeared, handed Tyler the gun, and stood waiting. Reynaldo leaned. "I told you he was given a gift."

Tyler had difficulty believing his eyes. The worn, hard rubber grips were gone. In their place were two wooden grips which fit perfectly and each was carved in an exquisite flower design. He looked up, and Frank smiled self-consciously. Reynaldo said: "He does it with a sharpened nail and his pocket knife."

Tyler stood up to reach in a pocket. Frank's big smile blinked out.

Again Reynaldo spoke. "Don't offer money. It upsets him."

Tyler remained standing. He shoved out a big hand. Frank gripped it briefly and released it. He looked at his brother, who spoke again. "He can hear better than I can. He just can't talk."

"He worked hours to do this?"

141

Reynaldo and Frank exchanged a long look before Frank nodded, and Reynaldo explained. "He . . . him an' God talk while he is carving. That's the only time."

Tyler fidgeted. "Can he write or read?"

"No. Neither can my mother."

Tyler faced the mute. "Frank, in all my life I've never seen such beautiful carving."

Reynaldo smiled softly. "Shake his hand again and only say *gracias*."

Tyler did both. Frank disengaged his hand, smiled into Tyler's eyes, then disappeared inside the house.

Tyler sat back down. Reynaldo offered the jug, and they both drank before Tyler spoke again. "I think I'd be off God for life."

Reynaldo relaxed in his chair and replied softly. "Do you know God?"

"What a hell of a question. No."

"They do, Francisco and my mother. Frank made them a carving of the Virgin. It is so beautiful in its hole in the wall that my mother cries every time she prays. Friend, *they know God*."

"And you?"

"No, but they talk to Him and He talks to them."

Tyler lifted out the gun. The day was ending, so he had to hold it up as he studied the carving. When he returned it to its holster, he said — "Beautiful." — and stood up. "I have to go."

Reynaldo accompanied Tyler to the barn, watched as the rigging out was done, and remained in place as he watched the big man ride off into the dusk.

Esmeralda materialized, also watched and sighed. Reynaldo turned. "Only outlaws ride at night," he said.

His sister leaned against an old, upright log, gazing

into the settling night where she could only see across the yard, and sighed again. Maybe only outlaws ride at night, but they shouldn't have to ride alone.

Chapter Thirteen

LINCOLNBURG

Tyler Heinz didn't go far. He and his animal slept in a grassy sump, but the following day they didn't stop even for water until past sundown. There were possemen scouring the countryside, different bands of them. Tyler saw them several times. Each band had a sign reader out front. Whoever they were looking for must have done something terrible for a small army to be hunting him — or them.

Tyler was returning to the kind of country he was fond of — the vast, inhospitable, poorly watered, and deadly country of caliche, wind, and blast-furnace summers. This particular summer was fading, and, while the days remained hot, the evenings turned cool, and a few hours before sunrise it was downright cold.

He watched a priest astride a big Missouri mule, riding blithely through the heat and dust of a north-south coach road and speculated why anyone in their right mind rode during the hottest time of the day, wearing a thick and heavy black robe from the neck to the ankles. He knew of *penitentes* who during their rituals carried a cross in rocky country, beating themselves and their companions on the back with chains. But this priest was not an Indian, or a Mexican, either. Tyler rode anglingly to make an interception where a stand of spindly paloverdes grew. The holy man saw him coming and halted. Where they met was not far from an ancient, roofless adobe house, long abandoned for whatever reason.

The priest called a greeting in accentless English. "Ride with me, brother," he said, smiling widely.

Tyler smiled, too.

As they went southward, the priest on Tyler's right side said: "I never saw such a beautiful gun."

Tyler told him the story of the carved grips.

The priest nodded sagaciously. "He works wonders. You never know where to expect them. My name is Father Hogan." The priest laughed. "Among the Navajos hogan means a house."

Tyler rode with the easy and comfortable judgment he had made. This priest was a friendly, likable man. He hadn't known many, but those he'd encountered seemed rarely to smile, to wear the mantle of humility, and to give of themselves even to animals. This one appeared to be different.

The priest said: "Do you know where the Mission of Carmel is?"

Tyler didn't. He wasn't familiar with the country they were riding through.

Father Hogan knew. "Two days ride, east of Lincolnburg." The priest mopped off sweat while speaking again. "On the outskirts of a town called Franklin. I know a good place where there is water and grass. We could reach Franklin tomorrow."

In the Southwest it was reasonable to assume a traveling holy man had a purpose. Tyler was satisfied with that.

When eventually they came to a stingy place of green grass in an otherwise drying, tan countryside, the priest reined in that direction. While riding, he explained: "I came onto this place years ago. Each time I'm down here, I spend the night. There's a trickle of water from some

145

rocks." Father Hogan smiled indulgently. "The only water hole for miles, so naturally animals of all kinds and sizes come here to drink."

Where Tyler hobbled his horse, there was ankle-high *alfilerera* with dark leaves and tiny lavender flowers. There was no finer horse feed. Because "filaree," as *gringos* called it, grew close to the ground, cattle with only one set of teeth looked for something that grew taller, but horses did well on it.

The priest's big mule with the sad, solemn expression of mules generally, scarcely heeded Tyler's horse. The priest emptied a saddlebag with the letters U S stamped on the flap. Tyler raised his eyes slowly, and the holy man shrugged. "It is the will of God that those who serve Him do so with vigor. To do that, my friend, His servants must eat well."

They ate well — cold beef roast, oranges, lettuce, and red wine.

Father Hogan didn't speak while eating. It intrigued Tyler Heinz that the priest produced a thin, double-bladed knife to slice food with and filled his face without a prayer before eating.

As daylight waned, they made a tiny, fat-wood fire. The priest produced a cigar, lighted up, and smacked his lips before saying: "These are the things which make life worth living, no?"

Tyler agreed after lighting his *cigarillo* and trickling smoke with his words. "A man don't need much . . . just enough, Father."

The stocky priest jerked the hem of his robe before a large beetle, armored and horned, reached the hem. The bug altered course and went lumbering out into the darkness. Father Hogan shifted the cigar from one side of his

146

mouth to the other. "You are a rangeman?" he asked.

"A livestock buyer, Father. Mostly cattle."

"And you drive them?"

"To the nearest railroad pens where buyers are like *zopilotes* waiting to cheat every way they can."

Father Hogan tilted his head, briefly considered the pin pricks of light high overhead, lowered it, and said: "I knew a man long ago who made a living stealing cattle and horses." He stopped to cross himself swiftly.

Tyler smiled. "He didn't live long, Father?"

"Well, he was in his fifties. There are easier ways to serve the Lord. They hanged him from a sour-apple tree."

Some coyotes padded into the firelight and faded. They did this several times. Tyler said: "Thirsty nuisances."

"God's creatures, friend," the priest said, and changed the subject. "Why do you suppose the posse riders were scouring the countryside?"

Tyler had no idea. "If they find the one they're looking for . . . I'd guess he did something real bad to get that many manhunters tryin' to get him."

The priest tipped ash into the dying, small fire when he spoke again. "They're everywhere, horse thieves, cattle rustlers, highwaymen. This part of the country offers little else in ways of making a living."

One of the coyotes made a mistake. As the pack withdrew, it went over to tease the mule. The large animal didn't even switch its tail in annoyance. It kicked. The coyote landed hard and ran. His companions yelped, and Father Hogan smiled.

"Traveler don't like coyotes."

Tyler said: "Traveler?"

"My mule. I named him after Robert E. Lee's horse. He's smarter than a horse . . . rough riding, but I've never

147

known a mule that wasn't . . . Mister Heinz, would you sell that gun?"

"Father, you wouldn't want it. It's different from other Colts."

"Doesn't it shoot straight?"

"Something like that, Father."

When the little fire was winking coals, they bedded down. Above was an array of tiny lights in all directions with no moon to help brighten the dark hours.

Tyler slept like a dead man. Twice lately he'd been fed so well he could sleep deeply — so deeply, in fact, that, while he may have heard sounds in the night, his brain recorded nothing.

Tyler opened his eyes slowly and not fully. The sun was high, immense, and too bright. He rolled onto one side, propped his head, and didn't move for about ten seconds.

The priest was gone as was his bedroll. The big mule was also gone.

Tyler shoved back the blanket and froze. Something else was missing — his trousers, shirt, hat, and the foul-weather jacket he had kept rolled and tied behind his cantle. The saddle, blanket, and bridle were where he'd put them the night before, but the coiled shell belt with the holstered six-gun on top were also gone.

He stood up, found his boots, and was stamping into them when horsemen came without haste from the direction of the road. They were unsmiling, heavily armed men. The foremost large man with the star on his vest had a drooping, dragoon mustache.

Tyler didn't move as the possemen stopped at the edge of the little grassy place, sat like statues without speaking, and gravely considered him. Still without speaking, one horseman raised an arm to point, and Tyler instinctively turned his head. There was a discarded soiled cassock near a thornpin bush.

Finally the mustachioed large man spoke. "Where's your gun?"

Tyler answered in the same curt manner. "It's gone, along with my britches, shirt, an' whatever else the son-of-a-bitch took. That's his robe yonder." Tyler considered the cassock. "A priest for God's sake."

The possemen dismounted. Two went where the animals had been. One of them hunkered, minutely studying the mule sign. He called to the lawman and pointed as he stood up. "Macky's mule."

The lawman returned to face Tyler. He asked Tyler's name, his occupation, and if anyone in the area knew him.

Tyler shook his head about the last question and explained. "I was ridin' through, met the priest, an' we bedded down here. It's new territory to me."

A tousled-headed tall man made a grating laugh, ignoring Tyler to address the man wearing the badge. "What they said up yonder was the truth." He paused long enough to look around at his companions. "Who'n hell would ever figure he'd be a priest?"

The lawman detailed a wiry, faded-looking individual to pick up the sign, and the wiry man reined his horse toward the place the hobbled animals had grazed, picked up the tracks, began following them, and did not once look back.

The lawman thumbed back his hat while regarding Tyler. "He's shorter'n you and thicker. Right?"

"Yes."

The mustachioed man looked Tyler up and down. "It's goin' to be embarrassin', you ridin' into town in your underdrawers."

Tyler asked what town, and the lawman told him to go saddle up as he also said: "Lincolnburg. We'll bunch up around you as best we can."

The lawman was not unpleasant, but neither was he right neighborly. He'd been in the saddle since the afternoon of the previous day.

His possemen were for the most part silent. The posseman carrying the abandoned priest's robe told Tyler the outlaw's name was Dan Macky. He shot three people for no reason during the robbing of the bank at Lincolnburg, and one of them had been a blind woman who was related to about half the local inhabitants.

Tyler asked for details. The posseman gave them to him. He was the blind woman's son. Her name had been Annie Dunn; the mustachioed large man was Michael Dunn. The woman had been blind for thirty-five years. It came on slowly until she had to use a stick to get around. She was tapping her way into the bank when she got shot. The posseman neither cursed, nor made threats, or raised his voice as he and the others, siding Tyler, rode together in a southerly direction.

Lincolnburg had exactly one reason for thriving, for existing — the railroad tracks came within a dozen yards of the town, and the twin rails shone like new silver. The town itself wasn't much. No one seemingly had ever done anything to make Lincolnburg attractive.

True to his word the lawman positioned his riders in a protective circle around Tyler, opened their ranks only at the plank walk in front of the general store where the sheriff growled for Tyler to get down and make a run for it, which he did. It wouldn't have had repercussions if, when he ran inside, the storekeeper and three matronly women weren't bartering at the goods counter.

150

His appearance in boots and underdrawers startled hell out of the storekeeper as his equally startled, and horrified, customers fled, one of the women shrieking.

Tyler went back, closed the door, and told the storekeeper he needed a shirt and a pair of britches.

The storekeeper was a rotund man in his fifties with a fringe of hair on both sides and an expanse of pink skin above. He got red as a beet as he moved toward a different counter and spoke sharply. "What'n hell's wrong with you, comin' in here in your underpants? I'll get the sheriff. He'll. . . ."

"Get the god-damned pants and shirt, an' it was the sheriff told me to come in here."

The angry storekeeper rummaged among boxes, found what he sought, and threw them atop the counter without facing around. Tyler got into the britches, then the butternut shirt. As he was buttoning up, the irate merchant said: "That'll be one dollar and thirty-five cents."

Tyler finished making himself respectable and told the pink-headed man he had no money, that he'd been robbed right down to his boots, and the storekeeper loosened slightly. He was about to speak when the big mustachioed lawman walked in. He considered Tyler and ignored the storekeeper. He said: "That's better. Enough folks saw you to feed the gossip mill for what's left of the year." The lawman jerked his head. "Come over to the jailhouse with me."

The storekeeper started to speak, and the lawman turned on him. "You'll get paid, you penny pinchin' son-of-a-bitch."

Halfway across the road Tyler said: "The storekeeper a friend of yours?"

The lawman turned his head. "No!" he said, and added nothing more.

151

Lincolnburg's jailhouse was large and commodious. There were five strap-steel cells. Sheriff Dunn motioned indifferently toward a bench. There were also several chairs. Tyler used one of them.

The sheriff wasted no time. "Tell me everythin'," he said, "while you 'n' him was together. Everything!"

Tyler recounted everything from his first encounter to the moment when he awakened to discover the priest had swapped clothing with him, had helped himself to everything he wanted, and had departed.

Dunn looked skeptical. "You a hard sleeper, Mister Heinz?"

"I was last night. I didn't hear a thing. Somethin' I don't understand, Sheriff. If I'd been in his boots, I'd have got away from here as far an' as fast as I could. He. . . ."

"He tried, Mister Heinz, but we got a telegraph. They dang' near cornered him up north before he got inside a mission, tied up the fellers, an' took that robe he was wearin'."

"Your tracker come back yet?"

Sheriff Dunn shook his head. "If he don't turn east or west, Mister Heinz, he'll make it over the border, an' most likely we'll never see him again."

Tyler considered the starch-stiff new shirt and pants. "I don't have two *centavos* to rub together, Sheriff. That deceivin' bastard took it all."

The unsmiling lawman wagged his head. "That storekeeper will get paid . . . that highway-robbin' bastard. Your horse is at the livery. It's over one street an' north. I told the liveryman you got robbed right down to your drawers. He said there wouldn't be no charge." The sheriff changed the subject. "I'd give five years' wages to get my hands on that measly son-of-a-bitch."

Tyler rose. Because he hadn't eaten since the night before, he said he hoped the caféman was an understanding individual, and the sheriff nodded. "He is. Him 'n' me are cousins." The lawman paused and looked up before also saying: "Dan Macky's also my cousin."

Tyler went in search of the café. It was at the extreme southward end of Lincolnburg. It was down there for a very good reason. Hungry trainmen could read the sign on the window from almost rifle range.

The proprietor came close to being a spitting image of the sheriff, except that he seemed to have an aversion to razors and had small, piggy, brown eyes. He knew who Tyler was. Everyone in Lincolnburg knew almost as much about Tyler Heinz as Tyler did. At the saloon they laughed. To anyone's recollection no victim of a highwayman had ever before arrived in town in his underdrawers.

The part no one laughed about was the relationship between the sheriff and the notorious local outlaw, Dan Macky. Those who knew had divergent opinions about what would happen when the sheriff met his cousin face to face. Tyler knew nothing of this. If he had, he would have willingly bet every penny he could beg, borrow, or steal that the man who was able to walk away wouldn't be the sheriff.

The caféman fed him, good-naturedly accepted his promise to pay, and watched Tyler walk northward on the opposite side of the road from the jailhouse.

At the saloon the barman offered a drink on the house, which Tyler accepted, and, after he'd downed that one, a leathery, old, pinch-eyed cowman bought the second drink.

Tyler repeated his story almost word for word to what he'd told the sheriff, and the squinty-eyed, thin cowman nodded to the barman and, as their glasses were being replenished, he said: "Dan Macky rode for me for three years. He was a tolerable rider, never rode out far enough to find tree shade an' sleep until close to supper time. He was a good horse-shoer." Several other regulars solemnly nodded without speaking. The cowman added a little more. "Damned shame what happened when he shot his aunt, the old blind lady, but I can tell you for a fact, an' I was there, he hit her only because he never could shoot worth a damn."

The barman put in his two-bits' worth. "Folks liked Danny. Him 'n' my boys used to bed down in the horse shed behind my house an' scare the whey out of each other tellin' ghost stories. He grew up. . . ."

Tyler interrupted. "He was an outlaw. From what I've heard. . . ."

"Mister," the old cowman interrupted to say, "ain't a man in this town hasn't done foolish things. I know for a fact three robbed stages an' one spent two years in prison for takin' mail sacks." The grizzled rancher then changed the course of what he had to say. "I can tell you, mister, shootin' his aunt will haunt Danny the rest of his life."

It was a shrewd observation by someone who knew Dan Macky. In fact, Macky's first stop after robbing the live-stock buyer was at the ugly, little, mud house of the priest over in Franklin, sixty miles almost due west from Lincolnburg.

Dan Macky and Father Silva had been friends since the holy man had arrived on the southwestern desert. It was Macky who explained to the newcomer priest the idiosyncrasies of not only the people who inhabited the Southwest, but also the country itself which could not in any way be compared to Cincinnati where the holy man had done God's work for eighteen years before being peremptorily sent to administer more than a hundred miles in three di-

154

rections of what early explorers in casques and carrying lances had said was purgatory.

The good father was slightly shorter than his friend, the outlaw. He was also not as heavy and was thirteen years older.

They sat in the high-domed, cool, old Carmel mission church with red wine as they talked. For Dan Macky, against whom the entire countryside was up in arms, the only recourse was to slip over the border, but, while he could not be pursued by *norteamericano* soldiers, he could be pursued by civilians, townsmen, stockmen, transients such as freighters, and lawmen — one lawman, in particular.

When the holy man suggested fleeing northward, Dan Macky shook his head. There were posse riders as thick as the hair on a dog's back. They were combing the country, and by now they would know about his ruse in a churchman's robe, and his robbery of the tall stranger he had plundered in the wee hours.

The priest threw up his hands. "Where then?" he asked.

Dan Macky answered without hesitation: "Here, Father."

"Here, in the mission?"

"Yes. If they come here, they wouldn't search. . . ."

"Dan, have you any idea what you're asking? I am a priest."

155

Chapter Fourteen

STAYING TO THE SECRET COUNTRY

"Sanctuary, Father."

For a moment the priest gazed at his friend in silence. It was his fault that during the course of their lengthy conversations he had mentioned the church policy of providing refuge. He had said it was called sanctuary.

He almost smiled in a bitter way. Words, he had been taught in three languages, were the Mother Church's shield and buckler. Words — and incense and solemn, resplendent ritual — were the blocks piled one upon the other that bound the millions to the sacredness of Christ's living personification. Words, he told himself, were symbolically a two-edged sword. Without speaking, he arose and led the way to a part of the old mission which hadn't been used in almost a century. For that long there had been no reason for anyone to go there, and for that long they hadn't.

There were rats who made scuttling sounds as Father Silva lighted a candle. There was also the mustiness that went with long abandonment, and the massive, narrow, and very heavy oaken door which hadn't yielded to pressure in generations and required the weight of both men to yield now.

The priest placed the candle on a small table, handmade with all the imperfections of its kind, and, while there was light, it scarcely reached into corners although the room was small. No more than fourteen feet square without a window for an excellent reason — the room was below ground level.

Dan Macky said nothing. In his profession hardship and inconvenience were enduring companions. As he sat on the edge of the crudely made cot, the priest said — "They won't find you." — and left after promising to bring food later. But he was wrong. The number of people who rode mules in a horseman's territory were less than minimal, and mule tracks were narrower than horse tracks.

The possemen from Lincolnburg didn't ride into Franklin, did not enter the village. There appeared to be no need. The mule tracks led to the mission, not the town.

Father Silva was at prayer before the magnificently carved altar below the equally stunning life-size Christ whose expression of anguish had been perfectly carved by the same Indian who had carved the altar. He was long dead, but the effigy's wounded side still showed bright blood, something perpetuated by the faithful.

Father Silva prayed less for forgiveness than he explained in prayer why he had given sanctuary to a thief and, so it was said, a murderer. The knuckles holding his rosary were white. His muttered explanation carried no distance in the high-domed, large room, but the sound of spurs carried. Father Silva arose to face around with a pounding heart. There were five of them. He recognized only one, the sheriff from Lincolnburg whose jurisdiction included Franklin and beyond.

Only one of the men accompanying the sheriff removed his hat, and he, like the others, stood in the doorway as still and silent as stone.

Father Silva made a brief obeisance, then walked along the eastern wall to face the bitter-faced man wearing a badge. He didn't smile, but inclined his head as he said: "Sheriff . . . ?"

157

Sheriff Michael Dunn did not attend church nor was he a particularly religious man, but as with others like him he would have preferred meeting the priest anywhere but inside the very old mission with its air of sanctity and timelessness. When he spoke, there was none of the customary gruffness. He told the priest he had followed mule sign to the mission, and let the words hang.

Father Silva would have died by his own hand before prevaricating on holy ground, so he herded the possemen from the building to a shady place overlooking the not always erect grave markers, whose inscriptions were scarcely readable except for those interred less than half a century ago. It was cool, and there were benches, but no one sat as the holy man faced Sheriff Dunn and began a long harangue which the lawman cut short curtly when he said: "Father, them mule tracks was fresh."

The priest was sweating. "There are many mules," he said.

The lawman rebutted him. "We followed the tracks, Father. They come here an' didn't go no farther."

Father Silva sat down in tree shade, looking up. Michael Dunn was an intimidating individual even when he was less motivated than he now was. The priest made a slight gesture before speaking. "And you think he is here?"

"I know you 'n' him been friends since you come here, an' the tracks led here."

Again the priest made his little gesture. "Do you want to search the mission? Is that it?"

The posseman who had removed his hat inside considered the grave markers. He was uncomfortable.

Sheriff Dunn barely inclined his head. "We got to be satisfied, Father."

Again the little gesture. "Search, Sheriff."

"I expect we will, but first tell me . . . have you seen Dan Macky lately?"

Father Silva sidestepped the direct answer the lawman wanted by arising from the bench and saying — "Search." — and would have walked away, but the sheriff stopped him.

"You can help us, Father."

The priest looked stonily at Michael Dunn and shook his head. When Dunn did not speak, the holy man walked away.

The mission of Carmel had been founded by Spain's zealous holy men who had corralled indigenous people, taught them to make adobe bricks, how to make rammed-earth walls and partitions, how to pray and make obeisance, which they did with correct humility, looking straight at the Christ carving and no higher. Like all missions, Carmel had been a busy center of civilization. There had been a tannery, a leather-working concern, a smithy, ovens for baking, a shoe shop for making shoes and boots, a series of places for females to learn, too.

When His Excellency, president, dictator, uncrowned emperor of Mexico, Antonio Lopez de Santa Anna y Lebron had secularized the missions, Carmel with the others had languished, its priests recalled, its herds gone wild. Ultimately nothing was left but its holy servitors, and in the borderland of the Southwest these became the elderly men who, for whatever reason, were sent to such places as the mission at Carmel. These holy men were to serve their communities and to keep the faith strong, while they were banished from usually metropolitan areas where a lack of magnetism made them incapable of increasing congregations.

Father Silva had been at the mission for six years. He

had explored its many nooks and tiny rooms. He thought he knew the mission. He was confident the possemen from Lincolnburg would not find the forgotten recesses, the below-ground grottos. So, instead of fretting or seeking divine intercession, he went to his two-room living area and sat down to complete his lengthy biannual report to the diocese, something he did in the form of a diary. This particular day he gazed at the paper, dark eyes troubled, and did not put down the Dan Macky matter.

He heard them rummaging and calling back and forth. When he could not hear them, he sat perfectly erect. They would be searching the cellar with its ancient wine pit and other things. For the second time since Father Silva had been at the mission men were exploring the cellar area, twice in the same day!

Someone approaching from the domed, long hall leading to his rooms was wearing spurs. Father Silva arose to stand, facing the door. There was no knocking. The door was flung inward, and Sheriff Dunn entered the room, kicked a small bench around, and sat down, looking steadily and stonily at the priest.

"Father, the son-of-a-bitch was here. I know that for a fact!"

Father Silva exhaled silently and sat at the small desk, closed the ledger, and said: "Let me say something to you. Do you suppose he left mule tracks to the mission to delay you?"

"Delay me?"

"Until he slipped into town, stole a horse, and ran away?"

Sheriff Dunn sat in stony silence for a long moment, then got to his feet. He left the room without speaking, and Father Silva went to the nearest window to watch the possemen ride in the direction of the town.

He returned to the desk, sat, and groped below for the crudely made earthenware jug which held red wine. He allowed the day to die, watched for a body of horsemen to leave Franklin, and, when he saw them riding back the way they had come, he allowed an hour to pass before descending to the area of the wine cellar and the little cells.

Dan Macky was gone.

He used a candle to search, found no trace, and went outside to do additional exploring. The hint of a sickle moon was rising before he abandoned the search, sat on a wall bench out back where grave markers were limned by what puny light shone from above, and for the first time since early in the day relaxed.

What a frustrated and bitter-eyed lawman hadn't found was either Macky's mule nor anyone in Franklin who had lost a riding animal, which meant, of course, that the renegade had escaped on his mule, and, since failing daylight precluded more tracking, the sheriff decided to return to Lincolnburg to his office and hope that, sooner or later, information would surface, and he could again take the trail.

Of one thing the lawman was certain. He could not expect the townsmen, and others he had dragooned to scour the countryside, to continue to do so. They had businesses, families, personal interests. The fact of a sixty-mile ride over and back in defeat would discourage them, as it also discouraged Michael Dunn. The exception was simply that they would give up, and he would not.

But it had been close, closer, in fact, than it had ever been before for Dan Macky. His escape hadn't been spectacular — he had simply waited until all the possemen were rummaging and searching upstairs and had fled from

161

the below-ground exit which had been a very old, worm-eaten, oaken door, had got his mule, and had ridden northward.

He continued to ride northward for two days, a route he reconnoitered carefully and was relieved to find that the mounted searchers were no longer searching. He had only a vague idea of the northward countryside, but what he did know was that, if he rode far enough, he would eventually arrive in country where no one had ever heard of Dan Macky. And he was right. No one ever had.

The sixth day he was following his routine of riding upland, sometimes sidehill country, a habit that had served him well since he'd stopped his first stage, but there were limits to the best strategies. After noon on the sixth day he was following a game trail high enough to be able to see clearly in three directions: south, north, and east. What prevented him from being able to see to the west was a jutting shoulder, or flank, of a massive out-thrust. It was timbered, rocky, and rugged. The mule picked his way which was the custom of his kind. There were no game trails, but, when Macky was at the easternmost bulge of the out-thrust, he saw a crooked set of ruts below which angled through timber around immense boulders, and passed from sight.

He continued northward until he reached the ruts, and about the same time he smelled smoke. Because the ruts had been made to avoid as much climbing as possible by angling on a gentle incline, Macky followed the ruts, with the smoke scent increasing. The ruts passed between two mammoth rocks. Beyond where they ended and a tendril of lazy smoke arose was a log house in a small clearing.

An old man, wearing red suspenders, a worn flannel shirt, trousers cut off above the ankle, and mucker's boots, was splitting kindling. The moment Macky came into view,

162

the old man's hand axe remained poised. Slowly he put it down, wiped his hands, and called: "Jigger!"

A second old man emerged from the cabin. He was holding a hexagonal-barreled rifle older than dirt.

Macky held his right hand aloft, palm forward. The hatchet man eased down on a fir round. The other old man did not move.

Macky dismounted as the hatchet man said: "Pardner, I ain't seen as good a-lookin' mule in thirty years. Is he broke to harness?"

Macky nodded. "Ride or drive."

He told the old men his name. They didn't reciprocate right then, but they showed him where to corral the mule and fork it feed, then they showed him their diggings. There were two shafts. One went straight down without a ladder; the second mine went into the side of the mountain behind the log house. Without a lamp or a candle a man couldn't see into either shaft. Macky asked if they made wages, and the hatchet man smiled. He had no teeth. He said: "We get by, friend. Come on inside an' we'll eat."

Macky followed the old man with the ancient rifle, who stepped aside for Macky to enter first, a mannerly thing to do, but Macky gestured for the rifleman to precede him, which he did.

Inside, the log house was everything needed for basic survival. Macky shed his hat and coat. The hatchet man sat sideways at a solid, homemade table, watching. When Macky dropped the coat, the old man brightened. "That's a real fine pistol, friend. I never seen grips carved like that before. Have you, Jigger?"

The rifleman turned from feeding fat wood into the stove's firebox, squinted, and wagged his head. "Never have, for a fact. You do that carvin'?"

Macky lied without a qualm. He was very good at it. "Done it a couple summers back with nothin' to do at a line shack."

Jigger dished food onto three plates, put them on the table, and gestured where Macky should sit. As they ate, Macky asked questions about the countryside roundabout and farther north.

The old miners had no difficulty answering. Where there were mountain ranges, they told Macky it was flat, livestock country. When he asked about cow outfits, they did the same thing. They mentioned several large ranches, called them by their brands, and whether they were truthful or not did not matter. What mattered was that the beefy, younger man believe them, and he evidently did.

They swapped stories after supper. The old men had no wine, but they had whiskey; not popskull but mellowed whiskey with hardly a taint of color to it. On a full stomach a man could drink a fair share, and Macky did. He didn't get drunk, but he loosened all over because the cabin was warm, and the whiskey helped. Jigger told him he and his partner made and sold whiskey when they ran into a dry spell. He also said their customers wouldn't touch any other whiskey — which, Jigger's partner added, was because they not only made the best whiskey, but they aged it until it looked like pure water. Almost like pure water.

Dan Macky had to go outside, not just to pee, but also to breathe in some chilly night air. Jigger and his partner remained at the table. After about ten minutes the hatchet man raised his eyebrows, and, when Jigger nodded, his partner left the house and paused long enough to pick up a slightly crooked oaken walking stick about as large around as a man's wrist.

164

Macky did not hear the old man. The only sound was when the crooked oak walking stick came down across the back of Macky's head.

Jigger came to the doorway, paused, then hiked ahead where his partner was leaning over the dead man. Jigger said: "You taken a fancy to the gun . . . keep it. Does he have a watch?"

"No, but, by God, I think we just got us a bank robber. Look at the money. He had it in his pockets. Go see what's in his saddlebags."

Jigger called from the shed. "I never seen so much money."

"Bring it over."

Jigger returned with the saddlebags flung over one shoulder. His partner had turned Macky's pockets inside out. He said: "Put the bags down, Jigger. Lend me a hand with Mister Mule Man."

They had a fair distance to drag the body. Where they stopped, with moonlight suddenly hidden by a passing cloud, was at the mouth of the first shaft the hatchet man had showed Macky.

As Jigger leaned, his partner said: "They're gettin' heavier."

When the body fell into the hole, the old men cocked their heads for the thud when it landed. It was quite a while before they heard it.

As they walked toward the cabin, the hatchet man said: "We got to fill that shaft, Jigger. Come real hot weather. . . ."

"I know. We got plenty of time. How many's that make, Ansel?"

"Six, countin' this one. Looka here, did you ever see such a pistol?"

Jigger took it, held it up, squinted, and said: "Maker's name's on the butt plate."

"Is it? I didn't see it. Gimme the gun."

"Hold it up so's starlight shines on it. You see what's wrote there?"

"G. Mars."

Chapter Fifteen

JIGGER, ANSEL, AND BEYOND

Jigger's concern was the saddlebags. He got an extra candle and lighted it before upending the saddlebags. For a long moment Ansel forgot the gun in his hand. "Jeee-zuz Christ," he whispered, and in a stronger voice asked a question. "Macky? I never heard that name before, did you?"

"No. The son-of-a-bitch was either a bank messenger or a bank robber."

Ansel put the gun aside as both old men began counting. Because they were limited in arithmetic, they made separate stacks for each fifty dollars. When they had finished, they sat back solemnly.

Eventually Jigger went after two cups of coffee. As he sat down and pushed one of the cups toward his partner, he said: "Well . . . in case he was follered, we'd best get our gatherings together and go a long way . . . as far as we can get from here. You know how much money is in them piles?"

"Three thousand dollars."

Jigger pushed the tin cup aside, lodged both elbows on the table, and slumped for a long time. Ansel went over to feed a scantling into the firebox. When he returned, he said: "Split two ways, we could live right well."

"You ever been to San Francisco?"

"No, an' neither have you."

167

"But I've heard about it. Wide open, lots of folks, an' lots of money."

Jigger dug out a small pipe, filled it, and lighted it from one of the candles. Ansel got their jug of white lightning. It was late. Outside the night was cold.

Jigger removed the pipe to speak. "I know a real pretty little town in Missouri."

Ansel put the jug down. "I know. I've heard about it for ten years . . . an' she's dead by now."

Jigger put an impersonal gaze upon his partner. "She likely is. Ansel . . . some decent place where there's a little house, plenty of winter wood, maybe a creek, with a medical man for your itchin' legs an' my sore back."

Ansel was fondling the Mars gun. As though he hadn't heard a word, he held the gun to sight down the barrel. "Bank robber, sure as hell," he said and passed the six-gun to his partner.

Jigger turned it over twice as he said: "I wonder who G. Mars is? He didn't make it. It's a Colt."

Ansel shrugged. "Maybe he's some cowboy. Maybe a storekeeper or a freighter."

Jigger shook his head. "No, sir. I'll tell you what I think. He was someone who lived with this thing. I think Mister Macky was a liar. Look at that carving." Jigger turned the gun toward his partner, and the explosion rattled cups and a dipper fell from a wall peg.

Ansel hadn't time to register astonishment. The front of his shirt blossomed red. He went off the bench like a man who'd been kicked by a mule.

Jigger didn't move for five seconds. He looked at the gun. His finger had naturally been inside the trigger guard, but he hadn't cocked the gun. It was on safety.

He put it down very carefully, leaned to peer over the

table, and settled back slowly. There was blood everywhere, and Ansel's face was turning grayer by the minute.

Jigger made two attempts to stand up before he succeeded. Outside, stars shone in an endless, twinkling array. A mule brayed. Jigger walked stiffly to the corral, pitched another flake of hay, and leaned on the topmost peeled pole, watching the big mule eat.

He didn't feel the cold until he went back inside where it was warm. He did not look at Ansel. He leaned on the table to pick up the six-gun. He squeezed the trigger and nothing happened. He curled his thumb to cock it, and the hammer would only come back about half or three-quarters of an inch. He went to the doorway and squeezed the trigger again. The muzzle blast spat red for a second. The sound was less loud than it had been inside.

He went back to the table, moved both candles closer, sat down, and methodically shucked out the two casings along with the four loads. He then tried to cock the gun a second time. It would only go to half cock, which was on safety. When he squeezed the trigger, the barely risen hammer came down so hard it jerked Jigger's hand.

He put the gun amid the stacks of greenbacks, looking at it. "A god-damned killer gun. Macky was a gunman." Jigger slowly shook his head. "A gunfightin' outlaw on the run. He'd've killed us in our sleep."

Jigger had three swallows from the jug, then rose, looking down at his partner. As he leaned to get hold of Ansel's ankles, he said — "It was an accident, partner." — and dragged Ansel to the straight-down mine shaft and dumped him. This time he didn't listen for the thud.

There wasn't much blood where he had dragged his partner, but inside the cabin it looked like someone had been butchering sheep.

* * * * *

When dawn arrived, its sickly gray light brought more cold. Jigger had fed the stove three times. He had also put all the greenbacks back into the saddlebags, and he had taken three more long pulls on the jug. He had fallen asleep on a long bench near the stove.

When he awakened, the house was frigid. The sun was climbing, and his head hurt. He had trouble getting the stove fired up because his eyes watered, but between mopping at his face and trying to set fire to the kindling he succeeded in prolonging a chore he had once been able to complete in a third of the time it took now that he was alone in the house.

He went to the wash basin. The water was colder than a witch's teat, and the mule had its long face over a corral stringer, solemnly watching everything he did. He and Ansel had had a horse. The light wagon was parked beside the corral. The damned horse had got out one night, and they'd never found it.

Jigger went over to the corral. He and the mule looked steadily at each other before Jigger said: "I hope Macky wasn't lyin' about you bein' broke to harness."

The sun was almost overhead before Jigger had let out every leather tongue as well as the collar pad and the collar. The mule did not move. The test was when a man led a harnessed animal out of a corral. The tugs dragging at its heels, bumping its legs, would tell. Macky's big Missouri mule didn't make a bobble.

Jigger led him among the rocks, through the big trees, and around the clearing. As he did this, he debated whether to try the mule on the wagon first, or load the wagon, then try him.

He left the mule out front. It took more trips in and out

170

than he figured, but eventually the wagon was loaded. Jigger climbed to the seat and set the binders. Two big ears were twisted backwards. Jigger eased off the binder and talked up the mule. It leaned into the collar and followed the ruts, being careful of rocks like it had never done anything else in its life.

When they reached flat ground, Jigger stood up to look back. Smoke was curling around the opened door. It was black smoke, the kind that arose where grease had been spread.

When they reached the road, Jigger lined the mule out in the direction of Sundown, the village where he and Ansel had sold whiskey, pedaled gold dust, and bought supplies.

It was a beautiful day by now, clear and warming. Jigger sat relaxed. He and Ansel had partnered for fifteen hard-scrabble years. They'd built the log house eight years back, and they had made their still and dug in their shafts. Jigger would miss the association, the company, more than the man. He had rooftops in sight when he shrugged off the numbness. How that damned gun had gone off still baffled him even though he now knew why it had.

He had the pistol atop the saddlebags on the seat beside him and was entering Sundown from the south when he twisted to look back. Dark smoke was rising into the clean, pure air like a giant discolored rope. People were standing on both plank walks and in the middle of the road, looking to the southwest. There wasn't another blemish of any kind on the horizon.

Jigger had intended to buy supplies, but changed his mind, and drove through the village and out the north coach road. He would have had explaining to do, particularly about his partner. He had never before driven into Sundown without Ansel on the seat, too.

171

There was a side road that led on an angling course toward some distant forested highlands. He turned off. If he hadn't been bothered by troubling thoughts, he would have appreciated how well the mule went along. Jigger had the Macky saddle, bridle, and blanket under the tarp in back.

By sundown he was near enough to poke along the foothills, looking for water. It was dark before he found a creek. The mule had picked up the scent long before the man detected the sound.

Making camp didn't take long. First, he hobbled the mule. It did not object. Rassling up a meal was simple. He used dry fagots. They burned hot and fast. After he had eaten a shriveled turnip and meat fried until it curled on the edges, he brought forth the jug.

He didn't like the idea of going to sleep with the saddlebags on the wagon seat, so he took them among some trees, shinnied up one, and draped the saddlebags over a high limb. There was always the possibility that salt-starved varmints would pick up the scent and climb to the cache, but in Jigger's opinion that was less likely to happen this way than having the saddlebags on the ground.

He hunched around the tiny fire. He had no relatives. Ansel had had none, either. He knew the north country from his buffalo-hunting youth. He also knew the areas east and west for a considerable distance.

Just before falling asleep, he thought again of that tidy little village in Missouri.

When he awakened the sun was in his eyes, and the mule was faunching. Jigger sat up, rubbed his eyes, and barely opened them to minimize the new day's brilliance. There were birds among the nearby timber and several deer watching. This was their drinking place. Jigger took a tin of

172

rolled barley to the mule, emptied it in the grass, and went back to make breakfast. The deer were motionless. He grumblingly told them to be patient, he'd leave directly, and ate.

The deer vanished among the trees. Jigger didn't notice it as he brought the mule in to be backed between the shafts. The last thing he did was go to the cache tree, shinny up it, retrieve the saddlebags, and climb down. He got to the seat with the saddlebags at his feet, kicked off the binders, and talked up the mule.

He was back on the coach road and again heading into an area where the road tipped and lifted. He didn't have much of a load, but nevertheless he frequently stopped to blow the mule. The last time was near the topout with forest giants growing right down to the edge of the road on both sides. Here, unless the sun was directly overhead, it wouldn't touch down. Here, too, an old stone trough which leaked from several places had a foot-deep area of mud. The mule had to be thirsty, but balked. There were mud daubers by the dozens. Only one flying insect stung harder, a bob-tailed hornet.

Jigger set the brake, climbed down, got a blanket, and went forward, swinging it. The daubers fled. Jigger led the mule up to drink, which it did for a long time, and only finished tanking up as the mud daubers returned.

The top-out was level for several hundred yards, and there were signs where previous travelers had camped. There was also something else, a mound of rocks about four feet wide and six feet long. There was no headboard.

Jigger left the road, drove far enough back to be in shade, set the brakes, hobbled the mule, and rummaged for something to eat. He didn't hear or see a thing. If he had been looking, he would have noticed the mule's twisted head and pointing ears. It wouldn't have made a difference. The arrow struck Jigger about eight inches below the neck, dead center.

He didn't fall. He crumpled against the wagon and slid down, dead before he touched earth.

There were three of them, one broncho Indian and two white-eyes — unwashed, ragged, vicious-eyed men. The broncho Indian admired the big mule. His people would rather eat white dog and mule than cattle, horses, or wild game.

One of the white men was red-headed with a full, round face and a bull-like build. His companion was taller, not as heavy, with an introverted expression and strange-looking eyes. They found the gun and the saddle-bags and were unbuckling the pouches when the Indian whistled. The sound was unmistakable. A heavy rig was coming at a steady trot.

The man with strange eyes ran for the timber. His companion ran, too, but, being heavier, he was the last to reach forest gloom.

It was the northbound, midday coach with luggage on top and four passengers inside. The whip hauled down to a stop. The gun guard raised a Winchester to his lap, studied the dead man, the laden wagon, and spoke to the whip. "Keep goin'. Damned war whoops again. *Get goin'!*"

A passenger called upward — "Maybe he ain't dead!" — and the whip answered. "Mister, he's dead. That arrer went through his heart."

When the last sound died and the dust settled, the Indian came forward, looped a rope around the mule's neck, twisted it into a squaw bridle, removed the hobbles, left them in the grass, and sprang onto the mule's back. He rode back where the pair of white men were sitting on pine needles, looking dumbfounded with greenbacks all around them.

The Indian slid off, considered the scattered money, and said: "I'll take the mule."

His companions exchanged a quick look before the red-headed man said: "Done. The mule's yours." He then leaned to stuff greenbacks into the saddlebags. Once he and the taller man exchanged a wink.

When they were ready to go back among the forest giants where their animals were tethered, the red-headed man cast a final look at the wagon. Their original intention had been to waylay such an outfit and make off with food. They'd been living hard for more than a month.

The taller man said: "Mark, we can't take it all. Come along."

Only the Indian made a sashay back to the wagon. There was an old, hexagonal-barreled rifle. It would be too heavy. He leaned to grab the earthen jug, then wheeled, and went after his companions.

They decided to camp two miles to the west in a virgin clearing where the mule stuffed itself until it could hardly move. The mule did not know how to lie down in hobbles. He'd seen it done but had never mastered the trick of kneeling first, legs touching, then dropping down behind. For animals who knew how, going down was a lot easier than getting up. The Missouri mule didn't have to worry about that. In fact, he didn't have anything to worry about at the moment. He was as full as a tick.

The men made a fagot fire, the kind that gave off no smoke, ate heartily of tinned goods from the wagon, and passed the jug around. Even the wild-eyed man smiled.

His name was Ned Forrester. There was a very large reward for him. He had butchered a family of four — had tied them to chairs and had slit their throats. His bounty was three gold watches, five necklaces, and sixty dollars from a can hidden in a wall. In order to find the hidden money he had taken the shoes and stockings off one of the women and held a torch from the fireplace to her feet.

After the description on the wanted dodger, it said: **Escapee From The Wyoming Prison For The Insane. Very Dangerous**. The reward was six hundred dollars, more bounty than had been offered for any other fugitive.

The red-headed man's name was Charley Young. His hair grew within four inches of his eyebrows. He was good with weapons. There were dodgers out on him under different names, but the description was the same each time. He was a coach robber who shot gun guards, whips, and outraged passengers out of hand.

Charley and Ned had picked up the Indian when he was falling down drunk in a village named Sweetwater near the Wyoming-Montana line. He knew very little English. He was a renegade Crow, but neither Ned nor Charley knew what kind of Indian he was. What they discovered was that he was good at holding horses and never missed with his arrows. They called him "Injun," never asked his name, and couldn't have pronounced it, if he'd told them. They counted out the money between them and gave the Indian two twenty-dollar greenbacks which he tucked away with a smile, got bareback atop the mule, and rode off, twisting and turning among the trees.

They never saw him again.

In the morning they first made certain the tomahawk hadn't taken their horses — which he hadn't — then had breakfast, and had a smoke while discussing several things, one of which was where the old man had got so much money. The second thing they discussed was where to spend some of it. Charley Young suggested backtracking to Summerville which had a decent emporium where they could get new clothes, a saloon, even a tonsorial parlor where they could get shaved, bathed, and haircuts.

Ned Forrester said — "Buttonwillow!" — and ignored the startled look on his companion's face, adding — "Pretty dance hall girls." — and widely smiled.

Charley looked steadily at Ned. They had stopped a mail coach on the outskirts of Buttonwillow where Ned shot both the driver and gun guard and a pompous damned fool who had climbed out and said: "See here! Do you know who I am?"

They didn't know and never found out. Ned had shot the pompous man from a distance of fifteen feet.

During Charley's consternation Ned also said: "They got a bank in Buttonwillow. You ever robbed a bank, Charley?"

Charley had, just once, and almost had got caught, and during the chase had been winged in the right shoulder. He made another suggestion. "Why not head southwest?"

"What's southwest? Buttonwillow's north."

"Southwest we can find a steam train an' go all the way to the Arizona Territory."

Ned's gaze came up to his companion's face. "Buttonwillow," he said, making a non-negotiable statement, and pulled forth the pistol from the man the Indian had killed. "I never seen such a pretty gun, did you, Charley?"

Charley hadn't, but his notice of the intricately carved grips at a distance was brief. He wasn't going within a hundred miles of Buttonwillow.

Ned palmed the gun, leathered it, drew it. His wasn't a very fast draw. He handed his old gun to Charley. "You can have it. I don't need two guns." Ned looked seriously at Charley. "If we're goin' to Buttonwillow, we'd best get to riding."

They had been together two years. Charley understood Ned Forrester as well as anyone did. He knew, for instance, that if he refused to accompany Forrester to Buttonwillow, Ned would throw one of his fits.

He rigged out slowly. Ned was already in the saddle. He was impatient. He was always impatient.

Charley swung up, took a deep seat, and the horse bogged its head. This was an everyday occurrence, and Charley didn't really mind. The horse didn't know how to unload a rider. He bucked in a straight line. When Charley got his head up, the episode was over.

They picked their way through close-spaced, ancient fir trees until they could make out the northward coach trace. Ned turned toward it. Charley followed several horse-lengths behind. A hundred or so yards before they reached the trace, Charley drew his six-gun without haste and fired. Ned's horse jumped out from under him and fled, head up and to one side to avoid stepping on the reins.

Ned Forrester was punched forward and tumbled awkwardly. Charley dismounted, kicked the dead man face down, emptied Ned's pockets, considered the gun with carved grips, dropped the gun Ned had given him beside the corpse, snugged up, swung astride, and turned back the way they had come. Sooner or later the crazy bastard would have tried to kill him, and there was the money, now all his. He had his holstered Colt, so he shoved the Mars gun into the front of his britches.

Eventually he turned south. He did not know the country he was passing through or the land he would see when he broke clear of the trees, but he was satisfied that, if he rode south long enough and far enough, he would see railroad tracks. In the end he was right, but it was a three-day ride and, when he found tracks, he had to parallel them for the better part of the fourth day before he saw the town through which they passed.

Chapter Sixteen

YANKTON

A respectable river ran north of the town. Charley crossed on a buttressed bridge stout enough to handle three or four hundred cattle without groaning. At the far end of the bridge there was a white painted sign nailed to a post that said **Welcome To Yankton**.

Red-headed Charley Young needed both a shave and a shearing. At the livery barn a crippled young man had pointed to the barber pole. To reach the tonsorial parlor, Charley had to cross the road and walk northward past a large emporium, a harness and saddle works, a bank with a front of red bricks, and the office of a fee lawyer named Alexander Short.

Yankton was a thriving, large settlement. Where there was a railroad terminal, most towns were large.

The barber wore pink sleeve garters with a small, embroidered, red rose in the center. He was a cigar man, but, while working on customers, he parked his stogie in a soiled, cracked dish on the counter where he kept his bottle of French toilet water, unscented patting powder, extra scissors, and razors. He had a high, squeaky voice.

When Charley Young mentioned a wash house, the barber nodded. Sometimes they smelled worse but not often. "Out back," he said. "Soap an' towels in there. Two bits, friend."

The hair cut was fifteen cents. Because Charley had no

coins, he handed over a fifty dollar bill. The barber's eyes widened, first at the greenback, then at Charley. He said: "I don't have no way to make change. If you'll set, I'll get it broke down over at the bank."

Charley didn't sit. He leaned beside the roadway window, watching the barber disappear inside the building with the impressive red brick front. He'd robbed one once and dang near got caught, in fact, did get creased over the right shoulder. He'd made away with six hundred dollars, an amount that offset the torn shirt and the scare. That had been seven years back. As he leaned in the shop, gazing across the road, he didn't remember the fright and the wound, just the six hundred dollars.

When the barber returned and laboriously counted out what Charley had coming, he said: "That's a lot of money, mister."

Charley Young handled that without hesitation. "Yeah, for a fact. I just sold some cattle."

Then he went out the back door to the bathhouse. He had to fire up a small stove to heat water. He also had to pump three buckets full before the water was warm enough. It was the first all-over warm bath he'd had in months. Creek bathing was all right, if a man had to get clean, but Charley thought the water was colder than a Jew's heart. He scrubbed with a rough chunk of tan soap and settled back. There was much to be said about town living.

The town marshal listened to the barber in stony silence. He was a man of average size with commonplace features. His name was Chet Holyfield. His close friends called him Preacher — everyone else called him Mr. Holyfield. He was fifty years old and had been a lawman for thirty of those years, and he was not only experienced, he was shrewd along with it. He told the barber to go back to his shop, to act normal, and the sheriff would manage to meet up with the stranger.

The usual place for casual meetings was at either the pool hall or the saloon. There was no red-headed man at the pool hall later when the sheriff entered, so he went up to the saloon. It rarely did much business in midday, but there were some patrons, mostly old men who nodded to the sheriff and went back to hunching over their little whiskey glasses. Some of these gaffers could make a jolt glass of whiskey last an hour, something the barman only objected to after sundown when business picked up.

The sheriff settled at the bar a short distance from the red-headed man. Even at this distance the red-headed man smelled like he had been three nights in a Turkish harem.

The barman had the essential garrulousness successful barmen were either born with or developed. He was black Irish, one of those gents who showed black shadow an hour after shaving. He was also dark-headed and dark-eyed. His name was Lucius Rourke, and he had a wisp of gray above each ear. Evidently he and the town marshal had an ongoing discussion about a recent horse race because, as the barman set up the glass and bottle, he said — "It was that close." — and the lawman delayed filling the small glass until he'd said — "An inch is as good as a mile, Lucius." — then poured, downed the jolt, and studied the stocky, red-maned stranger in the backbar mirror.

A wiry man wearing thick eye glasses and wearing black protectors from wrist to elbow walked briskly to the bar, and the barman put bottle and glass in front of the man as he spoke again to the sheriff. "They're goin' to set it up again for Saturday." As the lawman nodded, because he al-

182

ready knew this, the barman finished: "Same bet, Chet?"

The lawman was refilling the little glass and didn't look up as he said: "Double this time, Lucius."

The sheriff downed his second jolt and turned toward the red-headed stranger. "My name's Chet Holyfield. We got a horse race comin' up next Saturday, if you're a bettin' man."

Charley Young faced half around, smiling. "What're the odds?" he asked, and got blank looks from the lawman and the barman.

It was Rourke who answered. "No odds, friend. These horses been runnin' against each other since last year. First, one wins, then the other one wins."

"Which one won last time?"

Rourke almost smiled when he answered. The last race he had won seven dollars. "Dolly Lightfoot."

Charley Young removed a fold of greenbacks, selected a five, and put it beside his glass. "Five on Dolly Lightfoot."

Sheriff Holyfield snorted: "I hope you got money to throw away, mister."

Charley smiled, scratched inside the neck of his shirt, and carelessly said: "I have, Sheriff. At least that much."

Holyfield left the saloon, went down to the livery barn to examine the stranger's outfit, which was ordinary enough with scratches and worn places. Whatever the maker's name had been had been rubbed out on each fender, and it hadn't been put below the fork near the gullet. The liveryman was not exactly slow in the head, but close to it. He watched the sheriff make his examination and said: "Miles City saddle, sure as I'm standin' here. I seen dozens of 'em over the years."

Sheriff Holyfield nodded and left the barn to hike almost the full length of Main Street before he reached the hotel. The proprietor nodded his head. He had let out a room to the red-headed stranger, although at present he did not believe the man was in his room.

Sheriff Holyfield had one more call to make. He had to go back the way he had come, past the jailhouse, and down to an unpainted, small building with the name **S. Armour Livestock Bought & Sold**.

Steven Armour had three chins, a paunch convenient for catching cigar ash, and was somewhat less than average height. He wore a curly-brim derby hat day and night, and he wasn't bald. When the sheriff walked in, the livestock buyer was scowling over a lined ledger and looked up, scowling, but only for a moment. He pointed to a chair. Holyfield sat.

Armour said: "You hirin' deputies, Sheriff?"

Holyfield grinned. This was an exchange that had happened often between the men over the years. "I need to know if there's been any cattle shipped out lately."

Armour's three chins shook like jelly when he wagged his head. "Not from here an' not from up north, far as I know. There hasn't been no cattle cars, empty or full, pass through since last fall. I wouldn't expect there'll be any until later in the year." Armour fired up a cigar stub, leaned across the ledger, and raised bushy brows. "Sheriff . . . ?"

Holyfield asked another question. "Can you telegraph upcountry to other sidings and find out if anyone's shipped cattle lately?"

Armour's round, lineless face showed no expression before he finally nodded. "Yep. They all got telegraphs now. Is there somethin' botherin' you, Sheriff?"

Holyfield rose. "Yes, but it'll bother me more, if you get answers that no one's shipped cattle."

On his walk back uptown he met the red-headed man opposite his jailhouse and a few doors north of the general store.

The stranger smiled. "From what I've seen, Sheriff, a man could do worse than to settle in your town."

Holyfield's reply was genuine. "A man sure could, mister. We're growin', an' we got stores for just about whatever a body wants, an' a licensed medical doctor." Holyfield allowed moments to pass before speaking again. "You was in the cattle business?"

"And teamsterin' and stagecoachin'. I figured to talk to the feller who runs the passenger an' freight business. You wouldn't happen to know if he'd sell out?"

Holyfield couldn't even guess, so he said. "His name's Andy Driscoll. He's easy to get along with. His office is across the road an' part of the corral yard."

Holyfield wanted to keep this conversation alive but couldn't think of a way to do it, so, when the red-headed man departed in the direction of the general store, the lawman crossed the road toward his jailhouse office.

There was always something that had to be done, and for a while he forgot about the barrel-built, red-headed stranger. There was a dog fight in the center of the road. A large black and tan dog was wiping up the road with a smaller white dog. By the time Holyfield got there the little white dog showed blood as he cowered between the legs of a large man who waited until the big black and tan made a rush, and caught him in the ribs with a size-ten boot. The black and tan howled, fell, rolled over, got back upright, and ran in a dog trot between the emporium and the harness works.

A sturdily built man came into the roadway, heading for the man who had kicked his black and tan. Sheriff

Holyfield knew both men and got between them. The heavy-set man tried to shoulder past. Holyfield grabbed him by the shirt front and heaved him backwards.

That ended it. The large man, who owned the white dog, took his animal home. The short, muscular man who wanted to settle with the other man for kicking his dog yielded to the sheriff's pushing until he was back on the opposite plank walk. Holyfield said something to him, and he left, followed by his black and tan.

From the harness shop doorway the red-headed stranger said: "I guess a man had ought to figure a little dog'll belong to a big man an' a big dog'll belong to a smaller man."

Sheriff Holyfield nodded and smiled. "Except in this case . . . . that short, husky feller's a gunsmith by trade."

"An' the big one?"

"That's Andy Driscoll, the feller I told you about who runs the stages and does freightin'."

Charley took his time visiting the corral yard. He first had a meal and after that visited the lower end of town to see how his horse was faring. When he was satisfied about that, he struck out for the corral yard and missed his man by about fifteen minutes. Driscoll had taken a coach and four up north for a mile or two in order to satisfy himself about the wheelers, horses he had bought a few days earlier.

Charley returned to the saloon where business was even less worthwhile than it had been earlier. He took a glass of beer to the fly-specked front window and stood over there, sipping brew and gazing at the impressive red-brick façade of the bank.

Lucius Rourke joined him as a top buggy went past, and a thin shock-headed man waved in the direction of the window. As Rourke waved back, he said: "Doc Marlow. I don't envy him. They come all hours of the day an' night an', when they can't do that, they send for him." Rourke leaned slightly to follow the doctor's course, straightened back, and said: "It'll be another woman with a hung up baby."

Charley returned thoughtfully to the bar. It would be easy, much simpler than the last time. That time he'd walked in, waving a cocked six-gun. No thought in advance, no reconnoiter of the lawman's place, just walked in, got the money, ran out back, got astride, and ran for it. His horse had been fast enough, but among the angry townsmen there were men riding faster horses.

Charley nodded for a bottle and glass that the barman set up. Charley poured carefully, hoisted the glass which was full to the brim, opened his mouth, and dropped the whiskey straight down. Lucius Rourke applauded. Many tried; precious few didn't spill.

Charley had his last meal of the day, went up to his room at the hotel, groped for the saddlebags he had hidden, found them untouched. He pulled the only chair around, cocked his feet on the sill of the room's only window, and watched Yankton slowly wind down for the day. He smoked and relaxed. Somewhere a mule brayed. He remembered the last mule he'd seen. Two lovers strolled past, hand in hand. Charley killed his smoke, rose, and stopped stone still. Why in the hell would a man with three thousand dollars in his saddlebags even think of robbing a bank?

He'd pretty well botched it the last time, but he'd learned a lot since then. He went to bed, to do some figuring. From what he'd heard around town, that horse race Saturday was a genuine civic event. Everyone would be out

187

where the race would be run. It also crossed his mind that the bank might be closed, but he knew how to handle that as well as he knew to have his horse saddled and waiting in the back alley. It never occurred to him none of it would happen.

Charley Young went to sleep happy and did not awaken until he heard two men arguing in the hallway. One was waspish. The other one was argumentatively scornful when he said: "Alex, you're crazy. He sold a herd of cattle up north."

The waspish voice belonged to the barber. "I tell you, Ralph, I seen the dodger. Me 'n' the sheriff went through two boxes of dodgers. He was near the back of the second box."

The scornful man made the proper rejoinder. "Well, don't tell me it's up to the sheriff."

"I'm tellin' you because he might rob your store."

The argument ended when the scornful man said: "Leave it to Holyfield. You're the dangest nervous gent I know."

Charley came out of bed in one smooth glide, dressed in silent haste, dropped on his hat, swung the gun belt around, caught it in front, and buckled it. He raised and lowered the gun with the carved grips. It fit his holster perfectly.

The only window faced the roadway. He listened at the door, heard nothing, cracked it open to peek out, found the hallway empty, and, with saddlebags over one shoulder, crossed the hall, entered the opposite room which was empty, went to the back wall, hoisted the window, and climbed out. He was in the alley. The livery barn was at the south end of town. He fought the urge to run, walked normally the full distance, entered the gloomy runway, and was bringing his horse out to be saddled when the slow-thinking liveryman emerged from the harness room, watched, then turned back as he said: "I'll fetch your outfit."

Charley was not normally an excitable or nervous man, but it seemed to him the liveryman was taking too long, and, when he emerged from the harness room with the saddle over one shoulder, the blanket and bridle in the other hand, Charley yanked away the bridle first, buckled the throat latch, grabbed the blanket, flung it into place, and dumped the saddle atop it. He reached for the cinch, made it fast with the latigo, and faced around. The liveryman was staring in disbelief. He had never seen a man rig out so fast. Charley swung astride, made the horse lunge, and the horse hit the liveryman head-on.

Charley had seconds to make the decision. He reined southward. Northward would be where men would be hunting him. The horse was fresh the first two miles, but he had a gutful of morning hay that made him loggy. Charley had no choice but to favor the animal, so he sought cover, but the farther south he went the less cover there was, so he changed course, riding west with a slight, angling sashay northward.

The morning was cool. Charley made good time. So far he could detect no pursuit. By high noon the horse was dragging. Next he would begin stumbling. If Charley had had any idea where he could find another saddle animal, he would have made a fast trade and abandoned the one he was riding.

Chapter Seventeen

CORNERED!

Sheriff Holyfield's pursuit with a posse was at best half-hearted. When the fugitive left the road, he was difficult to track. The sheriff was satisfied the red-headed man was wanted. The dodger he and the barber had found was proof, and the reward was above average. But except for the dodger, which had been issued almost four years back, if Holyfield brought the fugitive back, because he had committed no crime that Holyfield knew about in his territory, all he could do was lock the fugitive up and begin a long exchange of letters with the authorities who had issued the dodger. And if Holyfield had learned one thing, it was that a prisoner would be a lot older before the governors and their flunkies who handled this kind of correspondence agreed to extradition, and there would be an even longer and reluctant exchange concerning the reward.

Holyfield's best tracker was an Indian, and he had been too drunk to sit a horse. But the sheriff persevered until dark before turning back.

No one in Yankton was disappointed. Some, like the barman, were not convinced the pursuit was legitimate. There were dozens of red-headed men. As he told the sheriff, when Holyfield arrived after dusk, tired and irritable, a real outlaw would have robbed the bank which had received a fresh shipment of crisp new greenbacks the day before the red-headed man had disappeared. Rourke knowledgeably added more. "Outlaws know about such things. One time back in Kansas some feller's folks said what was part of the James gang robbed a bank as two gun guards was packin' two bullion boxes into the bank. Each guard was carryin' a box. They couldn't do a damned thing."

The excitement passed, and within a week other events had replaced it. Most of the people of Yankton could not recollect even seeing the red-headed man.

For a fact, except for his carroty mane, Charley Young was only distinctive for his powerful build, but that was not especially unusual, either. What helped was the upcoming horse race. To this event Charley Young couldn't hold a candle.

All Charley knew from careful scrutiny was that the only cloud of dust he saw in the distance was not pursuing him. It was going in the wrong direction.

He still wanted to change horses. The one he'd been riding for the past couple of years was not fast. The reason Charley had kept him was because he had bottom and so could keep going long after most horses wore out.

His third day of wandering brought him to a thin, long land swell overlooking the yard of a cow outfit that had a wide creek hurrying past, the obvious source for the greenery in and around the yard. The buildings did not have a single dip in their roof lines, and the network of corrals, like the main house, were painted white.

It was not entirely unusual, but it certainly wasn't common, either. Cow outfits kept corrals and essential buildings in good repair, but seldom painted anything. The last time Charley had seen such a dude outfit, it had belonged to a man named Morgan, a wealthy investment banker from the East, and it had been a working outfit in name only. Its owner had been wealthy without running cattle.

191

Charley found a decent draw and settled in it. He hobbled his horse and flung the riding gear in tree shade. The place owned by Mr. Morgan up in Montana had not only upgraded beef but the best horses in the area. The yard Charley had spied out had horses in corrals and three fully rigged ones dozing at a tie rack in front of the main house.

The distance was considerable, but Charley Young knew horses. The tethered ones were leggy, fine-boned, quality animals. The kind someone took special care of. Charley could not determine whether they were shod or not. He would settle for a barefoot animal, but what he really wanted was a shod one.

He killed an afternoon recounting the money from the saddlebags, smoking, and dozing. His horse had good feed to its hocks and was making use of it. Something that had always intrigued Charley about his horse was the curlicue brand inside the left hind leg, which had clearly been made by an iron about the diameter of a thin pencil. When he'd been riding the animal for about half a year and it had cut its upper hind leg on wire in the grass, Charley had got down on his knees to doctor the wound. It was then he had found the brand. He had never seen one like it or in such a place. Most brands Charley was familiar with had straight lines, often connecting to other straight lines. The brand on his horse had curves, no sharp corners. He guessed it was someone's initials but couldn't make it out, and he had looked often.

It was a lazy, pleasant afternoon with larks in the grass and honey bees going and coming where an old oak had been darkened by their deposits of honey. Charley had plenty of time to consider the future. For one thing, he was never going north again, which left three directions. East, homesteaders were plowing and fencing, cutting trees, and dynamiting stumps so more land could be sowed into grain. South was Mexico. He'd never been down there, but from what he'd heard he dismissed the idea. West was open country, sparsely settled, with good graze, timber, and water. He knew men who had gone west. If they'd ever come back, he had neither seen them nor heard of them.

He would go west. With three thousand dollars he could buy a sizable stretch of land. Or he could settle in a town and maybe buy a saloon, or possibly even a hotel. He liked the idea of a saloon best. Saloonmen kept warm in winters, dry in summers, and, if he dyed his hair, maybe even took to wearing eye glasses and a close-trimmed beard which he could also dye, he could spend the rest of his life. . . .

The horse nickered. Charley came out of his reverie. The horse was standing, head up, little ears pointing. Charley followed out its line of sight and saw four unwashed, faded scarecrows on ridden-down horses on the thin ridge where he had been, studying the yard below. As he watched, they drew back and faded from sight northward among a stand of trees.

He remained in his arroyo. The strangers must have come from the north. Otherwise, they would most likely have found the arroyo with Charley in it. If he rode out of the arroyo and they were watching, they would see him. Very likely it would spoil his chance of stealing one of those breedy horses in the yard, but, if he remained in the arroyo and the strangers scouted even a little, they would find him. Possibly they were local riders, neighbors of the folks at the yard, but Charley Young had a sixth sense. He had ridden with men like those four. He had acted as they had acted.

He finally rode up out of the arroyo, breasted the thin ridge, and rode down the far side directly toward the yard. Three dogs greeted his approach with a hullabaloo of barking. Charley passed several big trees into the yard, stopped in front of the barn, and looped his reins through a stud ring.

A lean man appeared on the porch. He was not wearing a shell belt or holstered pistol. He called to Charley. "Half hour it'll be supper time. There's grain in the barn."

Charley threw the man a wave, unlooped the reins, and led his animal into a barn with grilled stalls, a raked runway, and four covered grain barrels in front of a saddle room.

Charley cared for his animal. As he watched it chewing rolled barley, he said: "If this is a working cow outfit, I'm a Dutchman's uncle." It was too much like the Morgan place up in Montana.

The man on the porch studied Charley as he crossed the yard. At the porch the man shoved out a hand. "Brad Hough."

As they shook, the red-headed man said: "Charley Long."

"Sit, Mister Long, supper's being made."

Brad Hough was dressed like a rancher, but his boots weren't scuffed, no one had ironed his shirt around a bunkhouse stove pipe, and his britches hadn't been worn until they could stand alone.

Charley said: "Mister Hough . . . ?"

"It'll be months before I'll be hiring again, Mister Long. I keep one man year around. Otherwise, I do seasonal hiring. I'd say from the looks of you, you know how that is."

Charley tried again, this time unwilling to be interrupted. "Mister Hough, do you have neighbors . . . four rough-lookin' individuals on rode-down horses?"

Hough turned. "My nearest neighbor is thirty miles away. I . . . where did you see them?"

Charley pointed, and his companion on the porch softly expelled a breath. "I don't know who they are. When you rode in, I thought you might be one of them."

"Who are they?"

"I just told you . . . I have no idea who they are, but they've been seen several times in the last week or so, by my wife and Ute, my year-'round hand. Did you see them up close?"

"Not very close," he said. "They been scoutin' you up for a week?"

"Something like that."

"Mister Hough, I'd like to ask you a personal question . . . do you keep much money in the house?"

Hough didn't answer the question. He asked one of his own. "Outlaws, Mister Long?"

"Mister Hough, I can tell you one thing . . . that's how they maneuver. They scout up first, then they come in like Comanches. They'll shoot anythin' that breathes. Is it just you 'n' your woman and the hired hand?"

Brad Hough faced Charley with signs of apprehension. He had known Charley about ten minutes. His first impression as Charley had been crossing the yard toward the porch had not been favorable, especially the six-gun in its worn holster with the beautifully carved grips. Personally, Charley was built like a bear, was attired in faded, unwashed clothing, and had a set of features that would only have inspired confidence in other men of his kind, and the lawman who sought them.

Hough straightened in his chair. "I'd like to ask you a personal question, Mister Long."

"Fire away."

"Those men . . . you said they would scout us up?"

Charley nodded, and Brad Hough blurted out the rest

of it. "Would they send a man in to get a closer look?"

Charley returned the other man's gaze and made a small, tough smile. "Mister Hough, if I was one of 'em, by now I'd have a gun barrel in the back of your neck, an' I'd wave my hat."

Hough neither moved nor seemed to be breathing.

Charley's smile widened. "Is your hired hand an Injun?"

"No. He told me his father named him Ute without telling him why. Mister Long . . . ?"

"I'd guess they scouted you up as good as they figure they have to. They know there's three of you, Ute, your wife, 'n' you. I expect they've already figured you're no more a rancher than they are. White fences, flower beds, breedy horses. Them things read like there's money around."

Brad Hough almost spoke when a handsome woman who didn't look sixty came out smilingly to invite her husband and the stranger inside to supper. Hough introduced his wife Alice to Charley Long, and, as they sat to eat, he also told her what the red-headed man had said about the wraiths she had seen. After that, there was very little conversation until the woman asked Charley to excuse them while she took her husband elsewhere for a talk.

Charley returned to the porch. Dusk was settling. He went down to the barn, ostensibly to look in on his horse, but actually to find dark places where he could blend while scanning the countryside. He wasn't looking for riders. He was looking for treetop reflections of a supper fire. He saw nothing like that, nor did he catch the scent of smoke.

Charley spent an hour watching and waiting. Some tomahawks wouldn't attack at night, but a man never wanted to wager good money on that. Some, like Apaches and Comanches, would attack after dark, seemed, in fact, to prefer it. The men Charley had seen weren't Indians. They would attack when they were satisfied it was time to do so. They were renegades, the worst, most ruthless of outlaws.

Charley knew their kind, and, if he'd thought of it, he'd have regretted riding into the yard earlier in the day. Normally, his sympathies would have been with the human wolves. The trouble was that they had seen him ride in, and no matter what he yelled to them about himself, their minds were set — there were three people. They would kill three people.

He returned to the main house by a route that fairly well shielded movement. When he got inside, the Houghs had compiled an arsenal. Some of the weapons, like a frail-looking rifle with a long barrel, wouldn't be of much use, but there were Winchesters, both rifles and carbines, and there were six pistols. Hough watched Charley's appraising gaze and said: "That one with the ivory grips was found on the Custer battlefield, and that nickel-plated one belonged to Belle Starr. I paid a price for them. Someday I'd like to open a museum. I've got Indian saddles, beaded shirts, lances, and two feather bonnets with double trailers."

Charley nodded. "You said they been around a week?"

Hough looked at his wife for verification before answering. "As far as we know. Ute and my wife have seen them in different places for about that long."

"Where's Ute?"

"He went to look for some springing heifers we've been worried about."

"Left this morning, did he?"

"Yes. He'll be along."

Charley said — "Uhn huh." — and dropped his hat on a chair seat. "That'll make five," he said.

Hough's wife spoke sharply. "Ute? Mister Long, he's been with us almost four years. He works hard and. . . ."

"How many of them breedy horses do you have, Mister Hough?"

"Eighteen head, mostly bred up, but four are pure Thoroughbred. Why?"

"They'll need good mounts, an' by now each of 'em's picked out the one he wants. You run cattle, too?"

"Sixty cows and two purebred bulls. The best quality I could buy."

Charley went to a lamp and hovered there as he asked another question. "What time do you folks usually bed down?"

The woman answered. "Between eight and nine."

Charley asked what time it was, and Hough drew forth a gold pocket watch, flipped it open, and said — "Ten after seven." — closed the watch, and pocketed it.

Charley sat down in a red-leather chair. "We got about an hour to wait. That is, if they're satisfied they know all they got to know. Renegades don't believe in takin' chances. They take their time, studyin' things out."

Hough softly said: "Tonight, Mister Long?"

"Damned if I know, Mister Hough, but I'd guess it'll be soon. Damned wonder they ain't struck before." Charley rose, considered the front wall window, and wagged his head. Glass windows cost a fortune. Most folks had perhaps two, most likely one, and they'd been smaller, double-hung windows. The window Charley was looking at cost a fortune and was at least five feet wide and about the same height. In daylight a person could see the yard and far beyond.

There was a drapery that worked on a pulley. Hough's wife asked if they shouldn't pull the drape, and Charley shook his head. "Not unless you been doin' it."

The woman shook her head. She looked young by lantern light. She also seemed to have lost color. She went to the kitchen, the refuge of troubled housewives, and rattled a dipper and a pot as she started to make coffee. While she was gone, Charley asked the man if his wife could shoot a gun. He offered a delayed reply. "She has done it. We've shot at targets. She's not a very good shot."

Charley pointed to the frail long-rifle. "It don't weigh much. Load it for her."

Hough didn't know how, so Charley charged the muzzle-loader as he told Hough it would shoot once, then have to be recharged.

Charley leaned the rifle aside as the woman brought three large mugs of hot black java. Charley set his aside and offered a reassuring remark for the woman's sake. "Maybe it won't be tonight. Maybe it won't be for several days."

Hough picked up on the last sentence. "We can send for help."

Charley tried the coffee. It was too hot. "Maybe," he drawled. "Tell me about your hired hand."

"Ute? He's a good man. He knows cattle and horses. He's good-natured, lives in the bunkhouse down near the barn. He's been with us about four years."

Alice Hough said: "He's very well-mannered."

"Does he have friends?"

"I don't think so. Not many. Occasionally on a day off he rides to a settlement northeast of here and returns the next day. We pay him forty dollars a month . . . good pay, so we've been told, for the area and the work."

Charley considered a small cedar box, and Brad Hough anticipated Charley, or thought he did, when he brought

199

the box over and opened it. "Georgia cigars. The best a man can buy."

Charley took one and pocketed it as he thanked his host. For a long time they sat in silence, until Charley got the squirrel rifle, handed it to the woman, and said: "Keep it snugged back when you shoot. They kick." He smiled as he added: "One shot, ma'am. Don't miss."

Brad Hough rose, went to the massive stone fireplace, and knelt to wrap fat wood in paper and lay the foundation of a fire. Charley asked if they usually did that after supper, and the woman answered. "If the house is cold."

Charley considered the woman. She was handsome with the wide eyes of a trusting person. He suggested that she go to bed. There was no assurance the renegades would come this night, or the next night for that matter. She neither put the rifle aside nor left her chair. She told Charley she would remain. The set of her jaw and the unwavering gaze she put on him told their story. She would not leave.

The fire blazed. Mr. Hough returned to a chair and sat forward, looking into the fire with both hands clasped between his knees. "They told me in New York I was insane to come out here. Since childhood I've read of the West." He shifted his gaze to Charley, who was examining his pistol. "That's a beautiful weapon, Mister Long. I've never seen one like it."

Charley leaned, pointing the barrel at the ceiling.

"You see what's engraved on the butt plate?"

"Yes. G. Mars." Hough settled back, and Charley also did.

Hough asked if G. Mars was the gun's maker, and Charley was disgusted. "It's a Colt's patent. That's engraved on the barrel."

"Then who was G. Mars?"

"I got no idea, but I can tell you, whoever he was, he was a gunsmith. Have you ever fired a Colt six-gun, Mister Hough?"

"Yes, indeed, quite a few times."

"Then you know you pull the dog back about an inch or such, an' it's on safety."

Hough nodded.

Charley held the gun gently in his lap. "An' you pull it full back to fire it."

"Yes."

"Well, Mister Hough, this gun's been worked so's you don't have to pull the dog all the way back, only to safety. If you're drawin' in a hurry an' the gun's on safety, you don't have to cock it. You just aim and squeeze the trigger."

"On safety, Mister Long, when you pull the trigger, the hammer goes down real gently."

Charley smiled. "Not on this Mars gun. The spring on this gun is maybe reversed from full cock. Whether that's what someone done or not, I don't know. What I do know is the spring for safety, or half cock, is stronger than the regular spring. On safety this pistol fires."

Hough and his wife exchanged a look. She looked longer at Charley with an expression of apprehension that was obvious.

Hough said: "I'll buy it from you, Mister Long. For my museum collection. The carved grips would attract people. I've never seen a gun like that, and I'd guess most other people haven't."

Charley hadn't lighted the cigar for a good reason. Although he enjoyed cigars, they didn't like him. Four or five stogies and he got hoarse. Now, he raised it to the lamp top and inhaled until it was burning. He considered Brad

Hough. "I don't think I'd ought to sell it. By the way, it's close to eight o'clock, ain't it?"

Hough consulted the gold pocket watch and nodded. He was unprepared for Charley's next question.

"Does your hired man often stay out this late?"

Again the Houghs exchanged a look before Mr. Hough answered. "No. But he could be down at the bunkhouse. Should I go see?"

Charley shook his head. "It don't matter a whole lot," he said, "but you openin' the door with light behind you might get you killed. Maybe not, too. Maybe not until to-morrow night or the night after."

Alice Hough abruptly rose, leaned the rifle aside, and went to the kitchen to return with the speckleware pot. She refilled three cups and lingered in the parlor.

Charley spoke quietly: "Sometimes you can make a trade. Let 'em plunder the house, take your money, get the best horses, an' leave. Sometimes they agree to trade, then kill you anyway."

Hough said: "I'd make that trade."

Charley considered the other man. "If it was just you 'n' me, maybe. But your woman's right handsome, an' rene-gades don't pass up no chance to get at a handsome woman."

Hough rose, poked another scantling into the fire, and stood watching sparks go up the chimney. Without facing around he said: "I shouldn't have done it. Lifelong dream or not. I shouldn't have brought either of us, her in partic-ular, to this god-forsaken country."

Charley could have agreed, but he rose, went to the door, and listened. A horse had whinnied. As he listened, two other horses whinnied. The last one to do it nickered, and Charley faced into the room. Whinnying horses were acknowledging the scent or sound of other horses. A nicker meant the other horses were close enough for the nickering horse to rub muzzles.

Neither of the Houghs had heard, but the man in front of the blazing fireplace had an expression of bitterness which could be read across the room.

Charley said: "Get away from the fireplace."

He had scarcely spoken when they all heard a squeaky gate being opened.

Chapter Eighteen

THE DEADLIEST, THE FASTEST . . .

Charley gestured for the woman to get the squirrel rifle, which she did, and then she stood like a statue awaiting the next order. Charley ignored her, went to the lamps, and blew them out. Dogs erupted into a frenzy of barking. When Mr. Hough asked if Charley thought the renegades were out there, he got a cryptic answer.

"I never knew a dog that could open a gate."

Charley told the woman to stay near the kitchen door and told her husband not to stand where the fire would background him. He then selected one of the Winchesters and went to the closed front door to listen, which proved to be a lesson in futility. Barking dogs would mask just about any other noise.

During this lull he saw the Houghs watching him and said: "They don't fight wars. They hit hard an' fast. If there's resistance, they might make a fight out of it. Depends on what they figure might be cached inside, like money an' valuables. If there's resistance, an' they want inside, they'll try to get alongside the house or out back an' set things on fire."

The Houghs were staring at Charley. They knew no more about him than he'd told, and what they'd guessed. They were both convinced, now, that their uninvited guest either was or had been as much a renegade as the ones out in the dark. Everything he'd been saying since the lamps had been put out had to come from a man knowledgeable about renegades and raiders.

Hough volunteered to go to the back of the house and watch. Charley told him to stay where he was. There'd be time to worry about the back after the renegades had attacked from the front.

What he had said was not an absolute, different raiders operated differently, but, if there was a fight, it usually started out front between the house and the barn. What Charley strained to hear was stampeding horses. When he didn't hear this, his heart sank a little. The renegades weren't just after horses. They had made the same appraisal Charley had made. This wasn't a working stock outfit. This was one of those dude places where wealthy Easterners settled in. This was not going to be a hit-and-run raid.

Time passed. The fire died to coals. The woman put aside her rifle and made a fresh pot of coffee. Charley almost smiled. Desperation worked differently with the sexes: men went for their armaments, while their wives got busy in the kitchen.

However, Brad Hough had fallen asleep in a chair when the coffee arrived. Charley went over and kicked his feet. As Hough awakened, he nodded to his wife, put the coffee aside, and went to brew up the fire.

Charley told him to get away from the fireplace and stay away from it. "Drink your coffee an' stay clear of the window. Go over to the far side of it an' stay there."

As the woman retrieved the rifle, she said: "Mister Long, is it possible we've made a miscalculation . . . that they aren't really out there?"

Charley looked long at the woman, showing no expression and not speaking. Somewhere he'd heard an adage about hope springing eternal in the heart, or something like that.

The dogs increased their furious barking until one gave a sharp howl, then whimpered as it slunk toward the house to disappear under the porch. It hadn't been shot. Something like a stone or a stick had struck it. Briefly the other dogs heightened their racket, but eventually they, too, left off barking and got under the porch.

Charley rummaged until he found a bottle of whiskey from which he took two long swallows before putting the bottle on a small table.

There was a creeping chill in the parlor. It might have been augmented by the unheated back rooms, perhaps even an open window.

Charley's attention was diverted when Brad Hough said: "I hear horses!"

Charley went to the wall west of the big front window, listened, and shook his head, but the sound became louder until Charley heard it. He yelled at Hough. "Kneel down. They'll come behind the horses. Shoot anythin' with two legs!"

Frightened horses do unusual things, especially if they're being crowded from behind. They had been known to climb steps onto porches. It was not uncommon for panicked horses to run over men, or to knock porch uprights loose so that overhangs collapsed.

Charley knelt with the Winchester butt on the floor. He risked a peek, saw thick dust and horses like ghosts, bobbing and weaving in several directions. Alice Hough left her doorway, went over behind her husband, and knelt. Charley saw her begin to raise the rifle and simultaneously yelled and shook his head. The woman continued to snug back the rifle but eventually lowered it. The only targets were stampeding horses. If there were renegades behind them, she could not make them out. It wasn't just because of darkness. It was also because churned earth sent up thick banners of dust.

Charley might have yelled at the woman not to kneel directly behind her husband, but he didn't. He was concentrating on the shadows, dust, and noise out front.

The horses veered right and left. Very briefly visibility improved and Hough yelled: "Ute!"

Charley risked another peek. During that brief moment of visibility he saw two horsemen about thirty feet apart. One was swinging a quirt. His companion yawed west in an effort to keep the horses in the yard. Above the noise Charley heard the woman loudly say: "Ute!" As her husband started to ease away from the window and bumped her upward swinging rifle barrel, she said something else Charley could not hear and roughly shouldered her husband aside.

Before the dust closed in, Charley saw four riders, spaced widely in an effort to prevent panicked horses from leaving the yard as long as they could. A large dapple gray collided with a horseman whose animal fought against falling as the gray horse passed. The rider had his hands full balancing to help his mount get upright; otherwise, he would have shot the gray horse.

Charley had a glimpse of a rider sitting tall in the saddle. It was the man the Houghs had recognized as their trusted hired man, Ute. The raiders were trying to bunch the horses as close to the porch as they could and, except that they were seasoned horsemen, they never could have accomplished it. Horses might not be brilliant, but even frightened ones will not charge directly into a visible, solid structure.

The dust and noise prevented the people in the house from using their weapons. Out of the corner of his eye Charley saw the woman settle the gun and pull the trigger.

Nothing happened. She tried a second time with the same result. She flung the rifle away, grabbed a big-bored Winchester buffalo rifle, leaned, and using a hand rest sought another target. Whether she actually saw a renegade, or thought she had, she fired. The buffalo rifle hadn't been tight against her shoulder; even so, the recoil would have flung her backwards, if her husband hadn't caught her. She dropped the rifle, moved clear, and rubbed her shoulder.

She hadn't hit a raider, but the lance of flame and thunderous explosion destroyed whatever chance the renegades had of forcing the loose stock close to the porch. The leaders whirled and raced blindly in the opposite direction. Another mounted man was nearly bowled over, horse and all, by a terrified thousand-pound animal.

A man screamed a scorching curse and fired at the front of the house, and the large, expensive, glass window blew inward in hundreds of pieces.

Charley felt the predawn cold as other raiders fired at the front of the house. Behind Charley, fireplace coals exploded out into the room. Neither Charley nor the Houghs knew this had happened. There was pandemonium inside as well as outside. The defenders were trying to find targets and avoid gunshots from outside the house.

The horses were long gone, and dust was settling. A sickly gray streak of dawn light was visible off to the east and, although visibility improved because the Hough buildings were in a wide, low swale, visibility only marginally improved for the defenders. Bullets shattered hanging pictures, lamps, even furniture.

There was no excuse for the renegades to continue to fight except for anger and a need for revenge. Charley was less surprised than were the Houghs that the attackers were

208

turning their hit-and-run raid into an all-out battle. He had told the Houghs it would be a fast, in-and-out raid. Maybe they would remember that later. At present, they were cringing, not daring to expose themselves to fire back. It would not have mattered much if they had tried returning the fire. The mounted men were sashaying back and forth as they fired, making difficult targets. Four men, firing steadily but with different patterns, made it possible for attackers to reload in the saddle while their companions kept up the shooting.

Even Charley's position beside the glassless window on the west side was not defensible. Anyone daring a peek for a moving target would be risking almost certain death. One raider was on the west side of the house, shooting out windows, creating havoc with whatever he hit. Because the sound of this gun was different, Charley yelled to the Houghs to stay where they were, to mind the yard, and belly-crawled toward a side room where a raider, using a saddle gun, was emptying his carbine.

Charley encountered red coals before reaching the doorless opening to a small room. Inside it was blacker than Toby's butt. There was broken glass and shattered wood everywhere. A roll-top desk had been splintered. The raider was passing southward along the west side of the house toward the rear. Out front the gunfire continued, but the raider Charley sought was no longer firing. Charley crept into the small office, crawled toward another broken glass window, and to avoid shards had to sweep the floor clear as he went.

If his guess was correct, the raider outside was reloading, which meant Charley had a little time to find the man. The firing out front was tapering off into intermittent gunshots.

At the window, Charley raised his free left hand to the

sill, brushed glass away, and began to rise up into a crouch. He took down a deep breath, raised up six-gun cocked, and looked out the window. There was no one in sight. He leaned farther and still did not see the raider. As he stood up to his full height and moved to one side of the window, a man out front yelled curses. "You'll come out! We'll burn you out!"

Charley was edging toward the doorless opening when he heard a shod hoof strike stone and stopped dead still. The sound was not repeated. Moments later gunfire erupted out front again.

Charley stood in the doorless opening until there was a lull in the firing, then swiftly crossed the room where fireplace coals were losing their color, reached the east side of the parlor, and entered another room as dark as the one he had left.

It was a storeroom with shelves of supplies lining three walls. He stumbled over a bootjack, reached to regain balance, and encountered some Mason jars full of meat. One teetered. He steadied it, groped along the wall using one hand to serve as a guide, found the latch of the back door, and halted. The firing out front was now down to an occasional shot. He could distinguish between the firing of raiders and that of the Houghs.

As he lifted the latch, he was careful that metal did not touch wood. When the door would swing free, he hesitated again, held his six-gun at chest level, and, using two fingers, eased the door open wide enough for limited visibility. He saw nothing.

Incoming air was chilly. He tried easing the door open farther. It offered minimal resistance and made no noise. Charley stepped closer, took down a big breath, and eased his head around with the six-gun poised. The horse raised its head, but the raider didn't. He was whittling shavings with a big, wicked-bladed boot knife.

The horse moved. The raider looked up — and saw Charley. He had been kneeling, skiving shavings with one hand, holding wood scraps with the other hand. Charley lowered his poised right hand, and the renegade hurled himself sideways as he groped for his holstered sidearm. He didn't stand a chance. Charley shot him high up through the body. The bullet's impact rolled the renegade. His hat came off, and the half drawn six-gun fell. The horse threw up its head and raced southward, stepping on its reins and breaking them as it ran.

Charley leathered his Colt, considered the unwashed, unshorn raider, listened briefly to the horse fleeing, stepped back, and closed the door.

He had no idea whether he had shot the Hough's hired man or someone else, and at the moment he didn't care. Charley returned to the parlor where the floor was scorched in a dozen places by dying coals, paused to shuck out the spent casing from his six-gun, and plug in a fresh load from his belt. Hough suddenly fired a Winchester empty and leaned to pass it to his wife to be reloaded. His wife took the empty weapon and rose slightly to pass him a fresh Winchester when a shot from the yard knocked her down.

Hough jumped over and knelt at her side. Charley made a guess. Whoever had shot Alice Hough had to have fired from the west side near the porch, if he was afoot, or from the same direction as he was riding west. If the raider was on foot, Charley might have time, but if he was on horseback. . . .

In general, the fighting seemed to have lost momentum. There was only an infrequent shot. The only way to find the raider who had shot Alice Hough was to open the bullet-riddled front door. Earlier that would have been lethal and still could be, despite the lessening of gunfire.

Charley reached the door about the same time Brad Hough called him to help with his wife. Charley crossed over, told Hough not to stand up, leaned, gathered the unconscious woman in both arms, rose, and walked toward a dark hallway. Hough would have followed, and this time, when Charley addressed the man, he swore. "Get back by the god-damned window. If they figure it's safe, they'll storm the front door. Use your damned head!"

The room where Charley eased the woman onto a bed was too dark to see. Charley groped, found a candle, and lighted it.

As he returned to the bedside, holding the candle, Alice Hough opened her eyes wide. Candlelight going upward from below made Charley's face a pantomime of dark and light. He looked indescribably evil.

He leaned and said — "Hold still." — and reached to turn her head. His hand came away with sticky fingers. He held the light as close as he dared, was still and silent for a long moment, then dryly said: "You'll live. Another couple of inches to the right, and it would have took off half of your head. It creased you and notched your ear." He made a death's-head smile. "You'll have a scar to tell your grandkids about. I'll fetch you some whiskey."

She sounded unsteady as she said: "There isn't any. We only had that one bottle, and it got smashed by a bullet."

"Stay here, lie quiet, and nurse the headache you're goin' to have."

The woman tried awkwardly to rise, and Charley pushed her back, kept the pressure until he felt her relax, then straightened up, smiled, pushed the candle close, and left the room.

Hough was back on the far side of the window, saddle gun grounded. As Charley appeared, Hough started to stand up. A bullet missed him by inches, and Charley caught Hough by the arm and hurled him half around. "Go set with your wife," he snarled, gave Hough a hard shove, and sidled over as far as he dared before getting belly-down to cover the remaining distance to the far side of the window where Hough had been.

Except for the sharpshooter somewhere west of the porch, none of the remaining raiders seemed to be in place to continue the fight. It would have helped, if there had been even a small window in the wall on the far side of the door. There wasn't. Charley did not risk a peek for an elemental reason: that sharpshooter west of the far side of the porch. So far he was the only renegade who had drawn blood.

There were scattered weapons on the floor. That big-bore old buffalo gun was closest, but Charley was satisfied, if he and the sharpshooter had it out, that it would be with hand guns.

A man yelled from somewhere near the barn. "Hough! Come out! If we got to come in, before we're through with you, you'll be beggin' us to kill you."

Charley couldn't resist. He called back. "You're sure mouthy, *pendejo*."

There was an interlude of silence before the raider called again, "Where is the Houghs? You the feller that rode in yestiddy?"

"Yeah."

"You kin or somethin'?"

"Never saw 'em in my life before yesterday."

Again the speaker hung fire before saying. "All right . . . walk out, get on your horse, and leave."

Charley laughed. "You want the son-of-a-bitch out back who's supposed to burn us out? He's still back there, deader'n a damned rock."

The caller from somewhere in the yard did not speak again.

Brad Hough came sidling along the far wall. With improving dawn light, Charley saw blood on his hands and clothing. He said: "You got some liquor? Anything that'll help her? She's goin' to have the granddaddy of all headaches directly."

"We have some laudanum."

It annoyed Charley that the woman had not told him this. He said: "Give her a good dose. An' stay with her. This ain't your fight any more . . . if it ever was. *Go on! Don't just stand there!*"

Chapter Nineteen

THE LAST MAN

The sharpshooter who had wounded Alice Hough obviously had a clear sighting of the window, which meant he also had the riddled front door in his line of sight, and there was no other way for Charley to find him. If he so much as cracked the door with improving dawn light, the sniper would see the movement.

Charley stood against the wall beside the door. If there were only a window, as there was in the little office — but there was no window, and the wall at his back was solid wood.

There was a way: leave the house by the back door and sidle along the west side of the house to the point where it junctured with the front wall. He considered this and remained where he was. With daylight approaching, anyone moving outside would make an excellent target.

That nasal-voiced, mouthy renegade called again. "You in there! You're alone. The Houghs is out of it . . . we'll make you a trade. Throw your guns out first . . . then come out, hands high."

Charley was disgusted enough to call back. "You silly son-of-a-bitch . . . come an' get me!" That ended the calling back and forth until Charley yelled again. "You better hurry up. The Army's on the way."

That brought taunting laughter. It sounded like two different voices. Charley wondered about it. There should have been three.

At the height of the derisive amusement Charley cracked the door several inches. The sniper fired, splinters flew, and the door shuddered. Charley pushed it farther open with his foot. Evidently the renegade thought the impact from his bullet had caused that. He did not fire again.

Charley ignored the brightening morning. If there were three of them, he'd die as sure as hell was hot if he sprang past the door to face the sniper. Three raiders would target him.

Hough came into the parlor but remained along the far wall. Charley saw movement and whirled. Hough made a little bleating sound. Charley shook his head and waited.

It was up to the renegades. Charley was bottled up. He wanted time which was now his only ally. Raiders rarely lingered. This bunch was doing more. They were digging in. They certainly knew how isolated the Hough yard was. A week or so of scouting had taught them all they had to know.

Hough picked up a Winchester and sidled to his former place on the east side of the front window. Charley watched him hunker for a peek, raise the Winchester, and pull the trigger. The sound of a hammer falling was clear to Charley. The damned fool had picked up a shot-out gun.

Somewhere a rider was spurring a horse into a belly-down run. Charley smiled. There were now two left, which made better odds, but not a hell of a lot better.

Hough, firing from the far side of the window, broke the silence. No one fired back. Charley thought the man who had yelled to him was somewhere east of the barn, a fair distance from the house. If the departing horse meant one raider had had enough, and if the mouthy renegade was distant from the porch. . . .

Charley reached to pull the door wider. Its hinges

grated. He had to use both hands. As he was widening the gap, Hough called to him. "Stay inside. We've got 'em thinned down."

Charley neither looked across the room nor heeded Hough's call.

Dawn light entered the room, which was a shambles. Hough watched without moving or seeming to breathe, as Charley braced himself. He would have scant seconds before the sharpshooter saw him. As for the brave soul down near the barn somewhere, that, in Charley's opinion, was the biggest risk.

He didn't move swiftly beyond the door; he moved slowly and warily. The sniper was beyond the west end of the porch. He was leaning a carbine aside when Charley appeared, and for two seconds the renegade froze before jumping sideways as he went for his hip holster.

He had the gun clear of its holster with a thumb pad pulling back the hammer when the Mars gun went off. The renegade went sideways clear of the porch before he fell. As with the man out back, his gun fell close to the body.

Charley turned to reënter the house when a mounted man ran at him from the direction of the barn. Hough yelled and fired. Charley whirled. The horseman had his hand gun raised and aimed. He fired as Charley was turning.

Charley was knocked back against the house. Hough fired, levered up, and fired again. The horse, stung across the rump by a wild bullet, reared straight up and fell over backwards. Normally a rider did not survive having the saddle horn driven through his chest. What saved the renegade was he was not straight in the saddle, and, when the horse reared, he went off sideways. Without weight on its back and with no restraining reins the frightened animal ran

217

blindly toward some cottonwood trees on the west side of the yard, but he hadn't reached the trees when his stunned rider scrambled to his feet about the time Hough fired again, and missed this time by two yards. The shot that downed the renegade came from the Mars gun in the hand of the man on the porch who had slid down the wall and had fired from a sitting position.

There were brief lingering echoes. Sunlight reached the length of the porch. Beneath it a dog whined in fright. Otherwise, there was not a sound until Brad Hough appeared in the doorway where Charley was struggling to rise. Hough froze. There was spreading blood on Charley's shirt.

It was Alice Hough, white as a sheet, caked blood on her dress and hastily bandaged head, who shoved past her husband to help Charley stand and who supported him past her husband and got him to a couch in the ruin of her parlor.

Charley felt very little pain. What he did feel was shock, and in its own way shock mitigated pain. He considered the haggard woman with the out-size towel bandage and the bright eyes. Laudanum worked wonders. Too much of it killed people; just enough bought them freedom from suffering.

Brad Hough went to the pair of dead renegades, appropriated their weapons, emptied their pockets, and put the contents into their hats. Then he returned to the house, leaned his Winchester aside, and placed the hats on a bullet-scarred small table.

His wife looked around from her kneeling position beside the couch. "He's been shot," she said, and her husband nodded. "I left the laudanum on the table beside my bed. Get it, Brad."

Charley and the disheveled woman eyed each other, and

Charley said: "You should have been wearin' the pants, ma'am."

Alice Hough couldn't force herself to open the shirt. She had never been able to avoid being sickened at the sight of blood. She said: "Does it hurt?"

"No, ma'am. Not much. It'll start hurtin' tomorrow. How bad is it?"

Alice Hough was a forthright person. She disliked liars, but she looked Charley in the eyes and lied with a clear conscience. "Bad enough, Mister Long. We'll get you to a doctor."

He made a mirthless, crooked little smile. "Ain't no town for miles from here, ma'am."

She turned as her husband reappeared and held out the little blue bottle. She took it and avoided eye contact with Charley as she said: "Open your mouth, please."

Charley closed his eyes and swallowed. One of the blessings of laudanum was that it worked fast. As the Houghs watched, Charley's color improved. When he opened his eyes, he looked up at the man. "I think one run for it."

Hough nodded. "It was Ute. He had to be the fourth one. The others are . . . out there."

Charley leaned to rise. Alice Hough restrained him with a bloody hand on his chest. Movement had increased the flow of blood. His entire shirt was soaked with it, the upper part of his trousers were also soaked. He smiled at the kneeling woman. "I got to take care of my horse."

She said: "My husband will do that. You sit back and rest."

Charley eased back. Blood was now spreading to the couch in several places and was also dripping on Alice Hough's skirt.

Brad Hough leaned and carefully removed the Mars gun

219

from its holster. Charley offered no resistance. He spoke to Hough in a voice whose words were beginning to slur. "Be careful with it. It'll fire on safety."

Hough went to stand by the shattered front window, examining the gun. His wife glanced only once in her husband's direction then used a sleeve to wipe cold sweat off Charley's face. "We owe you more than we can ever repay, Mister Long."

He gazed at her. "It was a pleasure, ma'am."

She sank back on her heels, reached with one hand to cover the hand in his lap, and softly said: "I'll never forget you, Mister Long. Never."

He neither answered nor looked directly at her, but fixed his eyes unwaveringly on the far wall. He was dead.

The sun was climbing. Every detail of the yard was clear as glass. A solitary horse wandered back into the yard, turned down past the barn, and entered the corral through a wide-open gate. It went to the leaky stone trough and drank. A long-haired dog with one blue eye came from beneath the porch, saw the open door, and walked in. It crossed to the side of Alice Hough and sat down.

Brad Hough turned. "Get the dog out of here," he told his wife. "You know they aren't allowed in the house."

She put her hand on the dog. It wagged its tail. She sank forward on the couch and cried. Her husband had never been able to stand hearing women cry. He went out onto the porch, considered the two sprawled men, slowly raised the Mars gun, aimed at first one, then the other, but did not fire.

It required three days for them to bury the dead renegades. When Hough stepped off a fair distance for the last grave, while his wife leaned on a shovel watching, he said:

220

"Here is where we'll bury Charley Long. And right there is where I'll make the museum. I'll get a good headstone for Charley. Folks'll want to see that. I'll have it chiseled on the stone . . . 'Here lies Charley Long, deadliest gunman of them all. Killed on this spot in the fight at Hough Ranch with renegades.' "

Alice Hough didn't work on the last grave. The headache that had been diminishing for the last day or so returned with a vengeance.

Brad Hough rode to the nearest town and didn't return for two days. His wife saw him coming a mile before he reached the yard. He was out front of eight or ten mounted townsmen. She watched him gesture without being able to hear what he was saying, but it was obvious. He was pointing to the places where attacking raiders had been, where the fiercest fighting had taken place.

When they rode into the yard, her husband invited them inside, introduced them to his wife, and stood aside as the awed townsmen gazed at the ruin of the parlor. One man approached the couch and said: "Is this where he died?"

Hough's reply was needlessly prolonged. "Right there on that sofa, shot through the chest. He got hit on the porch. My wife and I got him inside to the couch. He was dying. Would you like to see his gun?"

The strangers crowded around as Hough took the Mars gun off the mantle and passed it among them.

"It is a killer gun. I'm not exactly sure how it works, but it fired the moment Charley drew. The fastest draw and the deadliest gun in the West. After I get the museum built, I'm going to put it on a stand with a red velvet base under the gun and a glass box around it."

As one of the awed townsmen handed back the gun, he said: "Long? I never heard of a gunman named . . . you sure it wasn't Younger? I think Charley Younger rode with Jesse James."

Hough held the gun as he replied. "It could have been Younger. He said his name was Charley Long. Maybe he just shortened it." Hough put the Mars gun back on the mantle. "He was a gunman, gentlemen. He told me stories. He'd killed twenty-six men in fair fights."

One of the townsmen nodded about that. "If the gun was customized, he'd sure have an edge, wouldn't he? What kind of feller was he?"

"Average-looking, mannerly, but, when the fight started, he was like an army general. He gave orders, and he knew exactly what to do. I'd say he was maybe an officer in the war. Maybe a Union general."

An older man spoke quietly. "Maybe a Confederate gen'ral, Mister Hough."

Hough ignored that. Where Hough had been born and raised, there were only Union generals. He led them outside, showed them the graves, and explained that only one renegade had something in his pockets with his name on it. "A letter from a woman in Missouri. That's his name on the headboard. Frank Kandelin. The others were unknown, so that's what I put on the headboards, along with how they died, all of 'em except one named Ute who worked for us for four years. I couldn't believe it when I saw him riding with the raiders. He would be the one that rode away before the fight ended.

"Gents, right here is where I expect to build the museum. It'll hold evidence of the fight, the legend of Charley Long, the deadliest gunfighter of all time."

After the awed townsmen left and Hough returned to the house, his wife, wearing a smaller bandage, met him in the middle of the parlor. She had created as much order as

222

was possible. She tartly said: "We'll need a new floor. Coals from the fireplace scorched it badly." She turned, facing her husband. "I didn't hear him tell you stories, Brad. We don't even know if his name really was Charley Long."

Hough put an exasperated look on his wife. "Alice, I've always wanted to be a Westerner, to know gunfighters. We lived through a real gunfighters' war. My museum. . . ."

"Brad, just the truth should be enough."

"Alice, I'm going to hunt down other guns, other stories of gunfighting Westerners. Maybe even include Indians."

"Would you like something to eat?" she asked, heading for the kitchen. He answered as he followed. "We'll keep some whiskey around. They were drinking men. Charley sure was. How's your wound?"

She was working at the stove when she replied without facing him. "It's painful, but it's getting better. Sit down, Brad. When you get your museum established, maybe on tourist days I can come out of the house wearing a bullet belt with a holstered pistol and exhibit the top of my ear and the scar over it."

He beamed at her. "And boots with spurs, Alice."

She slammed a pan on the stove without facing him again until she was ready to put a platter on the table. "You could tell them I'm Belle Starr's sister."

He stared at her. "Wonderful, Alice."

That night she picked columbines and placed them on Charley's grave. "Whoever you were, I told you I'd never forget you, and I never will. Whatever my husband does for you, or to you, I'll never forget you as I knew you. Good night, Charley."

223